THE LOCATIVE ALTERNATION IN GERMAN

LANGUAGE ACQUISITION & LANGUAGE DISORDERS

Volume 15

Ursula Brinkmann

The Locative Alternation in German
Its structure and acquisition

THE LOCATIVE ALTERNATION IN GERMAN

ITS STRUCTURE AND ACQUISITION

URSULA BRINKMANN

JOHN BENJAMINS PUBLISHING COMPANY
AMSTERDAM/PHILADELPHIA

TM The paper used in this publication meets the minimum requirements of American National Standard for Information Sciences — Permanence of Paper for Printed Library Materials, ANSI Z39.48-1984.

Library of Congress Cataloging-in-Publication Data

Brinkmann, Ursula.
The locative alternation in German : its structure and acquisition / Ursula Brinkmann.
    p.   cm. -- (Language acquisition & language disorders : ISSN 0925-0123; v. 15)
    Includes bibliographical references and index.
  1. German language--Locative constructions. 2. German language--Prepositions. 3. German language--Verb. 4. German language--Case. 5. German language--Morphology. I. Title.
PF3369.B75   1997
435--dc21   97-26692
ISBN 90 272 2481 1 (Eur.) / 1-55619-778-0 (US) (alk. paper)   CIP

John Benjamins Publishing Co. • P.O.Box 75577 • 1070 AN Amsterdam • The Netherlands
John Benjamins North America • P.O.Box 27519 • Philadelphia PA 19118-0519 • USA

"Say me a sweet word"
" ... honey"

Gust
by Herbert Achternbusch

Acknowledgments

This book is based on my doctoral dissertation. The text of a dissertation is but the tip of the iceberg. What is hidden is the work of people who contributed to the thesis, either by their own work on the subject and related topics, or by the direct help they provided the Ph.D.-student. Here I want to name only those who helped me directly.

First of all, I want to thank Melissa Bowerman. She supervised both my M.A.-thesis and my Ph.D.-thesis, and with her patience, persistence, and guidance throughout these years, she taught me a lot about how to manage the strings that are attached to the balloons. I wish to thank her for her ingenuity in providing counterarguments to my claims, and for her insistence on forcing me to improve the structure of the thesis at all levels of its organization. The time and energy that she has invested will save you a lot of energy and time.

For their critical discussions and motivation, I want to thank Ingrid Kaufmann, Dieter Wunderlich, Barbara Stiebels, and Janet Randall, as well as Harald Baayen, Kees de Bot, Bernard Comrie, Sonja Eisenbeiß, Wolfgang Klein, Pim Levelt, Maaike Verrips, and Jürgen Weissenborn. Special thanks to Fp. and Norbert Groeben, for their mental wake-up calls before graduation.

My time at the Max Planck Institute for Psycholinguistics, first during the work on my M.A.-thesis, then as a Ph.D.-student, I thoroughly enjoyed. I owe a lot to the members of the reference project. Their discussions of the properties of spatial and temporal reference often confused me, and I am glad they didn't mind.

Several people were especially helpful when it came to do the experiments. First of all, I am indebted to all those curious and daring children who participated as subjects in my experiments, to their patient teachers and trusting parents, and to Marita Lange, who organized my various field labs. Inge Doehring kept friendly despite numerous revisions of the drawings that I needed, Harald Baayen helped me analyze the data with a statistical method yet unbeknownst to me, and Frauke Hellwig kept up the UNIX connection.

I am especially indebted to Misty Gaitens and Ted Struik, who turned the original version of the thesis into a book, and to Ted C. Struik, the concrete poet.

For keeping up my spirits, I want to thank Renée van Boxsel and Lily Sprangers. My special thanks go to Oscar van Weerdenburg and the Brinkmänner, Willy, Anna, Klaus, Renate *und Anhang*. My parents Anna und Willy often supported my decisions even though they didn't agree, and Oscar has been accompanying me in facing the consequences.

Contents

Chapter 1

Argument Structure Alternations and the No Negative Evidence Problem

On returning to the parking lot after a soccer game to find paint all over his car, a man is likely to be rather absorbed by what happened to his car, and so might exclaim *Vandals sprayed my car with paint!* But if he is an artist who wanted to paint the stadium in the sunset right after the game, he might be more concerned about what happened to his paint and so exclaim *Vandals sprayed my paint on a car!*

This study deals with the knowledge speakers must have in order to use a verb like *spray* in both of the syntactic frames exemplified above, and with how children acquire this knowledge. Verbs that may appear in both these syntactic frames participate in the LOCATIVE ALTERNATION. 'Locative alternation' refers to a change in the argument structure of transitive and intransitive verbs of motion, exemplified in (1a-b), and of transitive verbs of position, shown in (1c) (PFX stands for prefix, PV for preverb, SUBL for sublative, and INSTR for instrumental).[1]

(1) a.   Transitive verbs of motion
     English: The artist smeared paint onto the canvas.
                The artist smeared the canvas with paint.

     German: Der Künstler schmierte Farbe auf die Leinwand.
                the artist smeared paint-ACC onto the canvas-ACC
                'The artist smeared paint onto the canvas'

                Der Künstler beschmierte die Leinwand mit Farbe.
                the artist PFX-smeared the canvas-ACC with paint-DAT
                'The artist smeared the canvas with paint'

---

1. I use the term 'argument structure' to refer to both the semantic properties of a verb's arguments and how the arguments are expressed syntactically. This will be made more precise at the end of this chapter and in Chapter 3.

Hungarian: A müvèsz festèket kent a vàszonra.
             the artist paint-ACC smeared the canvas-SUBL
             'The artist smeared paint onto the canvas'

             A müvèsz bekente a vàsznat festékkel.
             the artist PV-smeared the canvas-ACC paint-INSTR
             'The artist smeared the canvas with paint'

b.   Intransitive verbs of motion
     English: Peter climbed up the mountain.
                 Peter climbed the mountain.

     German: Peter stieg auf den Berg.
                 Peter climbed onto the mountain-ACC
                 'Peter climbed onto the mountain'

                 Peter bestieg den Berg.
                 Peter PFX-climbed the mountain-ACC
                 'Peter climbed the mountain'

     Hungarian: Peter felmàszott a hegyre.
                 Peter PV-climbed the mountain-SUBL
                 'Peter climbed onto the mountain'

                 Peter megmàszta a hegyet.
                 Peter PV-climbed the mountain-ACC
                 'Peter climbed the mountain'

c.   Transitive verbs of position
     English: Phil hung pictures on the wall.
                 Phil hung the wall with pictures.

     German: Phil hängte Bilder an die Wand.
                 Phil hung pictures-ACC on the wall-ACC
                 'Phil hung pictures on the wall'

                 Phil behängte die Wand mit Bildern.
                 Phil PFX-hung the wall-ACC with pictures-DAT
                 'Phil hung the wall with pictures'

     Hungarian: Phil képeket akasztott a falra.
                 Phil picture-PL-ACC hung the wall-SUBL
                 'Phil hung pictures on the wall'

                 Phil beakasztotta a falat kèpek-kel.
                 Phil PV-hung the wall-ACC picture-PL-INSTR
                 'Phil hung the wall with pictures'

I will refer to verbs of motion and position collectively as LOCATIVE VERBS.[2] By combining with spatial prepositions (and/or particles), locative verbs specify a relation between an entity and a spatial region. The entity whose location is at issue is called the THEME. Locative verbs of motion combine with directional prepositions to specify that the theme moves or is moved away from a SOURCE, along a PATH, and/or to a GOAL; locative verbs of position combine with stative prepositions to specify the position (e.g., hanging, standing, lying) of the theme in a particular place. I will refer to all these spatial regions collectively as LOCATION and to the prepositional phrases that specify these regions as LOCATIVE ARGUMENT. The NP specifying the theme is the subject of the intransitive verbs and the direct object of the transitive verbs; the NP in the subject position of the transitive verbs specifies the entity who brings about the motion or position of the theme, usually called the AGENT.

The locative alternation affects the syntactic expression of the location: The location may be expressed either as a prepositional object or as the direct object of the verb. For transitive verbs, this means that the theme, which otherwise appears in direct object position, may optionally be expressed as a *with*-prepositional phrase (or equivalent phrase in other languages). In some languages, the alternation goes paired with a morphological marking on the verb, typically only when the locative argument is in object position. For example, in German and Dutch, the verb is usually prefixed with *be-* when the locative argument is in object position. In a few languages, like Hungarian (cf. (1)), the verb is marked — with different affixes — in both argument structures (Moravsik, 1978).

The locative alternation is one instance of a more general phenomenon — that in most languages, verbs may be used in a variety of syntactic frames. As will be discussed in more detail below, this variety of syntactic frames poses an interesting problem to researchers who want to explain how children determine the possible syntactic frames for a given verb. But let us first get a better idea of the phenomenon at issue by looking at some other cross-linguistically relevant alternations.

In most languages, the majority of transitive verbs may be used in both the active and in the passive voice, as shown in (2):

---

2. My use of the term 'locative verb' includes agentive verbs like *run* and *throw*, nonagentive verbs like intransitive *drop* and *hang*, and causative verbs like transitive *drop* and *hang*. Some locative verbs participate in the locative alternation, and some do not. Chapter 6 provides a discussion of the verbs that do not participate in the alternation.

(2)   Passivization
      English: Tom opened the window.
                    The window was opened by Tom.
      German: Tom öffnete das Fenster.
                    Tom opened the window-ACC
                    'Tom opened the window'

                    Das Fenster wurde von Tom geöffnet.
                    the window-NOM was opened by Tom
                    'The window was opened by Tom'

      Hungarian: Tom kinyitotta az ajtót.
                    Tom PV-opened the window-ACC
                    'Tom opened the window'

                    Az ajtót Tom nyitotta ki.
                    the window-ACC Tom opened PV
                    'The window was opened by Tom'

Many verbs may be used both transitively and intransitively. When used
intransitively, they often specify that the referent of the noun phrase in subject
position (the subject NP) undergoes a change of state. When used transitively,
they additionally indicate that the change was caused: The subject NP now
refers to the agent, while the direct object NP refers to the entity undergoing
the change, usually called the PATIENT. Cf. (3):

(3)   Causativization
      English: The pitcher broke.
                    Tom broke the pitcher.
      German: Der Krug zerbrach.
                    the pitcher PFX-broke
                    'The pitcher broke'

                    Tom zerbrach den Krug.
                    Tom PFX-broke the pitcher-ACC
                    'Tom broke the pitcher'

      Hungarian: A csésze eltörött.
                    the pitcher PV-broke
                    'The pitcher broke'

                    Tom eltörte a csészét.
                    Tom PV-broke the pitcher-ACC
                    'Tom broke the pitcher'

Passivization and causativization have in common that they determine which
of a verb's arguments is expressed as the subject, and both alternations
provide a particular means for speakers to express their attitudes about the

causal factors involved in the situation they want to describe. For example, by using a verb in the passive voice, a speaker can avoid specifying who initiated the action, which may be desirable if she doesn't know who it was or does not want to tell. Causativizing a verb has the opposite function: It allows speakers to introduce an agent in the subject position so as to be explicit about the causing party. Like all changes in argument structure, passivization and causativization may also be used to maintain discourse coherence by allowing speakers to make their utterances interlock with the topic-focus structure of preceding utterances. For example, if a speaker is asked *What did you do with the pitcher I bought yesterday?*, she is more likely to answer *I broke it* than *It broke;* but if asked *What happened to the pitcher I bought yesterday?*, she may as well answer *It broke.*

The DATIVE ALTERNATION has in common with the locative alternation that it affects the syntactic expression of a verb's internal arguments, as shown in (4).

(4) *The Dative Alternation*
    English: Rita brought some apples to Phil.
                Rita brought Phil some apples.

    German: Rita brachte einige Äpfel zu Phil.
                Rita brought some apples$_{acc}$ to Phil$_{dat}$
                'Rita brought some apples to Phil'

                Rita brachte Phil einige Äpfel.
                Rita brought Phil$_{dat}$ some apples$_{acc}$
                'Rita brought Phil some apples'

    Hungarian: Rita né-hà-ny almà-t hoz-ott Phil-nek.
                Rita some apple-ACC brought Phil-DAT
                'Rita brought some apples to Phil'

                Rita Phil-nek hoz-ott néhàny almà-t.
                Rita Phil-DAT brought some apple-ACC
                'Rita brought Phil some apples'

It applies to verbs of transfer that involve an agent, an object of transfer, and a recipient (who is usually animate). The alternation affects the syntactic expression of the NP that specifies the recipient, and in some languages also that of the NP specifying the transferred object. In the prepositional dative construction in English, for example, the NP specifying the transferred object is expressed as the direct object and the recipient NP as a prepositional object, while in the double-object construction, the recipient NP is expressed as direct object, and the NP specifying the transferred object as a secondary object.[3] In German, which distinguishes arguments with different case markings, the NP specifying the object of transfer always receives accusative case, while the recipient NP may either be expressed as the indirect object and be assigned dative case, or be expressed as a prepositional object. The case it receives when it is a prepositional object depends on the preposition: Some prepositions assign dative case, others accusative case.[4] Like the other alternations, the dative alternation allows speakers to tailor their utterances to the topic-focus structure of the discourse. For example, if a speaker is asked *What did Rita bring to Phil?*, he is more likely to respond *She brought him some apples* than *She brought some apples to him*; but if he is asked *To whom did Rita bring these apples?*, he'll probably say *She brought them to Phil* rather than *She brought Phil the apples*.

It seems plausible that, on observing sentences like those in (5), children see a relationship between the two argument structures the verbs appear in:

(5) a. Ted sprayed paint onto the garage.   b. Ted sprayed the garage with paint.
         Kim stuffed the shirts into his   Kim stuffed his suitcase with the
         suitcase.   shirts.
         The farmer sowed seed onto the   The farmer sowed the field with
         field.   seed.

Children learning English might assume that whenever a verb appears in the argument structure in (5a), it may also be used in the argument structure in (5b), and vice versa. Consequently, they might infer that *splash* and *pile* (for example) may take either their theme or their goal as direct object, as these verbs in fact do. But they would also be likely to conclude that *spill, coil,* and *pour*, for instance, alternate as well, and so might produce ungrammatical sentences like those in (6b):

(6) a. Paula spilled coffee over her suit.   b. *Paula spilled her suit with coffee.
         Joe coiled the dog's leash around   *Joe coiled the tree with the dog's
         the tree.   leash.
         Kim poured milk into his glass.   *Kim poured his glass with milk.

---

3. Evidence for the direct object status of the recipient comes from the passivized form of the double object construction – here, the recipient, not the transferred object, becomes the sentential subject; cf. *Phil was given some apples* with **Some apples were given Phil*.

4. Analyses of the acquisition of case-marking in German are provided by Mills (1985), Clahsen (1984), Tracy (1986), Eisenbeiß (1994), and Eisenbeiß and Penke (1996).

While *spill, coil,* and *pour* seem similar to *splash* and *pile* in that they specify that an object is caused to change location, they differ from them in that they may take as direct object only their theme and not their goal. In other words, there are restrictions on which verbs can participate in the locative alternation. The same is true for the passive, the causative, and the dative alternation, as is shown in (7-9).

(7) a. Phil resembles Paul.   b. *Paul is resembled by Phil.
         A kilo of lemons costs a dollar.   *A dollar is cost by a kilo of
                                             lemons.

(8) a. The dog climbed onto the hill.   b. *Bo climbed the dog onto the hill.
         The pen fell onto the floor.   *John fell the pen onto the floor.

(9) a. Sue pushed the car to Laurie.   b. *Sue pushed Laurie the car.
         David donated $1000 to Greenpeace. *David donated Greenpeace
                                              $1000.

How can children determine that the sentences in (6b-9b) are ungrammatical? A seemingly plausible answer might be that if children use a verb in the wrong syntactic frame, they will be corrected by adult speakers. But research indicates that children acquire language with little or no evidence about whether their utterances are grammatical. If this is correct, then the acquisition of argument structure alternations poses a learnability problem: If children acquire, for example, a rule according to which *strew* may take either its theme or its goal as direct object but that encompasses *spill* as well, how can they determine, without being corrected by adult speakers, that the rule does not apply to *spill*? Having to account for how children determine, without corrective feedback, constraints on a productive rule has become known as the NO NEGATIVE EVIDENCE PROBLEM.

The No Negative Evidence Problem

If children were corrected when producing ungrammatical utterances, they would have evidence — NEGATIVE EVIDENCE — that these utterances are not a part of the target language. The absence of negative evidence was first reported in a by-now classic study by Brown and Hanlon (1970; see also Bowerman, 1988, and Pinker, 1989, for reviews of the literature on the No Negative Evidence problem). Brown and Hanlon were interested in whether a necessary requirement of the then-still-current behavioristic theory of language acquisition was met: that children receive positive reinforcement ('reward') for their grammatical utterances and negative reinforcement ('punishment') for their ungrammatical ones. Such a feedback pattern was essential for the behavioristic claim that language acquisition results from the selection and shaping of the child's verbal output by appropriate reinforcement from outside. But Brown and Hanlon found that whether the parents of their subjects Adam, Eve, and Sarah approved ('rewarded') or disapproved ('punished') the child's utterance depended not on its grammaticality but rather on its truth. For example, Eve's mother responded positively to Eve's ill-formed "Mama isn't boy, he a girl" by saying "That's right". And Sarah's mother corrected Sarah's grammatically perfect "There's the animal farmhouse" because what Sarah was referring to was a lighthouse. No significant relationship was found between children's grammatical errors and parental correction, suggesting that parental reinforcement does not determine which constructions the child will continue to use and which ones she will eventually give up.

Braine (1971) also argued that negative feedback cannot guide children to an adult grammar. First, he pointed out, children seem universally to acquire language fairly rapidly beginning at around 18 months or earlier, even though cultural conditions and child-rearing practices differ widely. Second, in order to correct their children, parents would have to know how to explain to them what exactly is wrong with their utterances, and this may often be difficult. Third, even if children were corrected, they would have to be able to *use* this information, and Braine described several tutorial exchanges with children that suggest that they often cannot.

Braine used the lack of negative feedback to challenge the hypothesis-testing model assumed by researchers working within the framework of Transformational Generative Grammar (Chomsky, 1962, 1965). In this framework, it was assumed that the child develops and tests hypotheses about the rule-system underlying her target language on the basis of both her innate linguistic knowledge and the actual language data she encounters. When several hypotheses are consistent with the data, she compares them and selects the optimal hypothesis.[5] Braine showed that the hypothesis-testing

---

5. In more recent versions of Generative Grammar (Chomsky, 1981, 1986a,b, 1995), hypothesis-testing has been replaced by PARAMETER-SETTING (see Hyams, 1986; Wexler & Manzini, 1987; and Nishigauchi & Roeper, 1987, among others, for accounts of language acquisition in terms of parameter-setting; see also Section 2.4.).

model of Transformational Generative Grammar is problematic because it cannot account for how children reject a hypothesis that posits the existence of an OVERINCLUSIVE RULE. Overinclusive rules are rules that generate all the good sentences of the grammar but also generate ungrammatical sentences. (One example of an overinclusive rule has already been discussed above, i.e., a rule for changing the argument structure of locative verbs that generates sentences like *Paula spilled her suit with coffee*). Braine showed that in order to correct such overinclusive rules, children would need evidence about which of their sentences are not a part of the adult grammar. But since adults do not seem to correct their children, argues Braine, theories of language acquisition must be formulated in such a way that they do not rely on hypothesis-testing for explaining how the child restricts an overinclusive rule.

Baker (1979) was the first to point out that the acquisition of argument structure alternations poses a learnability problem (the more general learnability problem posed by language acquisition was first discussed by Gold, 1967), and he argued that the absence of negative evidence discredited the account of argument structure alternations that had been developed within Transformational Grammar (see Chapter 2). According to this account, children acquire productive rules for changing the argument structure of verbs, but, as Baker showed, the rules proposed were overinclusive in that they did not allow speakers to distinguish between verbs that actually do participate in an alternation and those that do not. Thus, the transformational rules posited to account for the acquisition of argument structure alternations could not be correct, given Braine's arguments — and Brown and Hanlon's empirical findings — that children must acquire language without the help of negative evidence.

Researchers have since then responded to the claim that children must acquire language without the help of negative evidence in two ways. Some researchers have tried to show how language can be acquired solely on the basis of POSITIVE EVIDENCE (evidence about which sentences are part of the language) (see, for example, Braine, 1971; Chomsky & Lasnik, 1977; Baker, 1979; Wexler & Culicover, 1980; Bowerman, 1983, 1987, 1988; Mazurkewich & White, 1984; Pinker, 1984, 1989; Berwick, 1985; Fodor & Crain, 1987). Others have argued that children do receive negative evidence after all: Even though parents may not provide *explicit* negative evidence, they often provide *implicit* negative evidence, in that they respond differently to ungrammatical utterances than to grammatical utterances. For example, parents seem to repeat children's grammatical utterances more often than ungrammatical ones (Hirsh-Pasek, Treiman, & Schneiderman, 1984), and they are more likely to expand an utterance (repeat it with small changes) when it is ungrammatical than when it is grammatical (Demetras, Post, & Snow, 1986; Penner, 1987; Bohannon & Stanowicz, 1988; Morgan & Travis, 1989).

But it seems doubtful that implicit negative evidence is sufficient for children to determine whether the generalizations they have made are correct. According to a recent analysis by Marcus (1993), implicit negative evidence is both too weak and too inconsistent. It is too weak because each parental response type, e.g., expansions, follows grammatical as well as ungrammatical utterances. Since the child cannot be sure that an expansion indeed indicates that her utterance was ungrammatical, she would have to produce the same utterance numerous times to see whether it is systematically followed by a similar response. Implicit feedback is too inconsistent because it is not provided by all parents or for all types of errors, and because it declines or even disappears with age, even though errors are still being made.

Theoretical and empirical arguments like these show that children indeed have to acquire language without negative evidence, whether explicit or implicit. This means that whenever we assume, for the particular part of the target language we are interested in, that children acquire a productive rule that has exceptions, we must either make sure that the rules we postulate are not overinclusive or show how children can cut back on their overinclusive rules. And since the problem of overinclusive rules arises whenever a rule can be applied to some but not all candidate lexical items, any approach to the acquisition of argument structure alternations that posits the acquisition of rules must take into account that children do not receive sufficient negative evidence to determine what the exceptions to an alternation are. Several solutions to how children acquire argument structure changes in the absence of negative evidence have been developed. Some of these approaches will be presented in the next chapter. The common goal of all these approaches is to determine what kind of knowledge underlies argument structure pairs such as those discussed earlier, such that this knowledge can be acquired without the help of negative evidence.

Motivation and Goals of this Study

I will attempt to contribute to this ongoing discussion by providing theoretical and empirical evidence about the acquisition of *be*-prefixation for locative verbs in German. The analysis of the locative alternation that I will present is motivated by the assumption that the alternation must be learnable without negative evidence.

The acquisition of the locative alternation in German is interesting for several reasons. First, *be*-prefixation — the means to bring this change in argument structure about — is both productive and constrained. Evidence that it is still productive (for both locative and nonlocative verbs) is given in (10).

(10) a. *Bereiten* der Wege verboten! '*Be*-riding the paths prohibited!'
(Prohibition sign in a park. Ralf Meyer, personal communication)

   b. Das Gelände wird *bestreift*. 'The area is being *be*-patrolled.'
   (Text from a handbook for frontier guards. Heike Behrens, personal communication)

   c. A zoo keeper, explaining the care that some animals require:
   "... die müssen dann ein bißchen *bekuschelt* werden."
   '... these ones then must be *be*-snuggled a little.'[6]
   (Rosemary Tracy, personal communication)

   d. ... und Rekonstruktionen archaischer Musik ähneln ganz merkwürdig den Sphärenklängen, mit denen sich die New-Age-Jüngerinnen nachmittags zu *bedudeln* pflegen.
   '... and reconstructions of archaic music resemble quite strangely those spherical sounds that the New Age apostles use to play to each other in the afternoon.'
   (lit.: '... with which the New Age apostles *be*-play each other')
   (Eva Demski: So leicht, einander zu erkennen. In: *art 12*, 1992, p. 65.)

   e. Die Runkeleien wurden das **comic to end all comics**: filigran gezeichnet, deliziös koloriert und literarisch *betextet*.
   'The Runkel stories became the **comic to end all comics**: filigree drawings, deliciously colored, and literarily *be*-texted.' (*Runkeleien* 'Runkel stories': Comic strips on the adventures of the knight Heino Runkel of Rübenstein; in 'Digedagse und Abrafaxe', ZEITmagazin 8, 1994, p. 9.)

Since the locative alternation *is* productive, we can assume that when children learn that locative verbs may express their locative argument either as an oblique or as a direct object, they learn something that goes beyond the

---

6. In contrast to English 'snuggle', *kuscheln* may take an oblique object, as in *Die Kätzchen kuschelten sich an ihre Mutter* 'The kitties snuggled themselves at/to their mother'.

memorization of individual lexical items. The productivity of the locative alternation in German gives rise, then, to the first question that I will try to answer in this study: How do children learn about *be*-prefixation and its effects on the argument structure of locative verbs?

The locative alternation in German is not only productive but, just as in English, it is also constrained. Some examples of verbs that may not participate in the locative alternation are given in (11):[7]

(11) schleudern 'fling'   –   *beschleudern '*be*-fling'
      schleppen 'drag'   –   *beschleppen '*be*-drag'
      stopfen 'stuff'   –   *bestopfen '*be*-stopfen'
      schieben 'push'   –   *beschieben '*be*-push'
      senken 'lower'   –   *besenken '*be*-lower'

If the locative alternation were not constrained, its acquisition would not pose a learnability problem: Each locative verb that takes its theme as direct object could then also take its goal as direct object, and the child would not need to discover any constraints. But since the alternation *is* constrained, it raises the question how children determine that verbs like *laden* 'load' may take either their theme or their goal as direct object, but that verbs like *schleppen* 'drag' and *schleudern* 'fling' take only their theme as direct object. More generally, how do they determine the constraints on the locative alternation? To answer this question will be the second goal of this study.

Since the locative alternation in German is both productive and constrained, it has all the necessary ingredients to make its acquisition a learnability problem. But it is intriguing for yet another reason — it involves the morphological marking of the verb. In the literature, several proposals have been advanced about how morphologically marked alternations in argument

---

7. The classification of these *be*-verbs as ungrammatical is mainly based on my own intuitions. To see whether others agreed with my judgments, I informally asked several other native speakers of German to evaluate the verbs; they generally agreed. I also conducted a pilot study with 10 adult native speakers of German, the results of which also support my intuition about which verbs do and do not alternate. The subjects of the pilot study were asked to evaluate the acceptability of sentences that contained either grammatical *be*-verbs like *beladen* '*be*-load' or *be*-verbs that I had classified as ungrammatical, for example, *beschleudern* '*be*-fling'. Both types of *be*-verbs have an unprefixed counterpart in which the theme is the direct object of the verb and the goal is expressed in a prepositional phrase. The sentences could be judged as *in Ordnung* 'okay', *etwas komisch* 'a bit strange', *sehr komisch* 'very strange', or *ganz schlecht* 'very bad'. In general, subjects agreed with my classification, judging sentences that contained verbs like *beladen* to be *okay* or *a bit strange*, while judging sentences that contained verbs like *beschleudern* to be *very strange* or *very bad*.

structure differ from unmarked ones, and how alternations of the two kinds are acquired (Marantz, 1984; Lebeaux, 1988; Pinker, 1989). Marantz (1984), for example, proposes that morphologically unmarked alternations are semantically constrained, while marked alternations are not. Pinker (1989), in contrast, assumes that both types of alternation are semantically constrained — in similar ways across languages — but that unmarked alternations have additional and often language-specific constraints. Up to now, researchers studying the acquisition of the locative alternation have focussed mainly on English, in which the alternation is unmarked (Pinker, 1989; Gropen, 1989; Gropen, Pinker, Hollander, & Goldberg, 1991a,b). An important goal of the present study will be to determine whether the claims they make about the acquisition of the locative alternation also hold for the alternation in German.

To summarize, I will propose a linguistic analysis of the locative alternation in German that can account for how children acquire the alternation and determine its constraints without evidence about whether they use a verb correctly. In particular, I will test whether the language-independent claims that have been developed on the basis of the unmarked locative alternation in English can account for the marked alternation in German.

The chapters are organized as follows. Chapter 2 starts by summarizing Baker's arguments against the transformational account of argument structure alternations and briefly presents his own solution to the problem, according to which children do not develop productive rules for the alternations. It then summarizes the evidence that children do develop productive rules, and presents and discusses four recent approaches to the acquisition of argument structure alternations that try to account for this: *Discovery Procedures* (Braine, 1971, 1988; Braine, Brody, Fisch, Weisberger, & Blum, 1990; Braine & Brooks, 1995), the *Criteria Approach* (Mazurkewich & White, 1984, and Pinker, 1984), the *Catapult Hypothesis* (Randall, 1987, 1990, 1992), and the *Lexicosemantic Structure Theory* (Pinker, 1989; Gropen, 1989; Gropen et al., 1991a,b) (my term).

Chapter 3 first provides some general information about *be*-prefixation in German, and then presents the linguistic analysis of the locative alternation (Wunderlich, 1987, 1992; Brinkmann & Wunderlich, 1996) that is the basis for the claims on which I build in the subsequent chapters.

In Chapter 4, I propose the NONINDIVIDUATION HYPOTHESIS. The Nonindividuation Hypothesis states that the direct object of a transitive locative verb may be omitted only when the quantificational properties of the corresponding argument are irrelevant. That is, it must be irrelevant how many objects or how much stuff changes location. This means that when the theme argument is not specified, the verb must allow speakers to interpret it as nonindividuated (as an unbounded or uncountable amount of stuff or objects). Speakers can then simply presuppose the existence of a suitable entity, i.e., the argument may be existentially bound. The theme then does not need to be expressed syntactically, which in turn allows speakers to interpret the (new) object NP as the goal once the preposition has been incorporated.

The quantificational properties of the theme can be taken to be irrelevant only if it is an INCREMENTAL THEME (Krifka, 1989a,b; Dowty, 1991). An incremental theme is an argument that is gradually involved in the event specified by the verb. An incremental theme allows the inference 'the longer, the more', i.e., the longer the action lasts, the more objects or stuff will be involved in the action. An incremental theme is therefore a major determinant of the temporal properties of the event: When the theme NP is individuated the sentence is interpreted as a temporally bounded event, and when it is nonindividuated the sentence is interpreted as a temporally unbounded process. Since the quantificational properties of the theme and the temporal properties of the event specified by the verb are interdependent, an incremental theme can be conceived of as nonindividuated when the verb is turned into a process predicate.

The Nonindividuation Hypothesis is a proposal about both the adult grammar and the acquisition of the alternation. With respect to acquisition, it predicts that a major difficulty in acquiring the alternation is learning how to *deindividuate* the theme of transitive locative verbs. No deindividuation is needed for what I will call MASS VERBS. Mass verbs are verbs of motion that — because they denote the motion of substances, e.g., *smear* and *spritzen* 'spray' — do not require the theme to be individuated in the first place. But deindividuation is needed for what I will call COUNT VERBS, i.e., verbs that are not subcategorized for substances, for example, *load* and *werfen* 'throw'. Since no deindividuation is needed for mass verbs like *smear*, the Nonindividuation Hypothesis predicts that children acquire the goal-object form earlier for these verbs than for count verbs like *load*. The claim that the goal-object form is acquired first for mass verbs was tested in two experiments, an elicited production experiment, presented in Chapter 5, and a comprehension experiment, presented in Chapter 7.

Some locative verbs in German do not alternate, or are at most marginally acceptable under *be*-prefixation. In Chapter 6, I offer an account of why the syntactic changes brought about by *be*-prefixation are impossible or only marginally acceptable for these verbs, and of how children can determine that the verbs are so restricted. I propose that the various reasons why a verb may show such a restriction can best be understood as a failure to meet one (or more) necessary conditions that are relevant to deriving the goal-object argument structure. My analysis of these verbs predicts that the verbs should differ in how easily they can be mistaken for alternating verbs. Testing this prediction for two classes of these verbs was the second goal of the comprehension experiment discussed in Chapter 7.

Chapter 8 summarizes the main claims and findings of the thesis and discusses their implications for future research.

Terminology

In the preceding sections, I have already introduced several notions that will be relevant for the discussions to come. In particular, I have used terms like *agent*, *theme*, and *goal* to refer to the various roles that a verb's arguments may play in sentences referring to typical situations of motion and transfer. These notions, which are also called the THEMATIC ROLES of a verb, have figured prominently in many theories of argument structure (cf. Gruber, 1965; Jackendoff, 1972, 1987; Keenan, 1976; Wunderlich, 1985; Kiparsky, 1989, 1992; Wilkins, 1988; Grimshaw, 1990, among others).

Theories of thematic roles differ in both the kinds of roles they postulate and in whether and how these roles determine the syntactic expression of a verb's arguments. In line with much recent theorizing (e.g., Levin & Rappaport, 1988, 1992; Jackendoff, 1990; Dowty, 1991; Wunderlich, 1992), I assume that thematic roles are convenient labels for characterizing the semantic properties of arguments that have particular positions with respect to the (sublexical) predicates that compose the meaning of a verb. For example, an *agent* may be characterized as the first argument of the predicate CAUSE, and a *theme* as the argument of the predicate MOVE. This view of thematic roles emphasizes the nature of the sublexical predicates that are hypothesized to compose the meanings of verbs (and of lexical predicates in general). One of its goals is to identify both a limited set of abstract and possibly cross-linguistically relevant predicates that determine the semantic and syntactic properties of verbs and a set of more specific predicates that represent the particular semantic contribution of individual verbs. Some candidate predicates of the two types will be discussed in more detail in the course of this thesis; for now, it is enough to point out that when I speak of agents, themes, and goals, I refer to arguments that have a particular position with respect to the sublexical predicates that compose the meaning of a verb. While this thesis is mainly concerned with the argument structure of verbs, in Chapter 3, the argument structure of prepositions will also become important.

This chapter should not end without some explication of the term 'argument structure' itself. The use of this term is often confusing, since it means different things in different theoretical frameworks. For example, Haegeman (1991) considers 'argument structure' to refer to just the *number* of arguments of a given verb. In contrast, Pinker (1989) treats it as 'a strictly syntactic entity, namely the information that specifies *how* a verb's arguments are encoded in the syntax' (Pinker, 1989, p. 71; emphasis added). In the framework I will adopt (Bierwisch, 1983, 1988; Bierwisch & Lang, 1989; Wunderlich, 1992, 1997), 'argument structure' refers to a complex set of information that is organized in terms of three different levels of structure, ranging from what is called the predicate-argument structure of a verb to the purely syntactic specifications of a verb's arguments (see Chapter 3). With these caveats in mind about the different definitions of 'argument structure', let us now turn to the proposals that have been put forward for solving the No Negative Evidence problem.

Chapter 2

Theories of the Acquisition of Argument Structure Alternations

When Baker (1979) brought the No Negative Evidence problem to the general attention of researchers studying language acquisition, the problem seemed to consist of only two components: the existence of grammatical patterns that have exceptions, and the lack of evidence available to the child about what these exceptions are. Baker's (1979) proposed solution to the No Negative Evidence problem, which will be presented and discussed in 2.1, did not yet recognize a third component: that children acquire productive means for assigning argument structures to verbs. The four other proposed solutions that are discussed in this chapter do take children's productivity into account.

2.1 The Conservative Learner

2.1.1 *Optional versus Obligatory Rules*

Baker (1979) realized that Braine's critique of Chomsky's hypothesis-testing model posed a serious challenge to the then-still-current transformational account of argument structure alternations, because it seemed that exceptions to the transformational rules the child was assumed to acquire could not be identified without negative evidence. In Transformational Grammar, argument structure alternations were accounted for by optional transformational rules. For example, the locative alternation would have been formulated roughly as follows (Hall, 1965):

(1) Paul sprays insecticide onto the roses.
     X   V   NP   *to*   NP
     1   2   3   4   5

(2)   1, 2, 3, 4, 5   >   1, 2, 5, 6, 3 / 6 = *with*

The rule in (2) transforms the sentence in (1) into *Paul sprays the roses with insecticide*; likewise, it transforms *Paul loads the boxes onto the wagon* into *Paul loads the wagon with the boxes.* Rules like those in (2) are called optional transformations because one may or may not apply them to obtain a grammatical sentence: Both *Paul loads the boxes onto the wagon* and *Paul loads the wagon with boxes* are perfectly acceptable.

The application of OBLIGATORY transformational rules, unlike that of optional rules, is prompted by specific elements in the sentence. An example of such a rule is subject-auxiliary inversion in English, which is triggered by an interrogative phrase like *why*, as illustrated in (3). When such a phrase is present, the subject must follow the auxiliary (Baker, 1979, p. 546):

(3)   a.   Why is he still here?   b.   *Why he is still here?

Both obligatory and optional transformational rules may have exceptions, but, as Baker showed, only exceptions to optional transformations pose a learning problem. An example of an exception to the subject-auxiliary inversion rule is the interrogative phrase *how come*, which does not trigger the inversion. Cf. (4) (taken from Baker, 1979, p. 545):

(4)   a.   *How come is he still here?   b.   How come he's still here?

Baker called exceptions to obligatory rules benign on grounds that children can identify them through positive evidence, i.e., sentences they actually hear. They can determine the exceptional status of *how come*, for example, by noticing that it differs from all the other interrogative phrases, which *force* the speaker to invert the order of subject and auxiliary. If the other phrases could appear with either the inverted or the uninverted word order, then the learner would not know whether *how come* was truly exceptional: Perhaps she simply had not yet happened to come across *how come* plus the inverted order. But since in all other interrogative sentences subjects follow auxiliaries, the learner is able to tell that the order in a question like *how come he's still here?* is exceptional.

The situation is different for exceptions to optional transformational rules. Some examples have already been discussed in Chapter 1: These were the verbs that do not participate in an argument structure alternation even though they seem similar to verbs that do. For example, if the rule in (2) were applied to the locative verbs *spill, coil,* and *pour,* it would yield ungrammatical outcomes:

(5)   *Paula spilled her suit with coffee.
      *Ted coiled the tree with the dog's leash.
      *Kim poured his glass with water.

Baker termed exceptions to optional transformational rules embarrassing. The transformational rule that changes the argument structure of alternating verbs does not have to be applied — nothing in the sentence indicates that one construction or the other should be used. The fact that the learner has not observed verbs like *spill* in the goal-object construction does not imply that *spill* may not appear in that form. Hence, she cannot determine whether *spill* is an exception.

Drawing on Brown and Hanlon's (1970) and Braine's (1971) studies, Baker argued that if learners extracted rules like those in (2) and used exceptional verbs in the wrong argument structure, adult speakers would not provide them with corrective feedback. Children would therefore have no way of knowing that the rule does not apply to *spill* and *pour,* and so, as adults, they should still accept sentences like *Paula spilled her suit with coffee* and *Kim poured his glass with water.* But since adult speakers judge these sentences ungrammatical, argued Baker, they must never have formulated the rule in the first place. Baker's solution to the problem of embarrassing exceptions was, then, to claim that the learner does not form rules for optional argument structure changes at all.

As an alternative learning procedure, Baker proposed that children carefully register the syntactic frames they have actually heard verbs appear in, as exemplified in (6). That is, instead of developing an optional rule for transforming one syntactic structure into another, they learn the possible syntactic frames for each verb one by one. This means that they learn the possible syntactic frames of a verb as part of the verb's lexical properties, i.e., they learn the possible PHRASE STRUCTURES in which a verb may appear.

(6)   spray: (___NP into/onto NP), (___NP NP)
      load: (___NP into/onto NP), (___NP NP)
      pour: (___NP into NP)
      lift: (___NP onto NP)

Importantly, children will not use what they know about the phrase structures of one verb to predict possible phrase structures for other verbs: They will include a given phrase structure in a verb's entry in their mental lexicon only if they have actually observed the verb with that phrase structure in the input. In consequence, they will not assign verbs a wrong phrase structure and so will not need negative evidence to arrive at the adult grammar. Note that Baker did not assume that learners would not formulate *any* productive rules; he proposed the conservative learning strategy only to obviate the need to postulate *optional* transformational rules.

2.1.2 *Overgeneralizations as Evidence against Baker's Account*

If children adhered strictly to the phrase structures observed in the input, they should not make any errors: Their inventory of phrase structures for a particular verb should always match that of adults. But Baker's proposed solution to the No Negative Evidence problem turned out to be untenable as it became increasingly clear that children do use verbs in phrase structures they are unlikely to have heard in the input.

Evidence for children's productive knowledge of argument structure alternations comes from two sources: errors recorded in diaries of children's spontaneous speech (Bowerman, 1974, 1982a,b, 1983, 1987; Lord, 1979; Mazurkewich & White, 1984; Gropen, Pinker, Hollander, Goldberg, & Wilson, 1989; Pinker, 1989), and experimental studies designed to test this knowledge (Mazurkewich & White, 1984; Hochberg, 1986; Maratsos, Gudeman, Gerard-Ngo, & DeHart, 1987; Pinker, Lebeaux, & Frost, 1987; Gropen, 1989; Gropen et al., 1991a,b; Braine et al., 1990; Naigles, Fowler, & Helm, 1992; Naigles, Gleitman, & Gleitman, 1992). The diary records show that children use existing verbs in argument structures that adults consider ungrammatical, and also that they are able to assign argument structures to novel verbs they have coined (by, for example, deriving them from nouns). The most extensive analyses of children's errors have been published by Bowerman (1974, 1982a,b, 1983, 1987), based on diary records of her two English-speaking daughters, Christy (C) and Eva (E), and comparable examples from other children. Examples of such errors, together with novel coinages and examples collected by other authors, are listed in (7-10).

(7)   Causative
a.   E   3;2   *Will you **climb** me up there and hold me?* (Wants mother to help her climb a pole.)
b.   E   3;7   *I'm gonna put the washrag in and **disappear** something under the washrag.* (Playing in tub with small toys and a container into which

she puts washrag.)

c. C   4;3   *It always **sweats** me.* (Refusing sweater.)

(8) Passive

a. C   3;6   *Until I'm four I don't have to be **gone**.* (=be taken to the dentist.)

b. C   3;6   *If you don't put them in for a very long time they won't get **staled**.*
(Reference to crackers in a bread box.)

c. C   4;3   *Why is the laundry place **stayed** open all night?* (=kept)

d. C   5;6   *I don't want to be **dogeared** today.* (Asking for her hair not to be
arranged in dogears.)

e. C   8;9   *A child wanted her doll to be **mummied**.* (=made into a mummy;
mummified.)

f. H   4;+   *He's gonna die you, David.* (Turns to mother.) *The tiger will come and
eat David and then he will be **died** and I won't have a brother any
more.*

(The examples in (8a-c,f) are passives of novel causatives; those in (8d-e) are
passives of novel denominal verbs)

(9) Dative Alternation

a. C   2;6   *Don't **say** me that or you'll make me cry.*

b. C   3;1   *I **said her** no.*

c. M   5+   ***Choose me** the ones that I can have.*

d. -   6;0   *Mommy, **open Hadwen** the door.*

(10) Locative Alternation

a. E   4;5   *I'm gonna **cover** a screen over me.*

b. E   5;0   *Can I **fill** some salt into the bear* (the bear = a bear-shaped salt shaker.)

c. E   2;11   (Waving empty container near mother.)

E: *Pour, pour, pour. Mommy, I **poured** you.*

M: *You poured me?*

E: *Yeah, with water.*

d. E   4;11   (Mother asks if E is going to finish toast.)
*I don't want it because I **spilled** it of orange juice.*

e. C   6;5   (Telling of TV episode.)

C: *Once the Partridge Family got **stolen**.*

M: *The whole family?*

C: *No, all their stuff.*

f. HS 2;+   *Besuppt.* (=souped (German). Referring to a spoon that has gotten soup
on it.)

(The children's age is given in years;months. Example (9d) is from Mazurkewich and
White, 1984; the examples of dative alternation and passives were first published in
Bowerman, 1983, the causatives in Bowerman, 1982a,b, 1983, and the locatives in
Bowerman, 1982b. Example (10f), produced by Hilde Stern, is taken from the diary records
of Stern and Stern, 1907/1928.)

Experimental evidence for productive knowledge of argument structure alternations comes from children's elicited production data and acceptability judgments (Mazurkewich & White, 1984; Hochberg, 1986; Naigles et al., 1992a,b). Elicited production studies, for example, have shown that children have productive knowledge of the passive (Pinker et al., 1987), the causative (Maratsos et al., 1987; Braine et al., 1990; Naigles et al., 1992a,b), the dative (Gropen et al., 1989), and the locative alternation (Gropen et al., 1991a,b). In one of these studies, Gropen et al. (1989) tested whether children would use novel verbs of transfer in the double object construction. The verbs, presented in a syntactically neutral form (e.g., *this is keating*), referred to novel actions in which various objects were transferred to either the child, a toy animal, or an inanimate object (the different recipients served to test whether children were sensitive to the requirement that the recipient in the double object form must be animate). The subjects were asked questions specifically designed to elicit double object constructions (e.g., *What am I keating to you?*). Children produced these constructions in about half the cases when they themselves were the recipients and in more than a third of the cases when the inanimate object or the toy animal were the recipients. Their willingness to use the double object construction with novel verbs can only be explained if we assume that they had acquired productive knowledge of the dative alternation (but not yet completely the animacy constraint), and were not just relying on the specific phrase structures they had heard verbs used in.

In sum, diary records and experimental studies provide evidence that children develop productive techniques for generating grammatical and often ungrammatical argument structures, and do not merely register the phrase structures observed with verbs in the input, as Baker had proposed. We now turn to theories that provide differing accounts of the nature of these techniques, and of how children determine restrictions on argument structure.

2.2 Discovery Procedures

2.2.1 *Identifying Patterns in the Input*

Braine (1971, 1988; Braine et al., 1990) has proposed that children determine the possible argument structures of a verb by acquiring verb-specific syntactic frames that come to stand before general syntactic frames.[1] His model predicts that overgeneralizations will occur in the *initial* phases of verb learning, when the child has acquired only very general means for generating sentences. Learning consists of acquiring more and more verb-specific syntactic frames; these come to take precedence over the earlier-learned general frames and so bring overgeneralization to a halt.

The key elements in Braine's account of verb learning are memory and its interaction with an input processor. The memory consists of several intermediate memory stores and a permanent store. The stores accumulate properties of the language input as analyzed by the input processor, which itself consists of a comprehension mechanism and a scanner (or parser in more recent terminology). The comprehension mechanism assigns utterances a predicate-argument structure and an illocutionary force, while the scanner has access to any categories and relations that are already stored in the permanent store. The scanner uses these categories and relations to classify the predicates and arguments provided by the comprehension mechanism in terms of categories like *action, possession, actor,* and *location.*

Memory and input processor develop together: The scanner observes patterns in the input and transfers them to the intermediate stores; once stored, the patterns help the scanner to analyze new data. The more often a pattern is observed, the more quickly its properties will travel along the various intermediate stores to reach the permanent store. When the scanner has learned the properties of a given pattern, it can start to analyse additional properties of the input.

General properties will reach the permanent store first because the more general a given pattern is, the more often instances of it will be displayed in the input and so be observed by the scanner. Assume, for example, that a child has already learned that some verbs may take the verbal complement [VP NP] or [*to* VP NP], as is shown in (11) for *help*:

(11) a. Ted helped her edit the text.   b. Ted helped her to edit the text.

---

1. Braine (1971) speaks of the acquisition of both 'rules' and 'property patterns'. In contrast, Braine et al. (1990) argue that children do not acquire rules for argument structure alternations, but rather CANONICAL SENTENCE SCHEMAS (e.g., agent-action-object) that allow them to assign argument structures to verbs by default (cf. below). Since Braine (1971) does not use the term 'argument structure' and Braine et al. do not use the term 'rule', I will use, when presenting Braine's general claims, the neutral terms 'syntactic frame' instead of 'argument structure' and 'means for generating sentences' instead of 'rule'.

Some verbs take both forms of complement, others only the [VP NP] complement (for example, *make* and *let*), and still others only the [to VP NP]
complement (for example, *permit* and *compel*). According to Braine (1971),
the child will first acquire a rule according to which complements may have
either form because the scanner is not yet able to distinguish the verbs that
take only one or the other form of complement. Once the general rule is
stored, the scanner can go on to analyze the particular complements that may
follow the verbs *make* and *let*, and *permit* and *compel* in more detail. These
verb-specific complement patterns will be stored and finally prevail over the
more general rule. Thus, when the child has learned that *make* takes the [VP
NP] complement, she will no longer apply the general rule.

The order in which specific and general means for generating sentences
are applied is decisive for avoiding a permanently overinclusive grammar
(i.e., one that produces grammatical as well as ungrammatical sentences).
While the child's grammar might be overinclusive initially, repeated exposure to positive evidence (grammatical forms) will lead to the registration of
more and more specific syntactic frames; finally, only the correct, verb-
specific information will determine the possible syntactic frames for a verb.

Braine (1988; Braine et al., 1990) has applied the theory of discovery
procedures to the acquisition of verb argument structure, proposing that
children first assign a DEFAULT ARGUMENT STRUCTURE to novel verbs and to
verbs for which they have not yet acquired sufficiently specific argument
structures. When first learning a verb — for example, *fall* — the child may
often fail to register the surface structure positions of the verb's arguments
and so may simply assign the verb a default argument structure on the basis of
CANONICAL SENTENCE SCHEMAS. For example, if the child applies the canonical
sentence schema AGENT-ACTION-PATIENT to *fall,* she will treat it as a transitive
verb (e.g., *He fell it down*), similar to the verb *drop*. Only after repeated
exposure to uses of *fall* in adult speech will she notice that *fall* may be used
only intransitively. An argument structure may be assigned by default when
the meaning of the new verb is taken to fit one of the canonical sentence
schemas the child already knows. Importantly, a child who assigns a default
argument structure to a verb on a particular occasion does not actually register
that structure as part of the verb's lexical entry.

Braine and his colleagues have provided empirical support for the claim
that children invoke default argument structures for verbs whose argument
structure they do not know (Braine et al., 1990). The default argument

structures they tested were the typical transitive sentence schema mentioned above, i.e., *agent-action-patient*, and the intransitive schema *thing-action*. The subjects (2- and 4-year old children and adults) were shown several actions. About half of these were described by the experimenters using existing English verbs — two intransitive (e.g., *fall*), two transitive (e.g., *throw*), and three both intransitive and transitive (e.g., *roll*). The remaining actions were described by novel verbs. One verb of each type was modelled by the experimenter in a neutral sentential context, for example, *this is kazing*. For the fixed intransitive and transitive verbs, the other verb was used according to its grammatical argument structure, and for the optionally transitive and novel verbs, one of the two remaining verbs was used intransitively and the other transitively. Each action-verb pair was followed by various probes (e.g., "What am I doing to the cow?") that focussed on the agent or the patient, or neither.

Subjects of all ages used the novel verbs spontaneously both transitively and intransitively, without having heard them in these frames. When the verbs were presented in a specific argument structure, subjects used them in the contrasting argument structure if the probe invited them to do so. For example, when the probe focussed on the agent for a novel verb that had been presented as an intransitive, subjects often used the verb transitively, and when it focussed on the patient of a novel verb that had been presented as a transitive, they often used the verb intransitively. The children differed from the adults in how they used the existing verbs of fixed transitivity. While the adults generally stuck to the only argument structure possible for these verbs, the children often used the ungrammatical argument structure when the probe encouraged them to do so. Thus, the adults seemed to have acquired specific argument structures for the existing verbs and so were no longer willing to resort to a default argument structure, but the children still assigned default argument structures. Since neither adults nor children had acquired any specific argument structures for the novel verbs, both groups of subjects were willing to assign them a default argument structure, as predicted by the theory.

In addition to testing the general hypothesis that children invoke default argument structures for verbs, the experiment also tested a more specific assumption concerning the source of children's errors with fixed intransitive verbs (e.g., *don't fall me down*). Bowerman (1982b,c; 1983) had proposed that these errors stem from children's recognition (and overgeneralization) of a rule that causativizes certain intransitive verbs (like those optionally transitive verbs used in Braine et al.'s study). If this account of the errors were correct, the subjects in Braine et al.'s study should have been more likely to transitivize novel verbs introduced as intransitives than to de-transitivize novel verbs modelled as transitives. No such unidirectional verb usage was found; the argument structures children assigned to the novel verbs depended mainly on the probe questions they had to answer.

2.2.2 *Evaluating Discovery Procedures*

Timing of the Errors

In her discussion of Braine's theory, Bowerman (1988) observed that the overgeneralizations in her data typically occurred after the verbs had already been used correctly for months or sometimes even years (that is, the children initially behaved conservatively, as Baker, 1979, had predicted). This, argues Bowerman, is at odds with Braine's assumption that children produce errors because they lack verb-specific argument structures and have to resort to a default assignment. Braine et al. (1990) responded by suggesting that the late errors in Bowerman's data may have resulted from discourse pressure. In their experiment, discourse pressure — in the form of the agent- and patient-oriented questions — did lead to errors: When the fixed intransitive verbs were followed by agent-oriented questions, and the fixed transitive verbs were followed by patient-oriented questions, children used the wrong argument structures in about a third of the cases.

Braine et al. note, however, that their hypothesis may seem to suffer from another problem of timing — that early errors do not seem to occur as often as they should if children indeed rely on default argument structures for verbs whose specific argument structures they do not know. The authors counter this by proposing that children hesitate to use verbs they do not really know yet. But this solution runs the risk of undermining the whole purpose of positing default argument structures in Braine et al.'s model: How could children who have only learned default argument structures know any better — why wouldn't they just take them to be the right ones for the verb in question? Even if they were aware of gaps in their knowledge, what use would the default argument structures be if they were not willing to draw on the little help they offer? Braine et al.'s solution to the unfavorable timing of errors for Braine's theory draws on discourse pressure to explain late errors, but presupposes that no such pressure operates on younger children. In order to solve the problems the timing of errors poses for their theory, Braine et al. would have to assume that discourse pressure either does not exist in the early years or is not perceived.

Cutting Back on Errors

According to Braine's theory, children make errors when they do not know the specific argument structures of a verb and so assign a default argument structure that is ungrammatical for that verb. They stop making errors because they eventually learn verb-specific argument structures. Relevant to this proposal are Braine et al.'s experimental findings on the existing verbs of fixed transitivity and on the novel verbs presented as either intransitives or transitives. Although the children did use the existing verbs in an ungrammatical argument structure, they were much more willing to assign a default argument structure to the novel verbs, i.e., to use them in the argument structure they were not presented in. This difference certainly reflects the effect of prior linguistic experience, but it does not show that repeated exposure suffices to constrain the use of a verb, nor does it explain why children should stop using default argument structures.

If repeated exposure to a (set of) argument structure(s) for a verb were indeed sufficient to constrain how children use the verb, they should be conservative speakers when they are grown up. But although adults are obviously more cautious than children in this respect (cf. the behavior of the adult subjects), they do not stick exclusively to existing argument structures. Consider the novel *be*-verbs listed in (10) in Chapter 1: *bekuscheln, bereiten, bedudeln,* and *bestreifen* are coined from the base verbs *kuscheln* 'snuggle', *reiten* 'ride', *dudeln* 'fiddle', and *(durch)streifen* 'patrol', respectively. The speakers who coined these verbs certainly knew the specific argument structure of the base verbs, but were nevertheless willing to assign the verbs a new argument structure. The novel verbs were probably not coined in response to discourse pressure either: Except for *bekuscheln*, the verbs appeared in written text, so the speakers/writers had all the time they needed to look for an existing verb that would meet the requirements of the text structure if they had wanted to.

But although adults are not completely conservative, they are more conservative than children (cf. the results of Braine et al.'s experiment), so Braine's theory must explain this shift. Put differently, why should learners stop applying default argument structures to a verb?

Braine and his collaborators suggest that they would do so when the specific argument structure is in conflict with the default argument structure. Unfortunately, the authors do not explain what they would consider a conflict; they propose only that nonalternating verbs will always be witnessed in only one argument structure, thus strengthening the link between the verb and this argument structure while never strengthening the alternative argument structure.[2] But is this a conflict?

Baker's (1979) notion of embarrassing exceptions is important here. Recall that when a child observes verbs like *pour* only in the theme-object construction, she cannot infer that the verb cannot be used in the goal-object construction — that construction may simply happen never to have been chosen. Hence, never observing sentences like **Kim poured the glass with water* is inconclusive with respect to whether *pour* may take its goal as direct object. And novel coinages like *bekuscheln* and *bereiten* show that the speakers did not experience a conflict between the specific argument structure they had observed for *kuscheln* and *reiten* and the argument structures available for *be*-verbs (i.e., [AG *be*-V BEN] in the case of *bekuscheln* and [AG *be*-V LOC] in the case of *bereiten*).

But if there is no conflict for these verbs, why do speakers experience as ungrammatical *be*-verbs like *beschieben*, and the goal-object form for verbs like *pour*? In the pilot study mentioned in Chapter 1 (see Footnote 7), for example, subjects refused to accept *besenken* and *beschieben* as possible verbs. But since — as *bekuscheln* shows — speakers of German are not averse to novel *be*-verbs in principle, the subjects' refusal to accept verbs like *beschieben* and *besenken* cannot be explained by their inexperience with these verbs. The problem with Braine's theory is that it cannot account for the selective productivity of argument structure alternations that lies at the heart of the No Negative Evidence problem. Merely registering the available argument structures in the input is not enough for developing this kind of linguistic choosiness.

---

2. The notion of 'strengthening a link' might suggest that Braine's theory is similar to connectionist approaches to language acquisition and learning (see, for example, Rumelhart & McClelland, 1986). But in Braine's theory, 'strengthening a link' simply refers to learning via repeated exposure.

Misleading Plausibility of CANONICAL SENTENCE SCHEMAS

At first sight, the idea that children use canonical sentence schemas to assign default argument structures to novel verbs may seem plausible. This plausibility comes from two aspects of English syntax, the language for which Braine's theory has been mainly developed. First, English has a strict subject-verb-object (SVO) word order, which makes it plausible that children have acquired schemas for formulating sentences. Second, it seems natural to describe events in terms of agent-action-patient, and the fact that English word order corresponds closely to this description again contributes to the plausibility of canonical sentence schemas.

What strikes me as problematic about Braine et al.'s account is the fact that the authors seem to simply rely on this plausibility instead of being precise about exactly what a (canonical or non-canonical) sentence schema is, and how children can derive default argument structures from canonical sentence schemas. Given that their arguments depend so heavily on the notions 'canonical sentence schema' and 'default argument structure', a more precise account would have been called for.

Moreover, sentence schemas lose much of their plausibility when we look at languages with a freer word order. They are particularly implausible for languages like German and Dutch, in which word order is not only freer than in English but also differs in main and subordinate clauses, with SVO order for the former and SOV for the latter. Do children have one schema for the SVO order in main clauses, which they manipulate to arrive at the SOV order in subordinate clauses (or vice versa)? Or do they have two schemas, one for each type of clause? If so, what are the connections between the two schemas? The notion of a sentence schema is, then, not plausible for languages like German — schemas are much too rigid to deal with the range of word orders displayed in the input.

In sum, Braine's proposal that specific syntactic frames come to prevail over general syntactic frames does not solve the No Negative Evidence problem. Even though it seems plausible at first sight, it cannot account for speakers' selectivity in using verbs in as yet unobserved syntactic frames, and the notion of 'default sentence schemas' is implausible for many languages. An approach to the No Negative Evidence problem that is able to deal with selective productivity is the Criteria Approach, which is the topic of the next section.

2.3 The Criteria Approach

The Criteria Approach exploits the fact that the verbs that participate in a given alternation have in common a number of semantic and sometimes morphophonical properties that are absent from the verbs that do not. Children can learn these properties on the basis of positive evidence, and when they have learned them, they can tell whether a verb alternates.

The Criteria Approach was proposed by Mazurkewich and White (1984) to account for the acquisition of the dative alternation and by Pinker (1984) for the passive, the causative and locative alternations, and *un-* prefixation. These authors reject Baker's conservative learner solution to the No Negative Evidence problem because it cannot explain children's overgeneralizations, but they agree with Baker that argument structure alternations are part of speakers' lexical knowledge, and not of their knowledge about syntactic transformation rules. The decisive difference between their proposal and Baker's is that they assume that speakers extract lexical rules for creating new lexical items.

In more recent publications, Pinker has modified the idea of criteria-governed productivity so much that it has become a completely different theory (Pinker, 1987, 1989; Gropen et al., 1991a,b; cf. Section 2.5). Therefore, I will focus here on Mazurkewich and White's account of how the dative alternation is acquired, while Pinker will be represented in the discussion as a critic of the approach.

2.3.1 *Mazurkewich and White's Account of the Acquisition of the Dative Alternation*

The English dative alternation is characterized by both a morphophonological and a semantic constraint. In order to appear in both argument structures involved in the alternation — [V NP1 *to/for* NP2] and [V NP2 NP1] — a verb of transfer must in general be of Germanic origin (receiving stress on the first syllable) and the noun phrase represented as NP2 above must refer to a prospective possessor (Green, 1974; Oehrle, 1976; Randall, 1992, among others).[3] These constraints apply to verbs like *give* and *bring*, shown in (12a),

---

3. For communication verbs like *tell*, possession is interpreted somewhat metaphorically; e.g., according to Pinker (1989, p. 48), "verbs of communication are treated as denoting the transfer of messages or stimuli, which the recipient metaphorically possesses." Verbs like *throw* meet

which take the preposition *to* in the first of the argument structures above, and to verbs like *bake* and *buy*, shown in (12b), which take the preposition *for*. Excluded are verbs like *donate* and *purchase*, shown in (13), which are of Latinate origin, and verbs like *open* and *drive*, shown in (14), which do not satisfy the semantic constraint. (However, the goal argument of verbs like *open* may sometimes be interpreted as a prospective possessor; the verbs may then appear in the double object construction; see Section 2.4 for discussion. Also, Latinate verbs that have been assimilated to the native stress pattern can appear in the double object construction, for example, *promise* and *offer*. Likewise, *donate* is accepted in the double object construction by some speakers provided it is stressed on the first syllable.)

(12) *Germanic verbs satisfying the semantic constraint*
    a. Pepe gave a statue to the museum./Pepe gave the museum a statue.
        Ted brought the training schedule to Lily./Ted brought Lily the training schedule.
    b. Anna baked a cake for Renata./Anna baked Renata a cake.
        Bill bought a lawn mower for Henry./Bill bought Henry a lawn mower.

(13)   *Latinate verbs*
        Pepe donated a statue to the museum./*Pepe donated the museum a statue.
        Bill purchased a lawn mower for Henry./*Bill purchased Henry a lawn mower.

(14)   *Germanic verbs not satisfying the semantic constraint*
        Sue drove the Peugeot 404 to the mechanic./*Sue drove the mechanic the Peugeot 404.
        Paul opened the door for Mary./*Paul opened Mary the door.

Recall that Baker equipped learners with knowledge of the phrase structures they have heard a verb used in. This knowledge involves subcategorization information of the kind shown in (6), repeated here for convenience in (15):

(15) send   (___NP to NP), (___NP NP)
     give   (___NP to NP), (___NP NP)
     say   (___NP to NP)
     report   (___NP to NP)

---

the possessor constraint because the constraint does not have to mean ownership. This is reflected in double object constructions like "Could you just give me your pencil for a second?", in which possession consists of temporary control of the transferred object (see also Pinker, 1989, p. 110, for discussion).

Mazurkewich and White agree with Baker that information about subcategorization is part of a speaker's lexical knowledge. But, following Jackendoff (1975), Oehrle (1976), Wasow (1981), and Pinker (1982), they propose that children develop a LEXICAL REDUNDANCY RULE on the basis of which they can generate novel phrase structures for verbs they have not yet observed with these structures.

A lexical redundancy rule is a mechanism for generating new lexical entries (e.g., *give NP2 NP1*) on the basis of an already existing entry (e.g., *give NP1 to NP2*). The rule specifies which properties are shared by the verbs that have already been observed with both entries and the properties that these verbs have in each entry. The rule Mazurkewich and White propose for the dative alternation is shown in (16) (Mazurkewich & White, 1984, p. 274. *Native* refers to what I have called *Germanic*):

(16) *The lexical redundancy rule for the dative alternation*

$$+V_i \ (+\text{native}) \qquad\qquad +V_i \ (+\text{native})$$
$$+\underline{} \ \text{NP1} \ to \ \text{NP2} \quad \Leftrightarrow \quad +\underline{} \ \text{NP2 NP1}$$
$$\qquad for \qquad\qquad\qquad \text{NP2 POSSESSOR of NP1 and NP2}$$
$$\qquad\qquad\qquad\qquad\qquad\qquad \text{GOAL or BENEFICIARY}$$

This rule relates only those verbs of transfer that are native (i.e., of Germanic origin) and whose goal or beneficiary argument is a prospective possessor. Like redundancy rules in general, it serves to organize a speaker's knowledge of related verbs in an economical way: Instead of having to list two entries for each verb, the speaker only has to know one of the entries and the redundancy rule, and this will allow him to generate the remaining entry. Thus, the rule enables him not only to reconstruct a phrase structure he has heard already but also to generate entirely novel lexical entries; in other words, it is a means for expanding the syntactic potential of verbs that satisfy the criteria specified by the rule.[4]

---

4. The rule proposed by Mazurkewich and White does not capture the possibility to derive lexical entries for novel verbs like *fax* and *email*, which is, however, possible (see Wasow, 1981, and Pinker, 1989, for discussion):

He faxed/emailed the news to Paul.
He faxed/emailed Paul the news.

The problem is that Mazurkewich and White specify the morphophonological property as native, thus excluding denominal verbs. That novel verbs like *fax* alternate shows that the constraint should rather be stated in terms of the relevant morphological and/or phonological properties of native or Germanic verbs. For example, Germanic verbs tend to be monosyllabic

According to Mazurkewich and White, a conservative learning of phrase structures holds only for the initial phase of acquiring the alternation. The phrase structures acquired during this phase lay the groundwork for the following step, in which the learner will take the similarities among them for defining a redundancy rule that relates the structures in a principled way. Based on findings reported in the literature (Carrow, 1968; Fischer, 1971), Mazurkewich and White propose that this happens around the age of five. (But see Roeper, Lapointe, Bing, & Tavakolian, 1981, referred to by Mazurkewich and White, who report that children older than five have still not mastered the alternation. See also Snyder and Stromswold, 1997, for evidence that children acquire the double object construction earlier than the prepositional dative construction.)

Overgeneralizations occur when children have developed a rule for dative alternation but are not yet sensitive to any constraints: They may therefore apply it to verbs like *open* and *drive*, which do not fulfill the semantic constraint, to verbs like *address* and *transfer*, which do not satisfy the morphophonological constraint, and to verbs like *recite* and *repeat*, which fulfill neither.

To constrain their rule, children must detect which properties are shared by the alternating verbs, but they can only realize the relevance of these properties when they are confronted with a triggering factor. Mazurkewich and White propose that the trigger is verbs like *cost* and idiomatic expressions like *give someone a headache* (cf. (17)). These constructions appear only in the double object construction, not in the prepositional form, because they involve inalienable possession and so do not specify transfer (Mazurkewich & White, 1984, p. 276):[5]

(17) *Triggers for the semantic constraint*
The book cost John five dollars.
The noise gave Mary a headache.

---

or, if polysyllabic, stressed on the first syllable. See Bresnan (1982), Pinker (1989), Randall (1992), among others, for proposals of how to distinguish Germanic from Latinate verbs in English; see also Pinker (1989, p. 118ff.), for evidence that certain semantically definable subgroups of Latinate verbs are infact grammatical in the double object construction.

5. However, one might argue that the verbs cannot function as triggers because the child cannot know for sure that they will never occur in the prepositional form.

On analyzing constructions like these, the child must recognize the relevance of the role of possessor for double object constructions.

The morphophonological constraint is triggered when the child becomes increasingly aware of the general differences between Germanic and Latinate verbs (as discussed in Chomsky & Halle, 1968; Siegel, 1974; Aronoff, 1976). These differences will tell him that there are two different classes of verbs, and will make him search for further aspects of the grammar that might be affected by this difference. On noticing that his list of alternating dative verbs contains only verbs of Germanic origin, he will install this property as a constraint on his rule.

Mazurkewich and White suggest that the semantic restriction may be acquired almost in parallel with the redundancy rule itself, i.e., about the age of five. From their data on judgments of acceptability, they conclude that the morphophonological restriction is mastered only much later. In their study, 12- and 16-year-old subjects judged a considerable percentage of double object constructions containing Latinate verbs as grammatical. This was especially true of verbs subcategorized for the preposition *for*: The 12-year-olds accepted 61% of the double object constructions rejected as ungrammatical by adults, and even the 16-year-olds accepted 28 percent. According to Mazurkewich and White, the constraint is acquired so late because Latinate verbs are not part of everyday language and so are known only to older children. If Mazurkewich and White's observations about the acquisition of the morphophonological constraint and their assumptions about the onset of a productive rule are correct, then children should possess productive knowledge of the alternation already around the age of five but should need several additional years for the finishing touch.

2.3.2 *Evaluating the Criteria Approach*

Incorrect Lexical Entries and the Timing of Errors

Until children have detected all the criteria that constrain the application of a given redundancy rule, they will be prone to overgeneralize the rule to verbs that fail to meet them. This is particularly likely to affect Latinate verbs: Until they have discovered the morphophonological constraint on the dative alternation, they may well use verbs like *demonstrate* and *select* in both the prepositional and the double object construction.

The Criteria Approach explains the timing of children's overgeneralization errors, which was shown to be a problem for Braine's theory (Bowerman, 1988; see Section 2.2.2). Mazurkewich and White assume that children are initially conservative, adhering to the phrase structures they have heard a verb appear in. They only begin to make errors when they develop a productive rule (see also Bowerman, 1977, 1982a,b, 1983, for a similar account of children's errors). This is in accordance with the onset of errors after an extended period of correct usage. In contrast to Braine et al. — who can account for late errors by referring to discourse pressure but cannot account for the absence of early errors — Mazurkewich and White can explain why errors appear only late: They propose that the child's knowledge becomes reorganized. The timing of errors suggests, then, that overgeneralizations are more than just a failure to respond appropriately under discourse pressure; instead, they reflect a step towards a more mature, productive mastery of the language.

The Criteria Approach also accounts for what I have called selective productivity (cf. 2.2.2): That some but not all candidate verbs can be assigned novel argument structures. According to the Criteria Approach, novel coinages like *bekuscheln* and *bedudeln* are perceived as grammatical because they possess the properties presumably relevant for the locative alternation in German (whatever these properties may be), while verbs like *senken* 'lower' and *rollen* 'roll' do not alternate because they lack these features. Perhaps the most appealing aspect of the Criteria Approach is that it traces out an interesting development that involves a qualitative shift in the child's organization of linguistic knowledge. Starting with a conservative adherence to the phrase structures observed in the input, the learner extracts from the stored entries a productive rule whose range of application is successively constrained by adopting criteria derived from the input.

It is precisely this last step — the restriction of the rule by successively adding criteria — that has been criticized most, both on theoretical and empirical grounds. Below, I present and comment on Pinker's critique (1987, 1989) of the Criteria Approach.

The Nature of the Criteria

Pinker's main criticism is directed toward the nature of the criteria proposed to constrain the various argument structure alternations. He aims at a theory of language acquisition that is shaped by the idea that the structure of language is caused by the structure of the learner (Pinker, 1989, p. 60), and he rejects the Criteria Approach in part because it fails to establish this causal link. In his view, the criteria often seem arbitrary, and, summed up across all alternations, rather heterogeneous: The morphophonological constraint on the dative, for example, depends on a verb's metrical feet, and the semantic constraints on the various alternations involve such diverse concepts as *prospective possessor* for the dative alternation, *hierarchy of thematic roles* for the passive, *direct causation* for the causative, and *holistic filling or covering* for the locative alternation (cf. Pinker 1984, 1989, for a summary). If the structure of language is indeed caused by the capacities of the learner, asks Pinker, why do the criteria seem to be so arbitrarily imposed on the various alternations? And, given such a diversity in kind, how can the child determine which criteria are relevant for which rule? The heterogeneity of the criteria also suggest that the total number of possibly relevant criteria the child must sample from might be too large. If there are infinitely many criteria, they are unlearnable, and, if their number is finite but very large, they cannot be learned in a reasonable period of time.

I agree with Pinker that the particular criteria proposed are problematic; however, I find the reasoning about whether there are too many or infinitely many criteria too hypothetical. I do not think that a theory should be discarded because of a hypothetical problem — we should first see whether it really *is* a problem. Moreover, Pinker does not base his criticism on empirical evidence that would tell us how easily children can determine criteria on rules (whether linguistic rules or rules that are independent of language). His critique is certainly sufficient to motivate searching for an alternative account, but it does not show that heterogeneous criteria pose an insurmountable problem to the Criteria Approach.

Why Complicate a Simple and Successful Rule?

Pinker's second argument takes up a problem first pointed out by Janet D. Fodor (Fodor, 1985, cited in Pinker, 1989; see also Randall, 1987): Why should children bother to learn criteria that constrain their rule, given that their unconstrained rule is not only simpler but also provides them with more expressive power (Pinker, 1989, p. 59)? Moreover, since the rule is fully compatible with the linguistic input, there is no evidence that would suggest they should change it. Pinker considers a possible solution to this criticism, according to which children are simply built to learn the language of their parents, but he rejects it on grounds that it does not explain why the parents themselves kept the constraint.

Pinker's argument certainly shows that a theory that does not require the child to add criteria to an overly general rule is preferrable to one that does. But again, I find the argument too hypothetical. It is mainly motivated by the goal of specifying the innate linguistic capacities the child is assumed to be equipped with. This is certainly a legitimate goal, but what if children *are* able to add criteria to their overly general rules? The idea that they are is appealing, and the argument that this ability is not sufficient to determine whether a verb alternates leaves open whether children have this ability and to what extent they actually use it.

The discussion so far has been based on the assumption that the alternating verbs children acquire actually display the relevant properties. This presupposes that children are able to distinguish phrase structures that they have heard in the input from those generated by their own imperfectly constrained rule. However, even the input might not be pure enough to allow them to formulate the relevant criteria, a problem to which we now turn.

Exceptions to the Criteria

The criteria proposed so far to constrain argument structure alternations have negative as well as positive exceptions. Positive exceptions are verbs that alternate even though they lack one or more of the required criteria (see Bowerman, 1987, 1988; Pinker, 1989; Randall, 1992, among others). Some positive exceptions to the phonological constraint to the dative alternation are shown in (18) ((18a-b) are from Pinker, 1989, p. 57, and (18c) is from Bowerman, 1988, p. 84):[6]

(18) *Positive exceptions to the phonological constraint*:
    a.   Dr. Bear referred Linda a patient.
    b.   I radioed Jim the news.
    c.   The teacher assigned John a desk in the back row.

---

6. I have changed the examples given by Pinker by using proper names instead of pronouns. The reason is that Mazurkewich and White discuss some similar examples in which a pronoun improved the acceptability of a Latinate verb in the double object construction, an effect which they explain by cliticization.

If there are enough verbs displaying the critical restrictions, positive exceptions are not devastating to the theory: The child can in principle learn them through positive evidence — i.e., by noticing that adult speakers produce sentences like those in (18). But the existence of positive exceptions does weaken the claims of the Criteria Approach, since exceptions make it more difficult for the child to determine the critical characteristics of alternating verbs.

A more critical problem for the Criteria Approach is the existence of negative exceptions — verbs that do not alternate even though they meet all the necessary criteria. The problem that negative exceptions raise for the criteria approach was first pointed out by Bowerman (1987, 1988). Some examples are listed in (19): Verbs that do not participate in the dative alternation even though they involve a prospective possessor and are of Germanic origin ((19a) is from Bowerman, 1988, p. 84, and (19b-c) are from Pinker, 1989, p. 59)); examples of children's overgeneralization of the double object construction to such verbs are given in (20) (from Bowerman, 1988, p. 79).

(19) *Negative exceptions to the semantic constraint*
     a.   *Her mother chose Mary a dress.[7]
     b.   *Sam shouted John the story.
     c.   *John pulled Bill the box.

(20) M 5+:   *Choose me the ones that I can have.
     C 3;1:   *I said her no.
     L 7;8:   *Shall I whisper you something?

The Criteria Approach gives no account of how negative exceptions could be discovered. Even if children correctly restricted their rule for the dative alternation to verbs of transfer involving a prospective possessor, they would have no way of determining that verbs like *choose, pull, shout, say,* and *whisper* — which satisfy the constraints — do not participate in the dative alternation.

The negative exceptions to the proposed criteria show that the criteria do not sufficiently constrain the child's rules for argument structure alternations. I do not agree with Pinker's additional criticism that the Criteria Approach

---

7. Some speakers find *choose* acceptable in the double-object construction. Variations in judgments like these, however, do not change the nature of the problem, as long as there are speakers that do not accept certain verbs in a particular construction even though the verbs meet all the relevant criteria.

should be able to explain why alternations are constrained as they are; in my view, this is the task of a linguistic theory, and not necessarily of a language acquisition theory. But since the Criteria Approach cannot explain how children end up with sufficiently constrained rules, it fails as a theory of how children acquire the alternations in the absence of negative evidence.

2.4 The Catapult Hypothesis

The Catapult Hypothesis, proposed by Randall (1987, 1990, 1992) as a solution to certain of children's argument structure alternation overgeneralizations, is based on a simple principle by which children can test their hypotheses about grammar: If A, then not B. If they discover that the target language contains constructions of type A, they can conclude that it does not contain constructions of type B — the existence of one type of construction provides them with positive evidence that certain other constructions are not part of their target language.

The idea that disjunctive principles guide the child in acquiring grammar originated in the theory of parameter setting (see, for example, Hyams, 1986; Wexler & Manzini, 1987; Nishigauchi & Roeper, 1987). According to this theory, Universal Grammar (i.e., the abstract set of grammatical principles that give rise to the specific grammars of individual languages) contains a small number of parameters, each with two (or possibly more) settings. The settings of the parameters specify only grammars that are consistent with the abstract grammar, i.e., that are possible instantiations of Universal Grammar. Knowledge of Universal Grammar is assumed to be innate; hence, children are able to acquire any possible instantiation of Universal Grammar. The setting of each parameter has a number of syntactic consequences, and these consequences constitute the evidence children need to determine how the parameter is set in their language.

The theory of parameters can explain the acquisition only of certain constructions: Those whose existence categorically rules out the existence of certain other constructions. An example is the direction of head government (Williams, 1981): The head of a phrase may govern elements to either its right or its left, but not both. (For example, the verb, as the head of the verb phrase, governs to the right in English, i.e., the verb precedes its internal arguments.) If, for whatever reason, children arrive at the wrong direction of government for their language, the various syntactic consequences head government has in the language (for example, whether and in which direction a constituent may move) will provide them with evidence to the contrary. The syntactic consequences of head government can provide this evidence because of the either/or logic of the parameter, according to which the presence of one direction of government rules out the other.

It has commonly been assumed that the lexicon does not obey an either/or logic. The information associated with individual lexical items is usually considered too unsystematic and idiosyncratic to be determined by parameter settings. A paradigm case of unsystematicity has seemed to be argument structure: Verbs with very similar meanings differ in their argument structures, for example, *give* and *donate*. Since it would be incorrect for children to predict, on the basis of their knowledge of how *give* behaves, that the semantically similar *donate* has the same syntactic flexibility, a single parameter setting for these verbs is impossible.[8]

2.4.1 *Using Syntax to Cut Back from Overgeneralizations*

Randall proposes that the either/or logic of parameters can, after all, be applied to the acquisition of argument structure: The crucial step is to show that a verb's inability to appear in more than one syntactic frame can be predicted on the basis of its other properties. If this prediction is possible, children can benefit from the either/or logic of parameters: If they have evidence that the verb has property A, they can conclude that it does not have property B, i.e., the ability to alternate. Randall formulates this either/or logic as the Catapult Hypothesis (Randall, 1992, p. 99):

(21) **The Catapult Hypothesis**
For every overgeneralization,
a.   the grammar contains a disjunctive principle P,
[either A or B (exclusive)]
and b.   the primary data exhibits A (or B).

Randall assumes that the crucial property differentiating alternating and nonalternating verbs lies in the verb's basic argument structure: Alternating

---

8. But see Juffs (1996), who has recently proposed a parameter setting account for some argument structure alternations, and Hale & Keyser (1993), who propose that lexical items have syntactic structures corresponding to those of sentences.

verbs take two obligatory postverbal (or internal) arguments, whereas nonalternating verbs take only one.

An obligatory argument is a constituent whose omission renders the sentence ungrammatical. The verb *give*, for example, takes two obligatory postverbal arguments, an NP and a PP, as shown in (22a). The sentences in (22b) and (22c) are ungrammatical because one of these arguments is omitted.[9] The verb *collect* may also appear with two postverbal arguments, as shown in (23a); but, in contrast to *give*, its PP is optional and may readily be omitted, as shown in (23b) (the examples are taken from Randall, 1992, pp. 102, 111).

(22) a.   Romeo gave those posies to Juliet.
     b.   *Romeo gave those posies.
     c.   *Romeo gave to Juliet.

(23) a.   Alice collected those recipes from her travels.
     b.   Alice collected those recipes.

When a constituent is not obligatory it can be either an optional argument or an adjunct. The difference between arguments and adjuncts may be described as follows: Arguments introduce participants in the event that have a relationship to each other, for example, the relationship between Romeo, the posies, and Juliet in the sentence in (22a), while adjuncts express a relationship between the event as a whole and other, more circumstantial aspects of the situation, such as place and time. Since arguments specify participants in the event, they are more relevant for the well-formedness of a clause than adjuncts; this difference in relevance is expressed formally by assigning arguments and adjuncts to different positions with respect to the verb phrase.[10] Both obligatory and optional arguments have the relationship of

---

9. What appears to be an obligatory argument can sometimes be omitted if a *specific* referent can be inferred from the context, as in *Being the richest man at the benefit party, Uncle Sam gave $1000*. Omissions like these are often called PRAGMATIC OMISSIONS. They differ from omissions of optional arguments, as in *Tom is eating*, in that the latter do *not* require inferring a specific referent — *Tom is eating* is most naturally interpreted as meaning that Tom is eating *some* food, but not necessarily any specific food identifiable from the context (see Bresnan, 1978; Mittwoch, 1982, among others, for analyses of constructions like these). I will return to the role of omissions in the discussion of Randall's theory.

10. Verb phrases are well-ordered chunks of information; how this information is structured is mainly determined by the verb, which is the head of the phrase. An important aspect of the phrase's structure is the number of arguments the verb needs for building the chunk. The way in which phrases may be structured is formulated in X-BAR THEORY (Jackendoff, 1977; *X* refers to the heads of phrases, and *bars* indicate different levels of complexity in a phrase).

SISTERHOOD to the verb, which means that they are integrated into the verb phrase (technically: that they are dominated by the same node that dominates the verb, i.e., the VP node). Adjuncts, in contrast, are attached outside the verb phrase, i.e., they combine with the verb phrase only after all the arguments of the phrase have been integrated.

In X-bar theory (Jackendoff, 1977), two principles are assumed to determine the order of optional arguments and adjuncts in a clause: The Order Principle and the Attachment Principle. In her Catapult Hypothesis, Randall proposes that children identify verbs that do not undergo a particular alternation by drawing on these two principles. I will focus here on the Order Principle, since the Attachment Principle is relevant only for specific properties of the dative alternation. Randall has developed her theory mainly on the basis of the dative alternation, so I present the Order Principle mainly by showing how it applies to this alternation.

The Order Principle

Randall formulates the Order Principle as follows (Randall, 1992, p. 101):

(24) **The Order Principle**
If an argument is optional, then it may not intervene between the head and an obligatory argument.

Randall uses the Order Principle to define a necessary condition that a verb must meet in order to participate in the dative and/or the locative alternation: To participate, the verb must at least take two internal obligatory arguments. The verbs *give, bring,* and *send* take two obligatory arguments, neither of which may be omitted (except for pragmatic reasons, cf. Footnote 9), as shown in (25). Since both arguments are obligatory, they may follow the verb in either order, and the verbs may participate in the dative alternation as long as other conditions such as animacy of the recipient are met:

(25) a.   The doctor gave some aspirin to the patient./ The doctor gave the patient some aspirin.
        *The doctor gave some aspirin.
        *The doctor gave to the patient.

      b.   The postman brought the letter to John./ The postman brought John the letter.
        *The postman brought the letter.
        *The postman brought to Mr Willis.

   c.   Carlo sent the secret papers to the ambassador./ Carlo sent the ambassador the secret papers.
       *Carlo sent the secret papers.
       *Carlo sent to the ambassador.

Deliver, report, and *explain* also take a direct object and a prepositional phrase, as shown in (26). But, unlike *give, bring,* and *send,* they can appear without the PP — their PP is optional. As predicted by the Order Principle, the prepositional object of the optional PP cannot follow the verb directly: Double object constructions are ungrammatical for these verbs, as shown in (26):

(26) a.   Pedro delivered the package to the client./ *Pedro delivered the client the package.
           Pedro delivered the package.
     b.   Alice reported the accident to the police./ *Alice reported the police the accident. Alice reported the accident.
     c.   Susan explained the solution to the professor./ *Susan explained the professor the solution.
           Susan explained the solution.

The Order Principle applies to the locative alternation in the same way. Locative verbs like *stuff* and *smear,* for which both the NP- and the PP-argument are obligatory, participate in the alternation, as shown in (27). In contrast, *fill* and *spill,* for which the PP is optional, do not, as shown in (28):

(27) a.   He stuffed his clothes into the bag./ He stuffed the bag with his clothes.
           *He stuffed his clothes.
           *He stuffed into the bag.
     b.   The baby smeared butter onto the wall./ The baby smeared the wall with butter.
           *The baby smeared butter.
           *The baby smeared onto the wall.

(28) a.   The waiter filled the glasses with wine./ *The waiter filled wine into the glasses.
           The waiter filled the glasses.
     b.   The child spilled the milk on her sweater./ *The child spilled her sweater with the milk.
           The child spilled the milk.

Randall proposes that children have knowledge of the Order Principle as part of their innate grasp of principles of Universal Grammar. This knowledge enables them to predict the syntactic potential of a verb: If they know that a verb takes only one obligatory internal argument, they can infer that it does not alternate. But why, then, do children make errors? According to Randall, children are sometimes mistaken about the correct argument structure of a verb — they may have erroneously classified as obligatory an argument that in fact is optional. In this case, they might assume that the verb alternates: After all, both of its arguments are obligatory, according to their analysis, so the verb satisfies the necessary condition for alternating.

To cut back from this overgeneralization, children need evidence about the true syntactic status of the argument. This evidence will be provided by adult speakers: Since the argument is optional, they will often omit it when using the verb. When learners discover that the verb takes only one obligatory internal argument, their built-in obedience to the Order Principle will bring an end to overgeneralizations. Notice that the evidence children need for this correction is *positive*: It is provided by adult speakers when they omit the optional argument.[11]

The learner's inferences, formulated in terms of the 'if A, then not B' calculus, are shown in (29)-(30) (cf. Randall, 1992, p. 112):

(29) a.   give   NP1   P-NP2   b. deliver NP1 (P-NP2)
           give   NP2   NP1

(30)   If A, then not B: A (A= P-NP2 of *deliver* is optional)
           _____

           therefore   not B (B= NP2 may intervene between
                                      deliver and the obligatory NP1)

The Order Principle applies on a verb-by-verb basis: For each verb, the child must distinguish between obligatory and optional arguments. In the next section, we will see that this distinction may be influenced by semantic factors.

The Problem of Benefactives

So far we have been concerned with verbs that take an obligatory or optional *to*-PP. But the dative alternation also involves verbs that take a *for*-PP, as

---

11. Pragmatic omissions of obligatory arguments may seem to pose a problem for Randall's account. On hearing sentences like *Being the richest man at the benefit party, Uncle Sam gave $1000* (cf. Footnote 9), learners may conclude that *give* takes only one obligatory argument, just like *deliver*, and they would then incorrectly exclude the double object construction. Randall (1992) points out, however, that learners will have positive evidence that double object constructions for *give* are grammatical, and that the recipient must therefore be obligatory, so they can correct their lexical entries.

shown in (31a-b). (The examples are taken from Randall, 1992, p. 104ff; (31b) has been slightly adapted to improve its acceptability in the double object construction.)

(31) a.   The architect is drawing a plan for the clients.
          The architect is drawing the clients a plan.
     b.   The art teacher bought pastels for his students.
          The art teacher bought his students pastels.

The syntactic behavior of these verbs cannot be predicted on the basis of the Order Principle alone. Like the *to*-PPs discussed in the preceding section, the *for*-PPs in (31) introduce the recipient of the transferred object. But these *for*-PPs — in contrast to the *to*-PP of a verb like *give* — are optional, as shown in (32).

(32) The architect is drawing a plan.
      The art teacher bought pastels.

If verbs like *draw* and *buy* indeed defy the Order Principle, their syntactic flexibility cannot be predicted by the child. Even worse, they may indicate that the Order Principle itself is wrong. But Randall argues that these verbs do not constitute counterevidence to the principle, because there are specific conditions under which optional arguments may be reanalyzed as obligatory arguments. In particular, reanalysis is possible when the recipient of the verb may be interpreted as a prospective possessor of the object transferred to him.[12] Take, for example, a sentence like *The teacher bought pastels for his students*. This sentence may be interpreted as meaning either that the students received the pastels only for use during their class and had to leave them in the classroom for the next class, or that they got to keep the pastels (and so could take them home). In the former case, *for his students* is optional and the double object construction *The teacher bought his students pastels* is questionable or ruled out. But in the latter case, *for his students* can be reanalyzed

---

12. Randall does not explain the difference between recipients and prospective possessors in much detail. For example, she does not comment on whether a prospective possessor is to be understood as a particular type of recipient or as an entirely different thematic role. Notice also that some researchers assume that specifying a prospective possessor is a general requirement for a verb to appear in the double object construction, regardless of whether, in the verb's prepositional form, the PP argument is specified as recipient or beneficiary (see, for example, Mazurkewich & White, 1984, and Pinker, 1984, 1989).

as an obligatory argument and the double object construction is acceptable.[13]

According to Randall, reanalyses like these lead to a new lexical entry for the verb; she assumes, for example, that there are two verbs *buy* — *buy1* and *buy2*. As represented in the argument structures for the two *buy*-s, given in (33), only the argument structure of *buy2* allows the double object construction.

(33) buy1:   NP1 (P-NP2)   theme (recipient)
              *NP2 NP1   *recipient theme
      buy2:   NP1 P-NP2   theme pros.possessor
              NP2 NP1   pros.possessor theme

According to Randall, reanalyses of optional arguments as obligatory arguments also explain why locative verbs like *spray* participate in the locative alternation, as illustrated in (34a-b). The theme of these verbs may be omitted, as shown in (34c), and so it must be optional. But by reanalysis, learners can create a new lexical entry for *spray* in which the theme is obligatory and so may precede the obligatory goal, as in (34a).

(34) a. Paul sprayed paint on the wall.
     b. Paul sprayed the wall with paint.
     c. Paul sprayed the wall.

How can learners, when trying to come to grips with the dative alternation (for example), determine the difference between ordinary recipients and prospective possessors, and how do they interpret a verb like *buy* when they notice it in double object constructions?[14] After all, they are likely to have classified the verb as taking a single obligatory argument, and so should not expect to find it in double object constructions. They cannot give up the Order Principle, since it is part of their innate linguistic knowledge. According to Randall, they might at first take double object constructions for *buy* and

---

13. See also Kirsner (1985, 1986) and Kirsner, Verhagen, & Willemsen (1985) for related arguments and evidence.

14. Randall discusses how learners can determine this difference for a verb like *buy* (see below). However, according to her analysis of the double object construction for verbs like *give* — *give* NP2 NP1: recipient theme — the child has no reason to assume that a prospective possessor is needed for verbs like *buy* to appear in the double object construction since no prospective possessor is required for the double object construction of verbs like *give*. It would therefore be preferrable to specify a prospective possessor as a general condition for verbs to appear in that construction, as is done in other accounts of the dative alternation.

similar verbs as evidence that the verbs do take two obligatory arguments after all, and that in sentences like *John bought groceries*, the recipient argument has been omitted for pragmatic reasons (cf. Footnotes 9 and 11). But, argues Randall, this analysis will be given up sooner or later: Since there is a version of *buy, buy1*, that really does take only one argument, learners will often hear *buy* without a *for*-PP, and so conclude, correctly, that there is a verb *buy1* that takes only one argument and is confined to the [NP (PP)] argument structure, and another verb *buy2* that takes two obligatory internal arguments and has both the [NP NP] and the [NP PP] argument structure.

So far, we have been talking about verb-by-verb-reanalysis. But Randall assumes that when the learner notices several apparent violations of the Order Principle, each one forcing him to create a new lexical entry with a prospective possessor argument immediately following the verb, he will develop a lexical rule. This rule will generate additional lexical entries for verbs like *buy* when these verbs can be interpreted as involving a prospective possessor. That is, a lexical rule that takes *buy1* as its input would create *buy2*, providing that the verb meets the semantic constraint that the recipient can be interpreted as a prospective possessor (cf. Randall, 1992, p. 122). Thus, in Randall's theory, semantic criteria become important mainly when the child must accomodate apparent violations of universal principles.

In summary, Randall has proposed a largely syntactic account of how children can determine which verbs participate in the dative and/or the locative alternation. Her account is based on the assumption that children have innate knowledge of the Order Principle, which states that an optional argument may not intervene between the verb and its obligatory arguments. Apparent exceptions to the Order Principle can be explained by assuming that optional arguments may — under specific semantic conditions — be reanalyzed as obligatory arguments. When the learner has noticed several of these apparent exceptions, he will develop lexical rules for creating verbs with two obligatory internal arguments from verbs with one obligatory internal argument; the new verbs may then participate in the dative and/or the locative alternation. The lexical rules are constrained by semantic criteria, which can be acquired on the basis of positive evidence.

2.4.2 *Evaluating the Catapult Hypothesis*

The simplicity of the Catapult Hypothesis is appealing: If the either/or logic of parameter theory can indeed be applied to the lexical properties of verbs, then the inferences that are needed for determining the constraints on the dative and the locative alternation may be straightforward. The child's main task is to determine whether a constituent is an obligatory argument, and X-bar principles will do the rest. In evaluating Randall's theory, I will discuss an empirical problem of the Catapult Hypothesis, negative exceptions to the Order Principle, and a theoretical problem, that of determining the syntactic status of a constituent.

Negative Exceptions to the Order Principle

Recall that negative exceptions to a proposed criterion turned out to be a major problem for the Criteria Approach (see 2.3): Since nonalternating verbs like *shout* and *pull* satisfy the morphophonological and the semantic criteria on the dative alternation, the child has no reason to think that these verbs cannot appear in double object constructions. There are also several negative exceptions to the Order Principle, as shown in (35)-(36) (pointed out by Pinker, 1989, p. 38ff.) and (37): The verbs do not alternate even though they take two obligatory arguments. (The sentences in which the recipient and goal arguments appear alone are ungrammatical regardless of whether the arguments are specified by a PP or by an NP.)

(35) *Candidate verbs for the dative alternation*
She entrusted her child to the daycare center./*She entrusted the daycare center her child.
*She entrusted her child./*She entrusted (to) the daycare center.

(36) *Candidate verbs for the locative alternation*
John slopped water onto the floor./*John slopped the floor with water.
*John slopped water./*John slopped (onto) the floor.
John encrusted the cake with walnuts./*John encrusted walnuts onto the cake.
*John encrusted the cake./*John encrusted the walnuts.

(37) He put the socks onto the bed./*He put the bed with socks.
*He put the socks./*He put onto the bed.

The restrictions on some of these verbs may be due to properties that distinguish the verbs from other verbs with two obligatory arguments. For example, the derivational history of denominal *entrust* and *encrust* may have to be taken into account (see Clark & Clark, 1979; Wunderlich, 1987; Jackendoff, 1990; Urbas, 1990; Labelle, 1991; Hale & Keyser, 1993, for analyses of denominal verbs); and *put* may be restricted to the prepositional form because of its semantic properties, i.e., it is a light verb like *make, do,* and *cause* (Randall, personal communication). But even if it is possible to account for the behavior of verbs like *entrust* and *put*, the existence of negative exceptions shows that the Order Principle is not sufficient to enable a child to predict whether a verb alternates.

Omission of Arguments

In her account of restrictions on the dative alternation, Randall (1987) invokes two kinds of optionality. When the PP is omitted for verbs like *buy*, no recipient should be inferred; in contrast, when it is omitted for verbs like *deliver*, a recipient must be inferred. The difference is represented schematically in (38) (where x stands for agent, y for theme, and z for recipient):

(38) a.   x buys y: z not inferred
     b.   x delivers y: z inferred

Recall that speakers may apply a lexical rule whereby they reanalyze the optional z of *buy* as an obligatory argument, provided that the recipient may be interpreted as a prospective possessor; the verb may then appear in the double object construction. *Deliver*, however, may not appear in double object constructions (cf. (26a)), which indicates that the optional PP argument of *deliver* cannot be reanalyzed as an obligatory argument. But why not? Randall (1987) argues that reanalysis is impossible because *deliver* and similar verbs imply a recipient even when they are used without a PP, whereas *buy* and similar verbs do not. Stated as it is, this acccount is implausible: If anything, the fact that verbs like *deliver* have an implicit recipient should make it easier to reanalyze the recipient as an obligatory argument.[15] Moreover, the account runs

---

15. In Chapter 6, I propose to account for the ungrammaticality of the goal-object form for directional verbs (e.g., *lower*) along similar lines. In particular, I will argue that these verbs cannot take the goal as direct object because they have incorporated an intransitive spatial predicate (e.g., *low*). The verbs always *imply* a reference location (typically, the source location of the theme), but cannot express a location syntactically as a direct object because the incorporated predicate is intransitive. I think, then, that Randall's account of why *deliver* does not participate in the dative alternation could in principle be correct but would have to be related to the morphological structure of the verb.

into conflict when it is applied to verbs like *spray* and *load*. When the optional theme of these verbs is not mentioned, it must be inferred, just like the optional recipient of *deliver*, so it should not be reanalyzable as an obligatory argument. Yet these verbs alternate.

The Order Principle also runs into trouble over the pragmatic omissions possible for verbs like *give*, as in *Being the richest man at the benefit party, Uncle Sam gave a $1000*. Again, an unmentioned entity must be inferred. Schematically, pragmatic omissions may be represented as in (39):

(39) x gives y: z inferred

To apply the Order Principle to *deliver* but not to *give*, the child must somehow determine that the omission of the optional recipient of *deliver* differs from the pragmatic omission of the obligatory recipient of *give*. So far, however, Randall (1992) has not shown how the child could do this.

In sum, Randall's proposal that syntactic principles may account for the acquisition of argument structure is not satisfactory. There are negative exceptions to the Order Principle: Some verbs do not alternate even though they take two obligatory arguments. The idea that optional arguments may sometimes be reanalyzed as obligatory arguments yields conflicting results with respect to the behavior of verbs like *deliver* and *spray*. Finally, Randall does not show how a child can determine whether an argument is omitted because it is optional or because — even though it is technically obligatory — its referent is immediately inferrable from the context.

2.5 Lexicosemantic Structure Theory

Pinker's (1989) approach, which I will call Lexicosemantic Structure Theory, is based on the assumption that the semantic properties of a verb determine the kinds of syntactic frames it may appear in. According to Pinker, the meaning of a verb is closely linked to its possible syntactic frames via a set of universal and innately known linking rules. Linking rules define regular ways of assigning arguments to syntactic positions (see Carter, 1976, and Ostler, 1980, for discussions of linking rules). In Pinker's theory, the rules operate directly on elements corresponding to variables in the decompositional semantic representation of a verb. For example, one linking rule maps the first argument of the predicate CAUSE (the agent) to the subject position, and another maps the second argument of CAUSE (the patient) to the direct object position.

On the assumption that the syntactic frames of a verb are closely tied to the verb's meaning, Pinker accounts for the acquisition of argument structure by proposing that children only need to know the meaning of a verb in order to predict the syntactic frames it may appear in. Alternations in argument structure are acquired by learning lexical rules for converting an existing verb into a new verb whose meaning differs from the old one in such a way that it can appear in a different syntactic frame.

Pinker has applied his theory to four major cross-linguistically common changes in argument structure — passivization, causativization, dative and locative alternation — as well as to several other alternations that are specific to English. The theory is designed so that it can cover both alternations that involve a morphological marking on the verb and those that do not, but it accounts for the properties of the two types differently, as will be discussed shortly. Since the locative alternation is the topic of this thesis, I will present Pinker's proposed solution to the No Negative Evidence problem with reference to this alternation. Pinker's analysis is based on the alternation in English, so we will first see how his theory works when the verb is not morphologically marked.

2.5.1 *How the Lexicosemantic Structure Theory Accounts for the*
Acquisition of the Locative Alternation

Recall that verbs that participate in the locative alternation may take as their direct object either their theme or their goal. The bidirectional lexical rule that Pinker proposes to account for this (based on Rappaport & Levin, 1985, 1988) is shown in (40):

(40) a.   X cause Y to go-to Z   ⇔   b.   X cause Z to change state
                                                  by means of
                                                  [X cause Y to go-to Z]

       Example:
       Paul smeared butter onto the bread ⇔   Paul smeared the bread with butter

A decompositional structure like X CAUSE Y TO GO-TO Z is called the THE-MATIC CORE of a verb. Each thematic core is associated with one argument structure by virtue of the operation of the universal linking rules. Thus, the thematic core in (40a) is associated with the argument structure V [NP_{theme} *into/onto* NP_{goal}], and the thematic core in (40b) is associated with the argument structure V [NP_{goal} *with* NP_{theme}]. The lexical rule shown in (40) takes a

verb with the thematic core in either (40a) or (40b) and converts it into a verb
with the other thematic core; the linking rules that apply to the new thematic
core then specify the syntactic positions of the new verb's arguments.

The Object Affectedness Linking Rule

In order to allow either its theme or its goal to be second argument of CAUSE,
the verb must be able to specify both some specific way in which the theme is
caused to change location and some specific way in which the goal is caused
to change state. Following Rappaport and Levin (1985, 1988), Gropen et al.
(1991a) assume that a single linking rule can then account for the change in
the argument structure of verbs of motion. The rule is formulated as in (41):

(41) **The Object Affectedness Linking Rule**
    An argument is encodable as the direct object of a verb if its referent is specified as
    being affected in a specific way in the semantic representation of the verb (Gropen
    et al., 1991a, p. 118).[16,17]

The proposal that an argument is linked to object position if it is specified as
affected accounts for the holistic interpretation that typically accompanies
arguments in object position. The term 'holistic interpretation' goes back to
Anderson (1971), who observed that goal-object sentences like *He loaded the
cart with apples* invite the inference that the cart is completely filled, while
theme-object sentences like *He loaded apples onto the wagon* do not.[18] The
proposal that the goal is affected in that it undergoes a change of state (cf.
(40b)) accounts for the holistic interpretation because it is natural to interpret
a change of state as affecting the whole object and not just a part of it (see also

---

16. Examples of what it means for an object to be affected in a specific way are given below. An
important aspect of the specificity restriction is that it makes the proposed linking rule
falsifiable (see Gropen et al., 1991b, for discussion).

17. Motion verbs like *smear* specify an argument as affected because they have the predicate
CAUSE in their thematic core. But Gropen et al. propose that the Object Affectedness Linking
Rule may be more general, applying also to arguments that are specified as affected for other
reasons, for example, the internal argument of *fear* and *see*. The Object Affectedness Linking
Rule is thus more general than a related linking rule proposed by Pinker, 1989, that links the
second argument of CAUSE to object position.

18. The holistic interpretation was later also observed for other kinds of direct objects; see
Green (1974), Moravcsik (1978), Hopper and Thompson (1980), Levin (1985), and Pinker
(1989).

Rappaport & Levin, 1985, 1988). Gropen et al. (1991b) argue that the proposal also accounts for the shift in perspective that is commonly associated with the locative alternation. In theme-object sentences, the location change of the theme is the main predication, and this means that the theme is in focus. But in goal-object sentences, the state-change of the goal is the main predication while the location change of the theme functions only as a means of bringing about this change; this means that the goal is in focus.

Examples of verbs that can denote both a specific manner of motion of the theme and a specific change of state of the goal are *sow* and *stuff*. *Sow* most basically specifies that the theme is caused to move in a widespread or nondirected manner, so it may take its theme as direct object, as shown in (42a) (cf. Pinker, 1989, p. 124ff., for a discussion of how to determine whether a verb most basically denotes a change of location or a change of state). But *sow* also describes a specific effect on the goal, i.e., that the goal is evenly covered with a mass. Thus, it may also take its goal as direct object, as shown in (42b):

(42) a. The farmer sowed seeds onto the field.
     b. The farmer sowed the field with seeds.

Stuff, on the other hand, most basically denotes that its goal undergoes a change of state by being filled to its limit, so it may take its goal as direct object, as shown in (43a). But it also describes a specific manner in which the theme changes location — it is forced into a container. So the verb may take its theme as direct object, as in (43b):

(43) a. He stuffed the bag with sweaters.
     b. He stuffed the sweaters into the bag.

In sum, verbs like *sow* and *stuff* participate in the locative alternation because they allow speakers to choose either the theme or the goal as the affected object.

Broad and Narrow Range Lexical Rules

To explain why some verbs participate in a given alternation while others do not, Pinker hypothesizes that there are two types of lexical rules, BROAD RANGE RULES and NARROW RANGE RULES. Broad range rules specify the necessary conditions a verb must satisfy in order to participate in an alternation; the lexical rule in (40) is the broad range rule governing the locative alternation.

In contrast, narrow range rules specify the sufficient conditions for alternating. Narrow range rules are more specific versions of a particular broad range rule: They apply to only a subset of the verbs covered by the broad range rule. For example, for the locative alternation in English, there is a narrow range rule that applies to verbs that describe a motion in which a mass is forced into a container against the limits of its capacity; this rule accounts for why the verbs *stuff, pack, cram*, and several others alternate. In contrast, there happens not to be a narrow range rule that applies to verbs that describe motions in which a mass moves via the force of gravity; this accounts for why the verbs *dribble, drip*, and *dump*, among others, do not alternate. Broad range rules are property-predicting: They predict what grammatical properties a verb would have if it were used in its non-basic argument structure. In contrast, narrow range rules are existence-predicting: They allow the speaker to create a fully specified novel version of a verb on the basis of the old verb (Janet D. Fodor, 1985; referred to in Pinker, 1989, p. 160ff.).

Both broad and narrow range rules are sensitive to only specific kinds of information in the semantic structure of verbs; these are termed the grammatically relevant meaning elements (cf. Pinker, 1989, p. 208ff., for an overview of these elements). The predicates shown in the thematic cores of the broad range rule in (40) are examples of such grammatically relevant meaning elements. The broad range rule that relates the two cores takes into account only these elements: It requires, for example, that a verb specify a change of location before it can convert it into a verb that specifies a change of state, but it is oblivious to the particular manner in which the change of location is brought about. Narrow range rules are sensitive to more subtle meaning elements than broad range rules, but not to all semantic aspects of a verb. For example, the narrow range rule that applies to verbs like *stuff* is sensitive to whether the verb specifies that a container is filled to its limits, but it does not distinguish between whether the container is filled by being stuffed or by being jammed with things. Hence, both *stuff* and *jam* must behave in the same way — they both alternate.

The two types of lexical rules define different reasons why a verb may not alternate. If a verb fails to meet the necessary condition for alternating, then the broad range rule cannot apply to it to provide it with an alternative thematic core. This is the case for *pour* and *fill*. *Pour* specifies only a particular way in which a substance changes location, and not a particular change of state of the goal. (Even though pouring may typically cause a container to change state from not being full to being full, it does not entail such a change — an action may also be called pouring even if the container ends up only half full; Gropen et al., 1991a,b). Therefore, *pour* may only take its theme as direct object. *Fill* also does not satisfy the necessary conditions for participating in the locative alternation, but for the converse reason: It describes a specific change of state of the goal, but no particular manner of motion of the theme. (An action may be called filling regardless of whether a substance is poured, dripped, or scooped into a container). Therefore, *fill* is confined to the goal-object construction. In contrast to *pour* and *fill, coil* does meet the necessary condition for alternation, but not the sufficient conditions. *Coil* — as in *John coiled the hose around the tree* — describes both a specific way in which the theme changes location (that it is moved in a circular fashion) and a particular change of state of the goal (roughly, that it ends up with a flexible object around it). But in English, there happens to be no narrow range rule that applies to verbs like *coil* to provide them with the thematic core needed for the goal-object argument structure — therefore, *coil* does not alternate.

Verbs that fall under the same broad range rule are said to be members of the same broad conflation class (a conflation class is a possible conjunction of predicates in a language; the notion goes back to Talmy, 1985), while verbs that fall under the same narrow range rule are members of the same narrow conflation class. The broad range rule associated with a certain alternation is more or less universal, assuming a language exhibits the alternation at all, while narrow range rules are more arbitrary and so tend to be somewhat language-specific. The narrow conflation classes associated with the locative alternation in English are shown in Table 1, along with other narrow conflation classes that might have alternated (because they fall under the same broad conflation class), but happen not to.

The role of broad and narrow conflation classes — and of the corresponding lexical rules — differs depending on whether an argument structure alternation changes the verb's morphosyntactic structure, for example, by marking the verb morphologically or by turning a finite verb into a participle (as is the case for the passive in English). For alternations with no such change, membership in a broad conflation class is a necessary but not a sufficient condition; in addition, the verb must be a member of an alternating narrow conflation class. But if the alternation involves such a change, as the passive does in most languages, then membership in the broad conflation

Table 1. Examples of alternating and nonalternating narrow conflation classes proposed for the locative alternation in English (Pinker, 1989, p. 126ff.) Content verbs most basically denote a change of location, and container verbs a change of state (see Schwartz-Norman, 1976, for the distinction, and Pinker, 1989, p. 124ff., on how to distinguish the two).

I. CONTENT VERBS	II. CONTAINER VERBS
Alternating. Simultaneous forceful contact and motion of a mass against a surface: *brush, dab, daub, plaster, rub, slather, smear, smudge, spread, streak.*	**Alternating**. A mass is forced into a container against the limits of its capacity: *pack, cram, crowd, jam, stuff, wad.*
Alternating. Force is imparted to a mass, causing ballistic motion in a specified spatial distribution along a trajectory: *inject, spatter, splash, splatter, spray, sprinkle, squirt.*	**Nonalternating**. Addition of an object or mass to a location causes an esthetic or qualitative, often evaluative, change in the location: *adorn, burden, clutter, deck, dirty, embellish, emblazon, endow, enrich, festoon, garnish, imbue, infect, litter, ornament, pollute, replenish, season, soil, stain, taint, trim*
Nonalternating. A mass is enabled to move via the force of gravity: *dribble, drip, drizzle, dump, ladle, shake, slop, slosh, spill.*	
Nonalternating. Flexible object extended in one dimension is put around another object (preposition is *around*): *coil, spin, twirl, twist, whirl, wind.*	

class is both a necessary and a sufficient condition. That is, when the alternation changes the verb's morphosyntactic properties, the broad range rules are both property-predicting and existence-predicting.[19]

This means that motion verbs in German, for example, in which the locative alternation is marked, only need to describe both a specific change of location of the theme and a specific change of state of the goal in order to participate in the alternation — which particular location- and state-changes they specify is irrelevant. This explains why the German verb *wickeln*, the translation equivalent of English *coil*, may alternate (if it is prefixed in the

---

19. As an example of an alternation that involves such a change, Pinker (1989) discusses the passive in English, which differs from the locative, the dative, and the causative alternation in that it changes the verb's morphosyntactic properties (turning the finite verb into a participle) and in that it applies to a much larger class of verbs. The broader applicability of the passive has often been taken as evidence that it is a syntactic operation, i.e., an operation that applies to all verbs with a direct object regardless of the verb's semantics (see Marantz, 1984, among others). Pinker (1989, p. 147ff.) discusses in detail his reasons for treating the passive as a lexical operation, his main argument being that not all verbs with a direct object passivize, for example, *cost, weigh,* and *contain.* I think his arguments are well taken; in fact, in the framework that underlies the analysis of the locative alternation adopted here (cf. Chapter 3), the passive is likewise considered a lexical operation.

goal-object form with *um-* 'around' rather than *be-*) — cf. *Er umwickelte den Arm mit einem Verband* 'He around-coiled the arm with a bandage'.

How can children determine the syntactic frames of verbs? They can do so, according to Pinker, by generalizing only within the limits of the conflation classes; that is, they are class-wise conservative. If the alternation is morphologically marked, the presence of the affix is the child's cue that the broad range lexical rule can be applied to any verb within the broad conflation class defined by the rule. That is, for morphologically marked alternations, the child associates the change in argument structure with the affix and will generalize within the limits of the relevant broad conflation classes, ignoring the intricate semantic differences between verbs of different narrow conflation classes within this class. If the alternation is unmarked, however, the child cannot associate the alternation with a particular morpheme, and so will generalize only within the limits of the narrow conflation classes. When a child has noticed that the content verbs *brush, dab,* and *smear,* for example, may take either their theme or their goal as direct object, she will automatically know that there is a narrow range rule that changes these verbs into verbs denoting a (specific) change of state, such that the verbs take their goal as direct object. She will then generalize this rule to verbs like *daub, plaster,* and *smudge,* because these verbs are similar to *brush, dab,* and *smear* in a particular way: They share the same grammatically relevant meaning elements and so are members of the same narrow conflation class (simultaneous forceful contact and motion of a mass against a surface). But the observation that *smear* and similar verbs alternate will not lead her to think that the alternation applies to verbs in a different narrow conflation class, such as *spray* (force is imparted to a mass, thus causing ballistic motion of the mass that results in the mass being spatially distributed on the goal). She will take *spray* to be an alternator only if she has observed either *spray* itself or another verb in the same narrow conflation class, such as *splash,* being used in both argument structures. Regardless of whether the alternation is marked, the child will never develop overly general rules for argument structure changes that later have to be constrained by adding criteria: Her productive knowledge of argument structure alternations will be appropriately constrained from the start.

But how, then, to account for children's errors? According to Pinker, errors occur for two reasons. First, the child may occasionally override the narrow range rules and use a verb that is compatible with a particular broad range rule in an argument structure she has not observed for verbs belonging to its narrow conflation class. This type of error need not be repaired — the child knows in principle that her utterance is not quite right. Second, the child may make errors because she has misunderstood the meaning of a verb. For example, if she erroneously assumes that *spit* specifies that force is imparted to a mass in such a way that it causes not only ballistic motion but also a specific spatial distribution of the mass on the goal, she will assume that *spit* alternates (provided that she has already developed a narrow range rule for members of the ballistic motion class, such as *splash*), so she might say things like *The baby spat the table with spinach.* She will stop using *spit* in the goal-object construction as soon as she learns that the verb says nothing about how the mass is distributed on the goal but rather highlights that something is expelled from inside an entity.

Empirical Evidence for the Object Affectedness Linking Rule

Recall that Pinker and his collaborators assume that only a single linking rule is needed to account for the change in the argument structure of locative verbs. For convenience, the rule is repeated in (44):

(44) **The Object Affectedness Linking Rule**
An argument is encodable as the direct object of a verb if its referent is specified as being affected in a specific way in the semantic representation of the verb (Gropen et al. 1991a, p. 118).

The Object Affectedness Linking Rule predicts that children will be more willing to express an argument as direct object if they understand the verb as specifying that the argument is affected. Pinker and his collaborators tested this prediction with children acquiring English in a series of experiments involving both existing and novel verbs (the experiments on existing verbs are reported in Gropen et al., 1991a, and those on novel verbs in Gropen et al., 1991b).

Gropen et al.'s first experiment involved the nonalternating verbs *pour, dump, empty,* and *fill. Pour* and *dump*, which take only their theme as direct object, were considered to specify a particular manner of motion of the theme and not a particular change of state of the goal; *fill* and *empty*, in contrast, which were both assumed to take only their goal as direct object,[20] were

---

20. *Empty*, however, turned out to be an alternator: The adult subjects did use it in the theme-object form (see below).

classified as describing a particular change of state of the goal and no particular manner of motion of the theme. Sixteen adults and 48 children, assigned to 3 groups with mean ages of 3;1, 3;11, and 5;0, participated in the study. The subjects were first tested to determine whether they were biased toward a manner or an endstate interpretation of the verbs, the prediction being that a bias toward a manner interpretation would make the use of the theme-object form more likely, whereas a bias toward an endstate interpretation would make the use of the goal-object form more likely. (Having a bias toward a manner interpretation of *fill* (for example) means that the subject erroneously assumes that *fill* specifies a particular manner of motion, and that this manner aspect is more important than any endstate the verb might also denote.)

In the test for bias, the subjects were shown several sets of drawings, each consisting of two panels much like a comic strip; the two panels were presented as showing successive phases of the same action. The first panel always showed a particular manner in which an object or some mass was moved, and the second showed the effect the action had on a goal object. The first drawing in each set was an introductory drawing showing an action that could be described by both *pour* and *fill*, or by both *dump* and *empty*. (It was assumed that if children attributed a particular manner to actions of filling, this manner would most likely be that specified by *pour*, since actions of filling a container typically involve pouring some stuff. Conversely, it was assumed that if children attributed an endstate meaning to *pour*, this would most likely be the endstate specified by *fill*, since actions of pouring typically involve filling a container.) For example, one introductory drawing — described as *filling* to half the subjects and *pouring* to the other half — showed a woman pouring water from a pitcher into a glass and the glass ending up full.

The introductory drawing for each set was followed by two similar test drawings, presented at the same time. One test drawing for *fill* and *pour* showed the woman again pouring the water, but this time it ended up spilled; the other showed the woman letting the water drip into the glass from a faucet, and then a full glass of water. The subjects were tested on their interpretation of *pour* (or *fill*) by being asked to decide which of the two test drawings depicted an action of pouring (filling). Each verb was tested by two sets of drawings, each set portraying a different instance of pouring (filling). Children who selected the dripping/filling pair were considered to be biased toward an endstate reading of *pour*, and were expected to use *pour* in the

ungrammatical goal-object construction more often than children who understood the verb correctly. Similarly, children who selected the pouring/spilling
pair were considered to be biased toward a manner interpretation of *fill*, and
were expected to use *fill* in the ungrammatical theme-object construction
more often than children who understood the verb correctly.

Immediately after a subject had selected a particular drawing as representing (e.g.) *fill*, he or she was probed with a question on the drawing selected. For
one of the two drawing sets for a verb, the question focussed on the goal (e.g.,
What is the woman doing with the glass?), and for the other it focussed on the
theme (e.g., *What is the woman doing with the water*?) (thus, each child had to
answer two questions per verb). Goal-focus questions were intended to invite
subjects to use a goal-object construction, and theme-focus questions a theme-
object construction. The purpose of the probes was to prevent children from
using only the theme-object construction, for example, because of an overall
response bias; such a bias would mask whether the subjects were in principle
willing to extend a verb to the goal-object construction.

Gropen et al. were mainly interested in whether children would use a
verb in a nonadultlike construction because they had misinterpreted its meaning. In general, children used both *fill* and *empty* in both goal-object and in
theme-object constructions, but used *pour* and *dump* only in theme-object
constructions. Since goal-object constructions are grammatical for *fill* and
empty, and theme-object constructions are grammatical for *pour* and *dump*,
only the incorrect theme-object constructions for *fill* and (to some extent)
empty were of interest. Let us look first at the data for *fill*. Here, the predicted
association between a manner bias and the theme-object form was found only
for the oldest children; the youngest and the middle age group of children who
used *fill* in the theme-object construction did so regardless of whether they
were biased toward a manner interpretation. *Empty* was used by adults as well
as children in theme-object constructions, so the children's use of *empty* in
these constructions could not be considered nonadultlike. Therefore, Gropen
et al. focussed on whether children who were biased toward a manner
interpretation for *empty* used the verb more often in theme-object than goal-
object constructions. This was found to be true for the combined child groups.
Children's use of the verb was also influenced by the query topic: They
produced more theme-object sentences for *empty* in response to the theme-
focus question, and more goal-object sentences in response to the goal-focus
question. The meaning children attributed to a verb was, then, not the only
factor that influenced their choice of a syntactic frame.

A follow-up study of only the verb *fill* was conducted with 16 adults and 48 children assigned to 3 groups with mean ages of 4;0, 5;7, and 7;9. The goal of this study was to test whether the first experiment had failed to reveal a significant association between verb interpretation and syntactic choice for the two youngest groups of children because the semantic test was too crude. The follow-up study tested both whether children were BIASED towards a manner interpretation and whether they were SENSITIVE to manner. Sensitivity to manner was defined more broadly than bias: Bias meant that a child judged manner (incorrectly) as more important than the endstate specified by *fill*, whereas sensitivity meant only that, regardless of what she thought about endstate, the child took *fill* to specify a characteristic manner. The subjects' sensitivity was determined by using pictures that established a contrast between pouring and dripping. The choice between a pouring and a dripping action as the referent for *fill* was presented twice to each subject, once when both actions resulted in a full container, and once when they both resulted in an empty container. (Thus, the sensitivity test did not force children do decide whether manner was more important than endstate.) A child who selected the pouring picture on both trials was assumed to be sensitive to, and to associate *fill* with, the characteristic manner in which something is moved in order to fill a container.

This change in emphasis was somewhat successful. When the data of the two youngest groups of children were combined, an association was found between sensitivity towards the pouring aspect of *fill* and the use of *fill* in the theme-object construction. But the behavior of a substantial number of subjects was at odds with the predictions of the Object Affectedness Linking Rule: Of the 34 children who used *fill* in the theme-object construction, 10 did so even though they did not show sensitivity to the pouring aspect of *fill*. To account for this, Gropen (1989) points out that the semantic test captured only one possible way in which children may (incorrectly) associate a manner aspect with the verb. The 10 children who used *fill* in the theme-object construction but who were not sensitive to a pouring manner may have associated some other manner with the verb. As in the first experiment, the children were influenced by the question focus: They used *fill* more often in theme-object sentences in response to a theme-focus question, and more often in goal-object sentences in response to goal-focus questions.

To achieve a better control over the meaning children attribute to a verb, a new set of subjects were taught a novel verb, *keat*. This verb was introduced in a syntactically neutral fashion, e.g., *This is keating*, and was presented as either a manner verb or an endstate verb. In the first experiment, the referent event consisted of an object (e.g., a package of marbles) that was moved to a surface (e.g., a piece of felt). When introduced as a manner verb, *keat* was paired with a situation in which the object was moved to the surface in a zigzagging manner, and when introduced as an endstate verb, it was paired with a situation in which the surface sagged down as the result of the objects being placed on it. Sixteen adults and 48 children, assigned to 3 age groups with mean ages 3;11, 5;1, and 7;5, participated in this study. After teaching the subjects the meaning of the novel verb, the experimenter tested how they would use it by focussing either on the moved object or on the surface (e.g., *Can you tell me, by using the word keating, what I am doing with the marbles/ with the felt?*). The experiment tested whether *keat* would be used in the theme-object construction when it was introduced as a manner verb, and in the goal-object construction when it was introduced as an endstate verb.

Subjects were indeed more likely to use the theme-object form when *keat* was presented as a manner verb than as an endstate verb. Surprisingly, however, they did not show a systematic preference for the goal-object form for the endstate verb: In general, they used theme-object forms much more often, and usually produced goal-object forms only when the query invited them to do so. Gropen et al. (1991b) discuss two possible sources for the infrequent use of goal-object forms for the endstate verb. First, children might have had a general tendency to interpret verbs as specifying manner. Such a tendency, first observed by Gentner (1978), showed up in Gropen et al.'s first experiments, described earlier, on existing verbs. Second, children might have mistaken certain unintended manner properties of the endstate action to be part of the verb's meaning. To make the surface sag, the experimenter had to nudge the moved entity a little against the surface, and this might have invited the children to think that the verb involved a particular manner of motion.

In a subsequent experiment the authors tried to overcome this shortcoming by creating a purer endstate verb. This verb named an action in which a surface changed color when an object, e.g., a sponge, was brought into contact with it. A second verb was introduced as a manner verb that (again) named an action in which an object was moved in a zigzagging manner to the surface, without causing the surface to change color. This time, the manipulation was highly successful: The middle age group of children (mean age 5;1) and the adults used the endstate verb exclusively in the goal-object construction, regardless of query; and the youngest and oldest children (mean ages 3;11 and 7;5) also used the goal-object form significantly more often than the theme-object form. In contrast, the manner verb was mainly used in the theme-object construction by all subjects.

Gropen et al. (1991b) also tested whether children were more likely to use the goal-object form when the goal could be interpreted holistically. If the holism effect (Anderson, 1971) indeed follows from a state-change undergone by the goal, and if children are guided in their syntactic choices by the Object Affectedness Linking Rule, then they should be more likely to use the goal-object form to name an action in which a surface becomes completely covered or filled than to name an action in which it is only partly filled. This hypothesis was tested in an experiment in which subjects (48 children assigned to 3 age groups with mean ages of 4;0, 5;7, and 7;10, and 16 adults) were taught a novel verb in either a partitive or a holistic condition. In the former, the verb named an action in which (e.g.) a single peg was inserted into a hole on a board, and in the latter, it named an action in which pegs were inserted until all the holes on the board had a peg. The subjects had to respond to questions focussing on either the theme or the goal. As predicted, they responded with more goal-object forms when the verb named a holistic action than a partitive action. This effect was due mainly to the tendency of subjects to avoid goal-object responses in the partitive condition, even when the query invited them to do so. Gropen et al. concluded that, as predicted, children were sensitive to the holistic interpretation because they were more likely to make the goal NP the direct object when the surface it referred to was completely rather than only partially filled or covered.

In sum, Gropen et al.'s experiments provide partial support for their hypothesis that children are influenced in their choice of syntactic frame by their interpretation of verb meanings, as predicted by the Object Affectedness Linking Rule. The subjects in the experiments were also influenced by the type of probe question they had to answer. An overall preference was found for the theme-object form over the goal-object form, which Gropen et al. explain by suggesting that children are generally biased toward a manner interpretation of verbs. But their subjects were also often willing to use a verb in the theme-object construction when they were not found to be biased toward, or had not been taught, a manner interpretation of the verb. Gropen et al. argue that these responses do not necessarily undermine the role of the Object Affectedness Linking Rule in children's acquisition of argument structure alternations, because the subjects in their experiments might have associated existing verbs with a manner that was not detected by the pretest, and they might have associated novel verbs that were intended to specify an endstate with a specific manner.

2.5.2 *Does the Lexicosemantic Structure Theory Provide an Adequate Account of the Locative Alternation in English?*

Pinker's (1989) theory of broad and narrow range rules offers an enormously rich and complex account of how children acquire verb argument structure and argument structure alternations. It neither underestimates the intricacy of the phenomena nor does it simply project theoretical principles of linguistic analysis onto the child's mind. By analyzing argument structure alternations in terms of an interaction between linking rules and broad- and narrow range lexical rules, Pinker offers an explanation for why argument structure alternations are so similar cross-linguistically (because they are constrained by the same innate linking rules), and why individual languages may be so puzzlingly choosy about which verbs they allow to participate in a particular alternation. The theory also provides us with a hypothesis about the difference between morphologically marked and unmarked alternations. In short, Pinker's theory is truly a psycholinguistic achievement, in that it offers both a general and plausible linguistic analysis of verb argument structure and an account of learning that is in touch with psychology.

The theory of broad and narrow range rules differs from the other approaches to the acquisition of argument structure alternations discussed in this chapter in that the proposed linguistic analyses are both specific enough and general enough to allow researchers to test whether claims similar to those made for English also hold for other languages. One of the main goals of evaluating Pinker's theory is therefore to discuss whether the Object Affectedness Linking Rule, which supposedly licenses the syntactic flexibility of verbs of motion, correctly predicts the behavior of such verbs in German. First, however, I will evaluate Pinker's (1989) theoretical claims about the locative alternation on the basis of the English data and the experimental evidence that he and his colleagues have presented in support of these claims. (For discussions of Pinker's theory, see also Naigles, 1991; C. Lee Baker, 1992, and Ingham, 1992.)

Neglecting Morphological Factors

By classifying locative verbs into narrow conflation classes entirely on the basis of semantic criteria, Pinker runs the risk of underestimating the effects morphological properties may have on argument structure (see Wunderlich, 1987; Baker, 1988, 1992; Jackendoff, 1990; Urbas, 1990; Hale & Keyser, 1993; Stiebels & Wunderlich, 1994, among others, and the discussion in 2.3.2, for analyses of these effects). The particular conflation classes he proposes contain underived verbs like *spray* and *pour* as well as a mixture of deadjectival verbs like *fill* and *dirty*, denominal verbs like *pile* and *cover*, and prefixed verbs like *entangle* and *intersperse*. But a verb's morphological derivation correlates strongly with its syntactic behavior. The narrow conflation classes contain about 29 denominal verbs, and only 4 of these alternate (*plaster, heap, pile,* and *stack*). The presence of a prefix is also a good predictor of argument structure: Of the 28 prefixed verbs in Pinker's list, only 2 alternate (*inject* and *bestrew*). There are 3 deadjectival verbs, *dirty, enrich,* and *fill* (*empty* is not listed), none of which alternates. These strong correlations between the verb's morphological structure and their syntactic properties are left unexplained in Pinker's semantic classification.

Problems with the Claim that the Goal Changes State

According to Pinker and Gropen et al., the goal argument of a verb must be specified to undergo a change of state in order to be expressed as the direct object. This claim is designed to account, among other things, for the two perspectives that are associated with the two argument structures of verbs like *load*: Theme-object sentences put the focus on the theme because its location change is the main predication, whereas goal-object sentences put the focus on the goal because its change of state is the main predication and the theme's location change is only a means to bring about this state-change.

This claim is problematic because it implies that the perspective focussing on the goal is brought about (caused) by the perspective focussing on the theme. But, as Wunderlich (1992) points out in discussing Rappaport and Levin's (1988) account of the locative alternation (on which the broad range rule for the alternation is based), it makes no sense to assume that one perspective causes another perspective. Perspectives are mutually exclusive ways of conceptualizing an event: If a speaker has chosen to conceptualize an event according to the change of state perspective (for example), the change of location perspective is ruled out.

Gropen et al.'s claim that the goal undergoes a change of state is problematic for yet another reason: A standard test for assessing whether a verb specifies a change of state, the choice of temporal adverbials, reveals that goal-object sentences do not necessarily involve such a change. Verbs denoting states (e.g., *be silent, be wide awake*) or processes (e.g., *grow, giggle*) combine with durational adverbials like *for two hours.* Verbs that denote temporally bounded events (e.g., *open, wake up*) combine with temporal frame adverbials like *within an hour* (Vendler, 1957; Dowty, 1972). Events may be bounded because they involve a transition from one state to another. Cf. (45)-(46):

(45) He was silent/wide awake for two hours/*within two hours.
      He was snoring/giggling for eight hours/*within eight hours.

(46) He woke up/opened the door *for five minutes (on the relevant reading)/within five minutes.

If a verb denoting a change of state can be combined with durational adverbials at all, the sentence may be interpreted in two ways. On one reading, it is interpreted iteratively, i.e., as describing a repetition of events of the same kind, as in *He kept opening and closing the door for five minutes.* On the other reading, it is interpreted as describing the post-change state (Klein, 1994), i.e., the state that obtains after the action has taken place, as in *He opened the door and it stayed open for five minutes* (see, for example, Croft, 1993, for an analysis of these interpretations). What a sentence like *He opened the door for five minutes* cannot mean is that the action of opening lasted for five minutes.

If it is correct that the ability of a motion verb to take its goal as object depends on the goals undergoing a change of state, then verbs used in the goal-object construction should combine only with frame adverbials, or should be interpreted iteratively or as referring to a post-change state if they are combined with durational adverbials. But neither of these two interpretations is required for the verbs in (47). These constructions do not, then, necessarily involve a change of state.

(47) He sprayed the lawn with water for hours/within an hour.
      The farmer sowed his fields with cotton seeds for days/within a day.
      She rubbed her leg with ointment for half an hour/within an hour.

This seems to be a serious problem for Pinker and Gropen et al.'s theory, since, according to the Object Affectedness Linking Rule, a goal must be specified as changing state in order to be expressed as direct object.

Evaluating the Experimental Evidence

Gropen et al.'s experiments leave a number of questions unanswered. First, why should it have been necessary to forestall an overall response bias by presenting children with a query focussing on either the theme or the goal? After all, the meaning of the verbs should have led children to choose one argument structure over the other anyway (Kay Bock, personal communication). Notice that the query often invited children to use a particular syntactic frame even though that frame was not backed up by the appropriate verb meaning, and they frequently accepted the invitation. For example, in the first of the experiments involving novel verbs, children generally used the theme-object form for the endstate verbs whenever the query focussed on the theme (Gropen, 1989; Gropen, 1991b).

Query focus and verb meaning were also dissociated in the other experiments. Recall that in the two experiments involving existing verbs (Gropen, 1989; Gropen et al., 1991a), children used the theme-object form for *fill* even when they did not show either a manner bias or — more inclusively — a sensitivity to manner. The authors argue that the subjects might have attributed a manner to the verb that was not captured by the semantic test. This is an empirical question (although one that is hard to falsify, since it might always be argued that the right manner interpretation was just not tested). However, notice that adults use the similar verb *empty* in the theme-object argument structure even though they presumably do not associate the verb with any particular manner of motion. (You can empty a bathtub by draining it or by scooping out the water.) Why, then, do we need to assume that some as yet undemonstrated nonadultlike attribution of manner underlies children's use of *fill* in the theme-object argument structure?[21]

Finally, the experiments raise the question why the goal-object form was so hard to elicit. If children determine a verb's syntactic frame on the basis of the Object Affectedness Linking Rule, then the subjects should usually have

---

21. Notice that the behavior of *empty* — like the failure of goal-object constructions to behave like state-changes discussed in the preceding section — casts doubt on the viability of the analysis proposed for the locative alternation: *Empty* does not, after all, specify a particular way in which the theme changes location.

chosen this argument structure for the endstate verbs. But, in fact, they used theme-object constructions more often than goal-object constructions for both endstate and manner verbs. The goal was made the direct object of an endstate verb more often than the theme in only one experiment, Experiment 4, in which the location changed color in the referent event. But according to the description the researchers give of the action leading to this color change (Gropen, 1989, p. 131ff.), the action did not seem to involve a change of location at all: The location was merely patted with the theme entity (e.g., a sponge), and thereby changed color. In my conception of such an action, I would classify the sponge not as a theme being moved to a location, but simply as an instrument. Thus, the verb naming such an action is not actually a verb of motion.

2.5.3 Does the Theory Explain the Properties of the Locative Alternation in German?

Recall that if an alternation involves the affixation of the verb, membership in the relevant broad conflation class is claimed to be both a necessary and a sufficient condition for alternating. I will show that this claim cannot account for the properties of the locative alternation in German. But first let us see whether the pattern of affixation in German and related languages is compatible with the claim that all verbs that take their goal as direct object are members of the same broad conflation class.

Affixation of the Verb

Recall that Pinker (1989) assumes that, regardless of whether the verb is a content verb (e.g., *spray*) or a container verb (e.g., *load*), it must belong to the change of location broad conflation class in order to take its theme as direct object, and to the change of state broad conflation class in order to take its goal as direct object. This predicts that in languages in which the verb is morphologically marked in one or both syntactic frames, the marking should apply equally to both content and container verbs.

However, in German and Dutch, in which the goal-object form of a verb is usually marked by the prefix *be-* (or equivalent marker), prefixation in general is required only for content verbs, as shown in (48) (but see Section 3.1.1, for examples of content verbs that need no prefix). Some container verbs may be prefixed with *be-*, but marking is almost never required, as shown in (49).[22] (I have classified the verbs as content or container verbs in accordance with Pinker's classification of the English forms that are cognate with them.)

(48) *Content Verbs*
   Die Vandalen spritzten Farbe auf das Auto. 'The vandals sprayed paint onto the car'
   Die Vandalen bespritzten/*spritzten das Auto mit Farbe. 'The vandals *be*-sprayed the car with paint'
   Lily schmierte Erdnußbutter auf die Tapete. 'Lily smeared peanut butter onto the wallpaper'
   Lily beschmierte/*schmierte die Tapete mit Erdnußbutter. 'Lily *be*-smeared the wallpaper with peanut butter'

(49) *Container Verbs*
   Sie luden/beluden den Wagen mit Heu. 'They loaded the wagon with hay'
   Sie luden Heu auf den Wagen. 'They loaded hay onto the wagon'
   Sie füllten/?befüllten den Tank mit Benzin. 'They filled the tank with gas'
   Sie füllten Benzin in den Tank. 'They filled gas into the tank'

That marking is required only for the derived form of content verbs, but not for the derived form of container verbs, suggests that different grammatical processes are involved in the two types of derivation. This is indeed what I will argue for in Chapter 3 (following Wunderlich's Preposition Incorporation account of the locative alternation). It is unclear to me how this asymmetry in marking could be captured in terms of broad range rule application, as is assumed in Pinker's theory. Moreover, how could children determine that both marked verbs like *bespritzen* and unmarked verbs like *füllen* belong to the same broad conflation class?

Is a Change of State Sufficient?

Recall that if an alternation involves the affixation of the verb, membership in a relevant broad conflation class is supposed to be both a necessary and a sufficient condition for alternating. This predicts that in German, content

---

22. An example of a container verb that sometimes requires marking is *packen* 'pack'. Thus, *den Koffer packen* 'to pack the suitcase' is fine without marking, but *den Tisch packen* 'to pack the table' is ungrammatical; it must be *den Tisch bepacken*. One possible explanation for the ungrammaticality of the latter example may be that *packen* functions both as a content and a container verb, and that the two variants behave differently with respect to the locative alternation. That is, the container verb variant of *packen* is fine only when the goal NP refers to a container-like object; whereas the content verb variant participates in the locative alternation just like many other ordinary content verbs, i.e., it may combine with goal NPs referring to surfaces when prefixed with *be*-.

verbs should participate in the locative alternation regardless of the specific manner in which the theme is specified to change location. But not all content verbs in German (i.e., those that take the theme as obligatory argument) participate in the alternation. Cf. (50):

(50) Die Schüler wirbelten ihre Taschen auf die Straße. 'The students whirled their bags onto the street'
      *Die Schüler bewirbelten die Straße mit ihren Taschen. 'The students *be*-whirled the street with their bags'
      Sie schleuderte die Müllsäcke auf den Hof. 'She flung the garbage bags onto the yard'
      *Sie beschleuderte den Hof mit den Müllsäcken. 'She *be*-flung the yard with the garbage bags'

In German, denoting a particular manner in which the theme changes location is clearly not a sufficient condition for participating in the locative alternation. This shows that the difference between morphologically marked and unmarked locative alternations is not appropriately captured by assuming that children only need to learn broad range rules to acquire the former, but both broad and narrow range rules to acquire the latter. Unfortunately, then, the elegant account that Pinker's theory seems to provide for the role of the morphological marking in argument structure alternations is not borne out by the data.

Is a Change of Location/Change of State Even Necessary?

If the Object Affectedness Linking Rule is indeed a universal constraint on direct objects of motion verbs, it should apply to all languages. However, in German, the theme can be the direct object even when it is not specified to change location in a specific manner, as shown in (51a) for the container verb *füllen* 'fill'. The same holds for its translation equivalent in Swedish, shown in (51b), and in Japanese, shown in (52). That is, these verbs behave like *empty* in English, which also specifies no particular manner in which the theme changes location but may take its theme as direct object.

(51) a.   Der Mann füllte das Glas mit Wein./Der Mann füllte Wein in das Glas.
      b.   mannen fyllde glaset med vinet./mannen fyllde vinet i glaset.
           (Example taken from Sjöström, 1990, p. 114)
           'The man filled the glass with wine'/'The man filled wine into the glass'

(52) Taro-ga mizu-de gurasu-o mitasita./Taro-ga gurasu-ni mizu-o mitasita.
      Taro-NOM water-with glass-ACC fill-PAST./Taro-NOM glass-LOC water-ACC fill-PAST.
      'Taro filled the glass with water'/'Taro filled water into the glass'
      (Example taken from Juffs, 1996, p. 102)

Similarly, but in the opposite direction, a goal can be the direct object in German even when it does not undergo a specific change of state, or even any change of state at all. With respect to specificity, note that in (53a), the verb does not specify that the cake necessarily undergoes any particular change of state, e.g., the sugar may end up on the cake in a thin or thick layer, or even in little heaps. As long as the sugar moves in a distributed manner, the action may be referred to as *bestreuen*. Similarly, in (53b), the paint may end up on the car in any pattern at all as long as it goes on with a brush or similar instrument.

(53) a. Donna bestreut den Kuchen mit Zucker.
'Donna *be*-sprinkles the cake with sugar'
b. Die Vandalen bestreichen das Auto mit Farbe.
'The vandals *be*-brush the car with paint'

In fact, the theme need not even end up on the goal at all, or leave any visible traces:

(54) a. Die Jungen bewerfen die Wand mit Kieselsteinen.
'The boys *be*-throw the wall with pebbles'
b. Ununterbrochen berieselt das Kind die Rutsche mit Sand.
'On and on, the child *be*-sprinkles the slide with sand'

That no state-change is involved can be shown by the distribution of temporal adverbials: Except for *werfen*, all the verbs in (53)-(54) can combine with durational adverbials without forcing an iterative or a post-state reading, as shown in (55). This is also true for *gießen*, which alternates, as shown in (56) (its English translation equivalent *pour* does not meet the necessary condition for the goal-object form).

(55) a. Minutenlang berieselte das Kind die Rutsche mit Sand.
'For several minutes, the child *be*-sprinkled the slide with sand'
b. Stundenlang bestreuten die Bäcker den 100m-Kuchen mit Zucker, um mit dem längsten Kuchen der Welt ins Guinness-Buch der Rekorde zu kommen.
'For hours, the bakers *be*-sprinkled the 100m cake with sugar, to make the Guinness Books of Records with the longest cake of the world'
c. Eine halbe Stunde lang bestrich Renée den kranken Gummibaum mit einer speziellen Nährlösung.
'For half an hour, Renée *be*-brushed the sick gum tree with a special nutrient fluid'

(56) Eine halbe Stunde lang begoß sie den Braten mit Butter.
'For half an hour, she *be*-poured the roast with butter'

Numerous examples could be added to show that in German, verbs of motion may take their goal as direct object even though they do not specify that the goal changes state. This supports the conclusion, drawn earlier on the basis of the behavior of adverbs with verbs like *strew* and *spray* in English, that the Object Affectedness Linking Rule does not correctly constrain the kind of arguments that may become the direct object of verbs of motion.

Let me summarize the main points so far of my evaluation of Pinker's theory. With respect to English, I have argued that the morphological structure of motion verbs should be taken into account and that temporal adverbials should be used to test whether the goal-object form requires that the goal undergo a change of state. According to this test, there are at least some verbs in English that may take their goal as direct object even when they do not specify a state-change of the goal. In discussing Gropen et al.'s experiments, I pointed out that Pinker's and Gropen et al.'s account of the locative alternation leaves unexplained why it was so difficult to elicit the goal-object form and why subjects often used the theme-object form of verbs even when they did not think that the verbs specified a specific manner in which the theme changes location. The predictions of the theory were then evaluated on the basis of German. In German (and Dutch), marking is needed only for the goal-object form of content verbs, never for container verbs; it is unclear how the claim that there is a single change of state broad conflation class for both types of verb can accomodate this difference between the verbs. Certainly the most serious empirical problem of the theory is that in at least one language, German, it is not a necessary condition for a verb to alternate that the goal change state, as it should be if the Object Affectedness Linking Rule indeed were a universal condition on when the internal arguments of a motion verb may become the direct object. Nor is it apparently necessary that the theme change location in a specific manner — cf. *füllen*.

A Possible Role for Affectedness in the Acquisition of Marked Alternations?

The discussion so far has shown that in German, a motion verb need not describe a state-change of the goal in order to appear in the goal-object construction. Is Object Affectedness then just irrelevant for German? Or might it be irrelevant only for the adult grammar but still be relevant, as Gropen et al. claim, for the acquisition of the alternation? I will consider this possibility by applying to the problem a theory that has been proposed by Lebeaux (1988) to account for the acquisition of the passive.

Lebeaux proposes that children start out using affectedness initially for acquiring the passive, but then learn that verbs may passivize even though they do not specify affectedness. Like Gropen et al., Lebeaux assumes that children are equipped with an innate linking rule on the basis of which they know that an affected argument is the logical object of a verb. Therefore, they are able to identify the subject of certain passive constructions, i.e, actional passives like *John was hit*, as the verb's logical object and so can learn that and how the argument structure of the base verb is changed under passivization. But, argues Lebeaux, to acquire the full range of passive constructions in their language, children cannot exclusively rely on their innate linking rule, since many verbs may passivize even though they do not specify affectedness — for instance *see* and *hear*. The passives of these verbs, e.g., *John was seen/ heard*, have been called nonactional passives. To acquire nonactional passives, children must learn that the crucial relationship between a verb and its internal argument is not the semantically determined relationship of affectedness but rather the syntactically determined relationship of case-marking.[23] In Government and Binding Theory, on which Lebeaux draws, it is assumed that in the active voice, the verb assigns case to its direct object. The argument structure change characteristic of the passive is explained by assuming that when the verb is marked by passive morphology, it can no longer assign case to its direct object; this means that the argument in object position must move to subject position in order to receive case (see Haegeman, 1991, for a summary and references). On the basis of this account of the passive, Lebeaux proposes that children have to learn how passive morphology affects the case-marking potential of the verb; when they have learned this, they will no longer restrict passivization to verbs like *hit*, which specify an affected argument, but also correctly extend it to verbs like *see*, which do not. By distinguishing between actional and nonactional passives in terms of affectedness, Lebeaux proposes to account for the finding reported by Maratsos, Kuczaj, Fox, and Chalkley (1979) that actional passives like *he was hit* are acquired before nonactional passives like *he was seen*.

According to Lebeaux, children can give up the affectedness constraint in acquiring the passive only because the alternation is marked. English also

---

23. Pinker (1989), in contrast, assumes that John is affected in some sense both by being beaten and by being heard, since both verbs specify that an agent affects or defines the state John is in. Thus, Pinker proposes to make the notion of affectedness abstract enough to cover not only *beat*, which accords with our naive understanding of what it means to be affected, but also *hear*.

has a means to passivize verbs that does not involve a marking on the verb, i.e., so-called nominal passives like *the city's destruction*; for these constructions, argues Lebeaux, the affectedness constraint still holds. *Destruction* is derived from the verb *destroy*, and *the city* can be interpreted as the logical object of *destroy* in the nominal passive because *destroy* specifies the argument in object position as affected. In contrast, in the superficially similar construction *John's perception*, John cannot be interpreted as the logical object of *perceive* since *perceive* does not specify an affected argument — *John* must therefore be the verb's logical subject, the perceiver. (This analysis of the nominals was first proposed by Anderson, 1979, and Fiengo, 1981.)

The morphologically marked locative alternation in German may differ from the morphologically unmarked alternation in English in the same way as passives differ from deverbal nominals in English. That is, in German, both affected and nonaffected goals may become the direct object, whereas English allows only affected goals in that position. On this assumption, Gropen et al. could accomodate the finding that in German the goal need not be affected to become the direct object by posing that children acquiring any language draw on the innate Object Affectedness Linking Rule initially, but, on discovering that the verb is marked in the goal-object argument structure in their language, look for a different criterion to decide whether a verb can appear in that construction, for example, whether it takes the goal as an obligatory argument.[24] When the alternation is unmarked in their language, children will not give up the constraint that the goal must be affected.

This modification of the theory, motivated by the need to account for the German data, comes at a cost: The restrictions on alternating verbs in German can no longer be determined, at least in part, on the basis of whether the verbs take an affected argument. That is, if Lebeaux's version of the Object Affectedness Linking Rule is accepted for German, the restrictions on the alternation, and how children determine these, must be accounted for without referring to affectedness. An experiment that tested both Gropen et al.'s and Lebeaux's version of the affectedness linking rule will be presented in Chapter 5. But let us first see whether it is possible to account for the locative alternation without invoking affectedness.

---

24. Notice that the criterion cannot be that the verb case-marks the goal in the theme-object form, since it is generally assumed that the *preposition* assigns case to this argument (see Haegeman, 1991, for a review of this issue).

Chapter 3

The Structure of the Locative Alternation

This chapter provides the linguistic analysis of the locative alternation on which I will build in subsequent chapters. A number of different analyses have been proposed in the literature, for example, the Change of State account of alternating verbs proposed by Rappaport and Levin (1985, 1988), on which Pinker (1989), Gropen (1989) and Gropen et al. (1991a,b) draw, and the syntactic incorporation analysis proposed by Baker (1988, 1992; cf. 3.2). (See also Eroms, 1980, and Günther, 1987, who analyze the alternation as a local phrase passive, and Olsen, 1994, who has offered an analysis similar to the one presented here. A detailed analysis of *be*-verbs is provided by Günther, 1974.) The analysis adopted here has been offered by Wunderlich (1992). Wunderlich proposes that the locative alternation results from the incorporation of a preposition into the verb, an operation that takes place in the lexicon. The Change of State account also posits a lexical operation that leads to a syntactic change. But the two accounts differ in that unlike the Change of State account, Wunderlich's does not posit that the verb changes its meaning. In view of the empirical problems of the Change of State account discussed in the preceding chapter, an account that does not draw on a semantic change is clearly preferrable over one that does (for a more detailed discussion of Rappaport and Levin's analysis of the locative alternation, see Olsen, 1994, 1995, and Brinkmann & Wunderlich, 1996). Wunderlich's analysis, then, offers a way to account for the acquisition of the locative alternation without appealing to the Object Affectedness Linking Rule.

Before presenting Wunderlich's analysis, I will provide some general information about *be*-verbs. This should enable the reader to gain a better idea of the linguistic context of the locative alternation in German, and to evaluate my proposals about the alternation and its acquisition.

3.1 General Properties of Expressing the Locative Argument as Direct Object in German

Recall that in German, the verb is marked morphologically when the locative argument is expressed as the verb's direct object. But marking is not always required, as has already been shown for the container verbs discussed in 2.5. I will summarize the main facts about prefixless goal-object verbs before turning to *be*-verbs proper. This will show what the prefix contributes to the alternation.

3.1.1 *Prefixless Goal-object Verbs*

One type of prefixless goal-object verbs is container verbs. Recall that in their basic argument structure the goal is the direct object: V [NP$_{goal}$ (*with* NP$_{theme}$)] (see also Pinker, 1989, p. 124ff., for discussion). Examples of container verbs in German are given again in (1). Some of these verbs serve double duty: They have the argument structure of container verbs, shown in (1a), and may also appear as true *be*-verbs, as in (1b). These *be*-forms are presumably derived from the (likewise derived) argument structure V [NP$_{theme}$ P NP$_{goal}$], shown in (1c); in general, the *be*-forms of container verbs behave like canonical *be*-verbs (cf. Wunderlich, 1992).

(1) a. Sie füllten die Kanister mit Benzin. 'They filled the cans with gasoline'
        Sie stopften das Loch mit Wax. 'They stuffed the hole with wax'[1]
        Sie luden den Wagen mit Heu. 'They loaded the wagon with hay'[2]
        Sie deckten das Dach mit Stroh. 'They covered the roof with straw'

    b. ? Sie befüllten die Kanister mit Benzin. 'They *be*-filled the cans with gasoline'
        * Sie bestopften das Loch mit Wax. 'They *be*-stuffed the hole with wax'
        Sie beluden den Wagen mit Heu. 'They *be*-loaded the wagon with hay'
        Sie bedeckten das Dach mit Stroh. 'They *be*-covered the roof with straw'

    c. Sie füllten Benzin in die Kanister. 'They filled gasoline into the cans'
        Sie stopften Wax in das Loch. 'They stuffed wax into the hole'
        Sie luden Heu auf den Wagen. 'They loaded hay onto the wagon'
        * Sie deckten Stroh auf das Dach. 'They covered straw onto the roof'

---

1. The simple goal-object form of *stopfen* is restricted to goal NPs referring to entities like holes and cracks. The verb may take other goal NPs as direct object, but only with a resultative predicate, for example, *Er stopfte die Tasche voll* 'He stuffed the bag full'. The theme-object form of the verb is not restricted in this way.

2. Labelle (1991) has proposed that English *load* is derived from a noun, and that the goal-object form of the verb thus incorporates the theme. This cannot be true for German, since *laden* is irregular whereas denominal verbs are always regular.

A second type of verb that need not be prefixed in the goal-object form are content verbs that, like English *spray*, have the basic argument structure V [NP$_{theme}$ P NP$_{goal}$], and may, under certain conditions, simply omit their theme and take the goal as object, as shown in (2). Verbs of this type differ from container verbs in that they appear only with limited types of goal NPs, such as those shown in (2); the constructions seem to be rather idiomatic. In many cases a *with*-phrase can only be added (according to my intuition) if it introduces a modified theme; for example, if it specifies that the wall was painted with *red* paint, but not simply with paint. (This may indicate that the verbs have undergone a semantic shift, for example, that *die Blumen gießen* has come to mean 'to water the flowers'.) When the verbs in (2) are combined with goals like those in (3), a prefix is required.

(2) die Wand/die Tür/das Fenster (mit roter Farbe) streichen
     'paint (lit.: streak) the wall/the door/the window (with red paint)'
     die Blumen/die Pflanzen (?mit abgekochtem Wasser) gießen
     'water (lit.: pour) the flowers/the plants (with boiled water)'
     die Einfahrt/die Straße/den Bürgersteig (mit Salz) streuen
     'sand (lit.: strew) the entrance/street/pavement (with salt)'
     Brote/Brötchen (??? mit Streichkäse) schmieren
     'make (lit.: smear) sandwiches/rolls (with spread cheese)'
     die Achsen (mit Spezialöl) schmieren
     'lubricate (lit.: smear) the axles (with special oil)'

(3) die Bruchstellen mit Kleber *streichen/bestreichen
     'to streak the sites of the fracture with glue'
     das Fleisch mit Butter *gießen/begießen
     'to *be*-pour the meat with butter'
     den Kuchen mit Zucker *streuen/bestreuen
     'to *be*-strew the cake with sugar'
     die Tischdecke mit Butter *schmieren/beschmieren
     'to *be*-smear the table cloth with butter'

Verbs that appear in constructions like *die Wand streichen* have a characteristic selectional restriction on their themes: The themes must be substances, not solid objects. Verbs with this selectional restriction will be relevant again in Chapter 4. Let us now turn to what the prefix *be-* contributes to the locative alternation.

3.1.2 *The Prefix* BE-

Historically, the prefix *be-* is related to the preposition *bi*, which no longer exists in this form in Modern German (Paul, 1920; Stiebels, 1991). In Gothic (around 300 A.D.), this preposition denoted spatial relationships equivalent to those specified by the prepositions *bei* 'near', *um* 'around', and *an* 'at' in Modern German. In Old High German (around 800 A.D.), *bi* specified roughly *around something* and later also *with respect to something*; it required the use of the accusative case. The existence of the preposition *bi* in former stages of German suggests that historically, *be*-verbs were derived by incorporating this preposition (Wunderlich, 1987).

In Modern German, many *be*-verbs have an idiosyncratic meaning so that it is no longer transparent what the prefix contributes semantically. But several subclasses of *be*-verbs can be distinguished (and will be discussed here) for which it *is* possible to determine the semantic contribution of the prefix.

Most *be*-verbs based on locative verbs provide an alternative for verb phrases that contain a prepositional phrase headed by a topological preposition (a topological preposition denotes a relationship between the to-be-located object and the neighborhood region of a reference object). Let me therefore briefly summarize the main semantic properties of topological prepositions in German. This will also show how *be*-verbs differ from container verbs and constructions like *die Wand streichen* 'paint (lit. streak) the wall'.

German has four topological prepositions, *in* 'in', *auf* 'on', *an* 'on/at', and *bei* 'at/near' (see Saile, 1984; Wunderlich, 1985, 1991; Herweg, 1988; Maienborn, 1990; Wunderlich & Herweg, 1991, among others, for semantic analyses of topological prepositions in German).[3] Like its translation equivalent in English, the preposition *in* denotes a relationship with the interior region of a reference object or relatum, regardless of whether there is a functional relation of containment between theme and relatum, as in *die Blumen in der Vase* 'the flowers in the vase', or a purely spatial relation of inclusion, as in *die Rosinen im Kuchen* 'the raisins in the cake'. *Auf* denotes a relationship with the outer surface of a relatum, and usually requires a relationship of support between theme and relatum, as in *die Vase auf dem Tisch* 'the vase on the table'. Sometimes it may also denote vertical relationships between objects, as in *das Etikett/die Fliege auf der Flasche* 'the label/

---

3. Constructions like *Eine Schlinge um den Hals* 'A rope around the neck' might suggest that *um* 'around' is a topological preposition, too. However, these constructions seem motivated by conceiving of the path denoted by *um* as a frozen path.

the fly on the bottle', but this seems to be restricted to cases in which the theme's underside is in contact with the relatum. The prepositions *an* and *bei* both denote a relationship with an unspecified neighborhood region of the relatum. They differ in that *an* can be used when the theme is in contact with the relatum — cf. *das Poster an der Wand* 'the poster on the wall' — as well as when it is not — cf. *das Haus am See* 'the house at the lake' — while *bei* can in general only be used if there is no contact between theme and relatum, as in *der Baum bei der Kirche* 'the tree near the church' and *die Vase beim Fernseher* 'the vase near the TV' (cf. Wunderlich, 1985; Herweg, 1988, and Maienborn, 1990, who offer different accounts of the semantics of *an* and *bei*). The preposition *bei* differs from the other topological prepositions in a fundamental way: It denotes only static spatial relationships, while *in*, *an*, and *auf* may also denote dynamic spatial relations, i.e., motion to a location.[4] The latter prepositions assign dative case when they express static relations, and accusative case when they express motion.

The phonological similarity between *be-* and the preposition *bei* might suggest that *be-*verbs derived from locative verbs typically paraphrase verb phrases containing this preposition, but they do not (cf. Wunderlich, 1987, and Stiebels, 1991, who discuss the semantic and phonological relationships between the former preposition *bi*, the prefix *be-*, and the preposition *bei* in Modern German). First, recall that *bei* cannot denote relationships of contact between the theme and the relatum, while *be-*verbs always denote relationships of contact; this is true of both *be-*verbs derived from transitive and intransitive verbs. Second, *be-*verbs cannot provide alternatives for verb phrases containing *bei* since *bei* cannot express motion, while *be-*verbs specify the transfer of a theme to a goal when the base verb is transitive (Wunderlich, 1987).

Be-, then, does not correspond semantically to the preposition to which it is phonologically most similar. Instead, *be-*versions of locative verbs correspond to verb phrases containing either the preposition *auf*, which, as noted above, specifies a relationship with the outer surface region of an object, or the preposition *an*, provided *an* describes a relationship of contact between theme and relatum, as shown in (4) and (5).

---

4. *Bei* may express dynamic relationships in some dialects of German, such as that spoken in the Rhineland.

(4) Bernd steigt auf die Mauer.
'Bernd climbs onto the wall'
Reiten auf den Wegen verboten!
'Horseback riding on the paths prohibited!'

Bernd besteigt die Mauer.
'Bernd climbs the wall'
Bereiten der Wege verboten!
'Horseback riding the paths prohibited!'

(5) Ted schmiert Butter auf die Tischdecke.
'Ted smeared butter onto the tablecloth'
Petra hängte Sterne an den Christbaum.
'Petra hung stars onto the Christmas tree'

Ted beschmiert die Tischdecke mit Butter.
'Ted smeared the tablecloth with butter'
Petra behängte den Christbaum mit Sternen.
'Petra hung the Christmas tree with stars'

In some cases, a *be*-verb can also replace a verb phrase that contains the preposition *in*, but this seems to be restricted to cases in which the base verb is intransitive, as in (6) (see also Stiebels, 1991, for discussion).

(6) Sie steigt in das Auto.
'She climbs into the car'
Sie tritt in das Zimmer.
'She steps into the room'
Zehn Familien wohnen in dem Hochhaus.
'Ten families live in the multistory building'
(Example from Stiebels, 1991, p. 67)

Sie besteigt das Auto.
'She climbs/enters the car'
Sie betritt das Zimmer.
'She steps/enters the room'
Zehn Familien bewohnen das Hochhaus.
'Ten families live in the multistory building'

Despite examples like (6), *be*-verbs usually specify spatial relations that exclude the interior of an object. This is clear for *be*-verbs derived from transitive base verbs: Except for *befüllen*, these verbs can only denote events in which the theme is moved to the exterior of the goal object. (*Befüllen* is not accepted by all speakers and — if acceptable at all — has a peculiar restriction on its direct object: The object NP must refer to a plurality of containers.) For example, the container verb *stopfen* 'stuff' and the content verb *quetschen* 'cram', which require that the goal object be a container, cannot be prefixed with *be-*, as shown in (7). Thus, German *be*-verbs are more restricted than their (unprefixed) English counterparts.

(7) Sie stopfte ihre Hosen in den Rucksack.
'She stuffed her trousers into her backpack'
Er quetschte seine Wäsche in den Koffer.
'He crammed his laundry into the suitcase'

*Sie bestopfte ihren Rucksack mit ihren Hosen.
'She stuffed her backpack with her trousers'
*Er bequetschte den Koffer mit seiner Wäsche.
'He crammed the suitcase with his laundry'

The semantic restrictions on *be*-verbs also hold for verbs that in principle alternate, e.g., *gießen* 'pour' and *werfen* 'throw': These verbs can only alternate and be prefixed with *be*- when they describe motion to the exterior of an object, as illustrated in (8):

(8) Ted bewirft die Wand/*den Abfluß (mit Dreck).
     'Ted *be*-throws the wall/*the outlet (with dirt)'
     Sue begießt den Braten/*das Glas (mit Wasser).
     'Sue *be*-pours the roast/*the glass (with water)'

(Notice that if *den Abfluß* and *das Glas* are interpreted as referring to the exterior of the corresponding entities, the sentences are grammatical.)

The topological restriction of *be*-verbs also influences how the referent of their object NP is interpreted. For example, the verb *packen* may take the goal as direct object without being prefixed with *be*-, as shown in (9a); in this case, the NP *ihr Auto* 'their car' refers to the car's inside. However, it may also be prefixed with *be*-, as shown in (9b); now, the NP *ihr Auto* is understood to refer to both the trunk and the top of the car. Obviously, it is the prefix *be*- that causes the different interpretations of *ihr Auto*:

(9) a. Wenn's in den Skiurlaub geht, packen Müllers ihr Auto immer als blieben sie ein halbes Jahr lang weg.
         'When leaving for the ski vacation, the Millers pack their car as if they will be away for half a year'
     b. Wenn's in den Skiurlaub geht, bepacken Müllers ihr Auto immer als blieben sie ein halbes Jahr lang weg.
         'When leaving for the ski vacation, the Millers *be*-pack their car as if they will be away for half a year'

To summarize, even though *be*-verbs that are derived from intransitive verbs may occasionally paraphrase verb phrases with the preposition *in*, *be*-verbs derived from transitive verbs in general paraphrase verb phrases with the prepositions *auf* and *an*. This topological restriction distinguishes *be*-verbs from both container verbs like *füllen* 'fill' and the content verbs in constructions like *die Achsen schmieren* 'lubricate the axles', in which the verb takes its goal as direct object without being prefixed. The restriction also shows that *be*- is more than a simple marker on the verb to indicate a certain argument structure — it is closely associated with specific independent prepositions. This supports an analysis according to which *be*-verbs are derived by incorporating a preposition, as Wunderlich (1987, 1992) has proposed. The topological restriction on *be*-verbs also contradicts a claim that is often made in analyses of argument structure changes: that argument structure changes involving a morphological marking on the verb are in general less restricted than argument structure changes that do not (Marantz, 1984; Lebeaux, 1988; Pinker, 1989). The topological restriction on *be*-verbs shows that the semantic effect of *be-* is not restricted to effects that have to do with the induced argument structure change, as seems plausible, e.g., for passive morphology, but that *be-* has a rather specific meaning and so introduces language-specific restrictions on the locative alternation.

In this section, the historical source of *be-* and its prepositional counterparts in Modern German have been discussed. But *be-* is not the only prefix that makes a verb take its locative argument as direct object. Some of the PREPOSITIONAL PREFIXES have the same effect on the argument structure of the verb.[5]

3.1.3 *Prepositional Prefixes*

A prepositional prefix (P-prefix) is phonologically identical to a semantically related preposition. German has several P-prefixes, for example, *hinter-* 'behind', *wider-* 'against', *um-* 'around', *über-* 'over', *unter-* 'under', and *durch-* 'through'. Of these, only *um-, unter-, über-*, and *durch-* are used productively with both intransitive and transitive motion verbs to make the locative argument the direct object (Wunderlich, 1983, 1987; Stiebels & Wunderlich, 1994), so I will limit my discussion to these. These prefixes have in common that they denote a path whose beginning and end point are not specified.[6]

P-prefix verbs derived from intransitive and transitive verbs of motion are shown in (10) and (11). The sentences in (11) show that P-prefix verbs derived from transitive base verbs may take an optional *with*-phrase.

(10) Das Schiff segelte um Kap Horn.   Das Schiff *um*segelte Kap Horn.
     'The ship sailed around Cape Horn'   'The ship *around*-sailed Cape Horn'
     Die Sportler joggten durch den Matsch.   Die Sportler *durch*joggten den Matsch.
     'The sportsmen jogged through the mud'   'The sportsmen *through*-jogged the mud'

---

5. Depending on the base verb, inseparable prefixes like *ver-* and *er-* may also cause the goal to become the direct object of the verb. The syntactic and semantic behavior of these prefixes is complex, and it is beyond the scope of this thesis to examine the conditions under which they bring about this change in argument structure. See Stiebels, 1996, for a recent and comprehensive analysis of prefix and particle verbs in German.

6. Some prepositions allow the speaker to infer a path by marking either the beginning or the (potential) end point of a motion, for example, *aus (dem Haus)* 'out of (the house)' and *zu (dem Haus)* 'to (the house)'. These prepositions can be used only as separable prefixes, cf. *Er goß das Wasser aus* 'He poured the water out' versus **Er ausgoß das Wasser* 'he *out*-poured the water'.

(11) Der Autoverkäufer malte rote Farbe über die Roststelle.
'The car dealer painted red paint over the rusty spot'
Der Bäcker mengte Kakao unter den Teig.
'The baker mixed cacao to-under the dough'

Der Autoverkäufer *über*malte die Roststelle (mit roter Farbe).
'The car dealer *over*-painted the rusty spot with red paint'
Der Bäcker *unter*mengte den Teig (mit Kakao)
'The baker *under*-mixed the dough with cacao' (meaning: He added cacoa to the dough.)

P-prefix verbs, like *be*-verbs, induce a holistic interpretation of the goal when it is the direct object of the verb. For example, the first sentence in (11) leaves open whether the rusty spot is indeed successfully covered, but the second sentence strongly suggests that the car dealer succeeded in hushing it up.

Another commonality between *be*-verbs and P-prefix verbs is that the denominal verbs among them are almost always derived by incorporating a noun specifying the theme. Cf. (12-13):

(12) Die Kinder machen Schmutz auf die Tischdecke.
'The children make spots on the tablecloth'
Ted tut Pflaster auf seine Knie.
'Ted puts plasters on his knees'

Die Kinder beschmutzen die Tischdecke.
'The children *be*-spot the tablecloth'
Ted bepflastert seine Knie.
'Ted *be*-plasters his knees'

(13) Sie bringen ein Dach über der Terrasse an.
'They install a roof over the terrace'
Sie bauen eine Mauer um das Grundstück.
'They build a wall around the property'

Sie *über*dachen die Terrasse.
'They *over*-roof the terrace'
Sie *um*mauern das Grundstück.
'They *around*-wall the property'

Some further examples are *bebildern* (lit. *be*-picture) 'illustrate', *durchbluten* (*through*-blood) 'supply with blood', *übertünchen* (*over*-varnish) 'white-wash', and *unterkeilen* (*under*-wedge) 'drive a wedge under something'. That *be*-verbs derived from a theme nominal are especially productive has often been noted in the literature (Kühnhold & Wellmann, 1973; Günther, 1974; Wunderlich, 1987; see also the novel denominal verbs in Chapter 1). Although there are fewer denominal P-prefix verbs than denominal *be*-verbs overall, they show the same pattern.[7]

---

7. A rough estimate of the proportion of denominal *be*-verbs and P-prefix verbs that incorporate a theme can be made by comparing the denominal verbs of both types listed in a dictionary. The Wahrig (1982) dictionary, for example, lists 199 denominal *be*-verbs, of which 157 or 78.9% are derived by incorporating the theme. Of 57 denominal P-prefix verbs prefixed with *um, unter, über,* and *durch,* 46, or 80.7%, are derived by theme incorporation, a very similar proportion. The remaining denominal *be*-verbs and P-prefix verbs have incorporated a noun denoting the instrument of an action (e.g., *durchschiffen* 'through-ship'), the goal of a motion (e.g., *beseitigen* 'remove'; lit.: 'bring to a side'), or a noun denoting a kind of person (e.g., *behexen* 'bewitch'), among others.

But there are also differences between *be*-prefixation and prefixation with a prepositional prefix. First, P-prefixes are less restricted in the type of intransitive verb they may combine with: While the prefix *be-* can combine only with intransitive verbs that have an agent in subject position, P-prefixes can combine with some intransitive verbs regardless of whether their subject is an agent or a theme. Cf. (14) and (15):

(14) Die Bierfässer rollten über die Straße.   Die Bierfässer *über*rollten die Straße.
     'The beer barrels rolled over the street'   'The beer barrels *over*-rolled the street'
     Die Steine schlugen durch die   Die Steine *durch*schlugen die
     Bretterwand.   Bretterwand.
     'The stones hit through the boarding'   'The stones *through*-hit the boarding'

(15) Die Murmeln rollten über den   *Die Murmeln *be*rollten den Bürgersteig.
     Bürgersteig.
     'The marbles rolled over the sidewalk'   *'The marbles *be*-rolled the sidewalk'
     Die Steine schlugen auf die Mauer.   *Die Steine *be*schlugen die Mauer.
     'The stones hit against the wall'   *'The stones *be*-hit the wall'

The prefix *be-* also differs from the P-prefixes in that it can combine with verbs other than motion verbs, as shown in the next section.

3.1.4 *Other Semantic Classes of BE-Verbs*

Apart from *be*-verbs with a locative meaning, there are several other semantic classes of *be*-verbs. Some of these can be distinguished in terms of the type of verb the *be*-verbs are derived from: verbs of active perception, verbs of material manipulation, verbs of speech, and verbs of emotion (Wunderlich, 1987). In their base forms, all these verbs take a prepositional phrase, the argument of which appears as the direct object of the corresponding *be*-verb. Examples are given in (16) to (19). Note that for these verbs, *be-* sometimes replaces prepositions other than *an* and *auf*, especially the prepositions *um* and *über*.

(16) *Verbs of active perception*
     Der blinde Firmenchef tastete/fühlte   Der blinde Firmenchef
     auf dem neuen Mazda herum.   betastete/befühlte den neuen Mazda.
     'The blind director of the company   'The blind director of the company
     touched/felt around on the new Mazda'   *be*-touched/*be*-felt the new Mazda'
     Der Hund roch/schnupperte/schnoberte   Der Hund beroch/beschnupperte/
     an der Wurst.   beschnoberte die Wurst.
     'The dog sniffed at the sausage'   'The dog *be*-sniffed the sausage'

(17) *Verbs of material manipulation*
Der Bildhauer arbeitete an dem Marmor.   Der Bildhauer bearbeitete den Marmor.
'The sculptor worked at the marble'   'The sculptor *be*-worked the marble'
Das Mädchen schnitzte an dem Ast.   Das Mädchen beschnitzte den Ast.
'The girl cut at the twig'   'The girl *be*-cut the twig'

(18) *Verbs of speech*
Man sprach/redete über das Rauchen   Man besprach/beredete das Rauchen im
im Büro.   Büro.
'One spoke about smoking in the office' 'One *be*-spoke smoking in the office'
Man schwatzte/kakelte über dies und das. Man beschwatzte/bekakelte dies und das.
'One waffled over the news'   'One *be*-waffled the news'

(19) *Verbs of emotion*
Sie staunte über das zersägte   Sie bestaunte das zersägte
Fahrradschloß.   Fahrradschloß.
'She gaped at the sawn-apart bicycle   'She *be*-gaped the sawn-apart bicycle
lock'   lock'
Sie trauerten/weinten um den Tod ihres   Sie betrauerten/beweinten den Tod
Onkels.   ihres Onkels.
'They mourned/cried about their uncle's 'They *be*-mourned/*be*-cried their
death'   uncle's death'

However, there are a few examples of P-prefix verbs in these classes that have taken on idiomatic readings, for example, *durchschauen* 'see through' and *umschreiben* 'circumscribe'. A literal meaning is available for some of the P-prefix verbs derived from a verb of emotion, as in *Sie durchschluchzte sieben Taschentücher* 'She *through*-wept seven handkerchiefs'. But, unlike the object NP of the corresponding *be*-verbs, the object NP of these verbs does not refer to the source of the emotion.

There are two further semantic classes of *be*-verbs: *be*-verbs that paraphrase prepositional phrases with a dative/goal or benefactive argument and a few lexicalized *be*-verbs with a privative reading. For these latter verbs, the theme cannot be expressed in an additional prepositional phrase:

(20) Andrea schenkt ihrem Vermieter rote   Andrea beschenkt ihren Vermieter mit
Rosen.   roten Rosen.
'Andrea gifts her landlord$_{dat}$ red roses' 'Andrea *be*-gifts her landlord$_{acc}$ with red
roses

(21) Oscar kochte Suppe für die Familie.   Oscar bekochte die Familie mit Suppe.
'Oscar cooked soup for the family'   'Oscar *be*-cooked the family with soup'

(22) Er erbte von seinem Großvater die   Er beerbte seinen Großvater (*mit der
     vollständige Münzsammlung.   vollständigen Münzsammlung).
     'He inherited the complete coin   'He *be*-inherited his grandfather (*with
     collection from his grandfather'   the complete coin collection)'
     Er raubte der Frau die Handtasche.   Er beraubte die alte Frau (*mit/*von der
     'He robbed the old woman of her purse'   Handtasche/ihrer Handtasche$_{gen}$).
                                              He *be*-robbed the old woman
                                              (*with/*of her purse/her purse$_{gen}$)'
(Examples (20) and (22) are from Stiebels, 1991, p. 67ff.)

To summarize Sections 3.1.3 and 3.1.4, both *be*-verbs and P-prefix verbs can
be derived from intransitive and transitive verbs of motion, and most of the
denominal verbs of either type are derived by incorporating a noun that
specifies the theme. When the base verb is transitive, these verbs usually
imply a holistic interpretation of the goal, and the speaker can express the
theme in an optional *with*-phrase. Only the P-prefixes combine with intransitive verbs whose subject is a theme, and only the *be*-prefix may combine with
verbs other than locative verbs.

Two restrictions on the locative alternation in German have been mentioned: that the goal must not be a container and that the subject of a *be*-verb
must be an agent. I will discuss a number of additional restrictions in Chapter
6, and will try to show how children can discover them. Let us now turn to the
linguistic analysis of the locative alternation.

3.2 The Locative Alternation: Incorporating the Preposition

This section presents the Preposition Incorporation account of the locative
alternation proposed by Wunderlich (1992; see also Brinkmann &
Wunderlich, 1996, for a recent discussion); this analysis will be the basis for
the claims to be made in the subsequent chapters. While the Preposition
Incorporation account has been developed mainly on the basis of German *be*-
prefixation, it is meant to account for the locative alternation in other languages as well.

According to Wunderlich, the locative argument becomes the direct
object of the verb when the verb incorporates a preposition. The incorporation
takes place through FUNCTIONAL COMPOSITION, a procedure developed within
the framework of Categorial Grammar. In this procedure, two otherwise
independent predicates — here the verb and the preposition — are combined

to form a complex predicate that now expresses jointly all the arguments of the two previously independent predicates. This predicate may be learned as part of the input language or it may arise through on-line incorporation as a speaker invents a new word. Either way, the predicate projects its argument structure into syntax. The way in which this is done is accomplished by independent principles, which will be discussed below.

Preposition Incorporation: Lexical or Syntactic?

According to Wunderlich, Preposition Incorporation is an operation that takes places in the lexicon, leading to the formation of a new lexical unit. His account thus differs from the incorporation account proposed by Baker (1988, 1992) within the framework of Government and Binding theory — which is probably the best known incorporation account. Let me therefore state my reasons for preferring Wunderlich's account over the one proposed by Baker.

Unlike Wunderlich, Baker proposes a syntactic incorporation account in which the locative alternation results from HEAD-TO-HEAD MOVEMENT. This means that the preposition, which is the head of the prepositional phrase, is incorporated into the verb and leaves a trace in its original position. This trace is governed by the verb but, unlike the (unincorporated) preposition, cannot assign case to the argument of the preposition. The argument must therefore be assigned case by the complex verb. This is possible because the incorporated preposition no longer prevents the verb from governing the prepositional argument; thus, this argument can receive case from the verb and so be realized as direct object. However, the former direct object NP now cannot receive case from the verb any longer; therefore, its head noun is reanalyzed as incorporated. In contrast to the incorporation of the preposition, this reanalysis, termed ABSTRACT INCORPORATION, does not lead to a morphological fusion between verb and noun. Importantly, head-to-head movement is a syntactic operation, so the complex verb need not form a stable part of the speaker's vocabulary: The incorporation of the preposition takes place in the process of forming an utterance.

There are several reasons for preferring Wunderlich's lexical account of preposition incorporation over the syntactic account proposed by Baker. The verbs that take the goal as direct object in German clearly form a new lexical unit — many *be*-verbs are listed in common dictionaries of German. Accordingly, a syntactic incorporation account like the one proposed by Baker needs an extra mechanism for explaining how syntactic incorporation may lead to the formation of new lexical units. No such additional assumptions are required by a lexical incorporation account. More serious problems of Baker's account have been observed by Stiebels (1991), who shows that the empirical motivation for the proposed abstract incorporation of the theme NP's head noun is unclear. First, the theme NP can usually still be expressed independently of the verb (for example, by an independent *with*-phrase), so Baker needs two types of incorporation in order to explain why some incorporated elements are excluded from appearing outside the incorporating element while others are not. Second, it is hard to see how abstract incorporation — proposed to deal with an NP that supposedly cannot receive case — could explain why we find case-marking on determiners and attributive adjectives that specify the theme NP in the goal-object structure. An example from German is given in (23):

(23) Sie lud d*as* vergammelt*e* Heu auf den Wagen.
     she loaded the-ACC rotten-ACC hay onto the wagon
     'She loaded the rotten hay onto the wagon'

     Sie belud den Wagen mit d*em* vergammelt*en* Heu.
     she loaded the wagon with the-DAT rotten-DAT hay
     'She loaded the wagon with the rotten hay'

To explain this pattern of case assignment, Baker would have to assume that abstract incorporation applies not only to head nouns, but also to more complex phrase structure levels, i.e., to N'- projections (*vergammelten Heu*) and N"-projections (*dem vergammelten Heu*) (Stiebels, 1991).

The lexical incorporation account presented in the following makes no reference to an abstract incorporation of the theme, so the appearance of the *with*-phrase in the sentence and the case-marking pattern within the phrase are unproblematic. (How the *with*-NP is dealt with in this analysis will be discussed in 3.2.2) Given these problems of Baker's account, then, a lexical incorporation account like the one proposed by Wunderlich is clearly preferrable.

Wunderlich's account has been developed within the theory of Lexical Decomposition Grammar (see Wunderlich, 1992, 1997), which draws on the theory of Semantic Form (Bierwisch, 1983, 1988; Bierwisch & Lang, 1987) and proposals by Kiparsky (1989, 1992). What is relevant for our purposes is the theory's account of argument structure. The following is mainly based on Wunderlich's (1997) elaboration of the theory and on related work that deals with the locative alternation (Wunderlich, 1987, 1992; Brinkmann & Wunderlich, 1996).

3.2.1 *The Analysis of Argument Structure in Lexical Decomposition Grammar*

Lexical Decomposition Grammar distinguishes two levels of argument structure, PREDICATE-ARGUMENT STRUCTURE (P-A structure) and THEMATIC STRUCTURE. P-A structure consists of predicate constants and argument variables.[8] It is a strictly binary structure, which means that a predicate combines with its arguments one at a time. Its semantic properties are expressed in terms of logical types, as defined in Categorial Grammar. The particular nature of the predicate constants (hence simply predicates), as well as the relations holding between them, yield a hierarchical ranking of arguments in P-A structure. This ranking at P-A structure is then translated into an ordering of the verb's arguments at the level of thematic structure, where the ordered arguments are specified for their syntactic functions.

An argument's rank in P-A structure depends on the type and position of the predicates of which it is an argument. Basic predicates may be one-place and two-place predicates; the arguments of the latter are intrinsically ranked. When there is more than one predicate in P-A structure, then argument ranking further depends on the position of the corresponding predicate in P-A structure: The more EMBEDDED the predicate, the lower the argument's rank in the hierarchy.

A metaphor proposed by Jürgen Weissenborn (personal communication) is helpful for understanding what is meant by embeddedness. According to this metaphor, the different predicates in P-A structure are like the layers of an onion. In the P-A structure of the verb *open*, for example, shown in (24), the predicate OPEN, which specifies the state of an entity y, is, so to speak, the center of the onion. The next layer is the predicate BECOME: BECOME takes a proposition (P) as argument, thereby expressing that non-P changes to P; in

---

8. The P-A structure is an essential part of the semantic form of a lexical item and is therefore often referred to as 'semantic form'. In the present context, I use the term 'P-A structure' since it indicates more clearly the content of this level that is relevant for our purposes.

this case, that y changes state from not being open to being open.[9] Since BECOME takes a proposition as argument, it adds no new individual argument to the P-A structure. The outermost layer, CAUSE, does introduce an individual argument, the agent, represented here as x, and specifies that the agent causes the process. s stands for situational argument, which in Lexical Decomposition Grammar is assumed to be an argument by virtue of which verbs can refer to situations. Like referential arguments in general, s is not linked to a syntactic position.

(24) P-A structure:
    [CAUSE (x, BECOME (OPEN (y)))] (s)

Notice that the argument y, which is caused to change state, recursively takes part in more and more complex predications. It is therefore the lowest argument, and x, which is an argument of the least embedded predicate CAUSE, is the highest argument. The hierarchical ranking of the arguments determines their syntactic expression, as will be shown below.

At the level of thematic structure, the predicate constants drop away, and information is given only about the order of arguments, as determined by their rank in the P-A structure. Information about this ranking is transmitted to the thematic structure by the Hierarchy Principle (Bierwisch, 1988):

(25) **Hierarchy Principle**
    In the thematic structure, the hierarchy of arguments in the semantic form is preserved in the inverse order. ('Semantic form' refers to what is called the P-A structure in the present context.)[10]

The Hierarchy Principle constrains the semantic operations available in Categorial Grammar to those that leave the order of arguments unchanged — functional application and functional composition (Wunderlich, 1992). For our purposes, we only have to consider functional application, which refers to the application of a predicate to its argument. Because of the Hierarchy Principle, the verb is applied to its complements in an order that reverses the argument

---

9. Individual arguments denote entities; they are realized as noun phrases in the sentence. Predicate arguments denote properties or relations and are realized as adjective or prepositional phrases. When not specified otherwise, the term 'argument' refers to individual arguments.

10. The Hierarchy Principle shows that the thematic structure captures the same information about arguments as the P-A structure, but represents it differently. As an independent level of representation, it can also encode information that is not captured by the P-A structure about idiosyncratic properties of lexical items (see also Footnote 13).

hierarchy: The first complement it applies to functions as the lowest argument, and the last complement it applies to functions as the highest argument.

With respect to the example above, this means that the verb *open* first applies to the argument y, which thus functions as the lowest-ranked argument; the corresponding lambda abstractor λy (with λ indicating which variables will be replaced in the course of applying the predicates) will be placed on the left-most side in the verb's thematic structure. Next comes the argument x, which therefore functions as the highest argument, with λx being placed on the right-most side. (Recall that BECOME takes a propositional argument, not an individual argument, so there is nothing to place to the right of λy.) The result of these steps is shown in (26): The thematic structure of the (transitive) verb *open* now represents the hierarchy of the arguments in the P-A structure in terms of an ordered sequence of lambda abstractors. As required by the Hierarchy Principle, the order of λy and λx in the thematic structure is inverse to that of x and y in the P-A structure.

(26) Thematic structure   P-A structure
     $\lambda y \, \lambda x$ CAUSE (x, BECOME (OPEN, y))

The ordering of lambda abstractors in the thematic structure determines the syntactic function of each of the arguments. Languages differ in their devices — sometimes called 'linkers' — they use to express arguments syntactically; German, for example, uses case marking, and English uses word order. The purpose of each linking system is to express which argument is the highest argument in a verb's P-A structure, which is the lowest, and which is intermediate. An important advantage of Lexical Decomposition Grammar over alternative accounts of argument structure is that it can account for word order systems as well as for morphological case marking systems.

To ensure that each argument will be associated with the appropriate linkers in clausal phrase structure, Wunderlich proposes a set of binary features for capturing the order information in thematic structure. The features specify whether there is a higher argument role [+/-hr] and whether there is a lower argument role [+/-lr]: Linkers 'look for' the order information in the encoded form.[11] In our example, the feature [+hr], defined as *there is a*

---

11. A similar system of binary features was proposed earlier by Kiparsky (1992). Kiparsky defines the features [+HR] and [+LR] as *this is the highest role* and *this is the lowest role*, respectively. Accordingly, the plus- and minus-values of the features are the opposite of the ones in Wunderlich's feature system. The present system of relational features has been developed by Bierwisch and Wunderlich in collaboration with Kiparsky (Dieter Wunderlich, personal communication).

higher role, is assigned to λ*y*, since λ*x* is a higher role (i.e., *x* is less embedded in the P-A structure). Conversely, the feature [+lr], defined as *there is a lower role* is assigned to λ*x*, since λ*y* bears a lower role. The opposite feature specifications [+lr] and [-lr] are needed as well, i.e., to account for verbs with three structural arguments (cf. below). Thus, λ*x* and λ*y* in the thematic structure of *open* are represented as in (27):

(27) Thematic structure   P-A structure
     λy   λx   CAUSE (x, BECOME (OPEN, y))
     [+hr] [-hr]
     [- lr] [+lr]

Sometimes an argument in the thematic structure cannot be assigned features by default as just described, for example, because the verb assigns lexical features to its arguments (cf. Footnote 13), or because an operation like passive is applied, which modifies the arguments' feature values at the level of thematic structure (Wunderlich, 1997). Features also cannot be assigned by default if a verb marks an argument for being oblique, since feature marking is restricted to a verb's direct arguments. Such an argument can only be expressed by an oblique NP — for example, by a pre- or a postposition. How prepositional arguments come into play will be explained when we turn to the locative alternation.

With the arguments being marked by binary features at the level of thematic structure, they can now be linked to syntactic functions. This is possible because each linking mechanism in a language is specified for a particular position in thematic structure. Let us see how this works for German.

German has three structural cases, accusative, dative, and nominative.[12] (28) shows which features are relevant for each case.

(28) nominative [ ]
     accusative [+hr]
     dative   [+hr,+lr]

Case assignment can proceed only if it adheres to the SPECIFICITY PRINCIPLE,

---

12. Whether dative case can be considered a structural case has been the topic of much discussion in the literature on the German case system. Haider (1984, 1985, 1986) proposes that dative case is always lexically assigned, whereas Reis (1985), Wegener (1985, 1991), Czepluch (1987, 1988), and Fanselow (1987) argue that it may be structurally or lexically assigned, depending on the verb.

which means that an argument always receives the most specific case compatible with its features. The most specific case is dative case. An argument can be assigned dative case only if there are two other arguments in the thematic structure: a higher and a lower argument.[13] The lowest of these three arguments will receive accusative case, since in the presence of two higher arguments, it can be assigned the feature [+hr]. Accusative case can also be assigned if there are only two arguments altogether — the one with the feature [+hr] will receive accusative case. Nominative case is not specified for any particular feature, so it can be assigned regardless of whether there are three, two, or one arguments. But it will always be assigned to the highest argument because only then can the remaining cases be assigned appropriately. (For example, for a verb with two arguments, accusative case can be assigned only to the lower argument ([+hr, -lr)], since only this argument has the feature [+hr]; nominative case must then be assigned to the higher argument ([-hr, +lr]), since it is the only case compatible with these features.) Let us now turn to how the locative alternation is dealt with in this system.

3.2.2 *The Locative Alternation*

The argument structure of a typical alternating verb is given in (29), and a sentence pair including the verb is shown in (30):

---

13. Some verbs in German assign dative case even though they take only two arguments, for example, *helfen* 'help' and *gefallen* 'please':

(i)   Der Lehrer$_{nom}$ half dem Schüler$_{dat}$ 'The teacher helped the pupil'
(ii)   Der Aufsatz$_{nom}$ gefällt dem Lehrer$_{dat}$ 'The essay pleases the teacher'

In Lexical Decomposition Grammar, this is accounted for by assuming that these verbs assign lexical features to one of their arguments, an assignment which is motivated by the particular semantics of the verbs. In the case of what Wunderlich (1997) calls CONTROLLER DATIVE VERBS like *helfen*, the lower of the two arguments (*dem Schüler* 'the pupil'; [+hr, -lr] by default) is marked with the lexical feature [+lr]; this 'reference' to a lower argument invites the inference that the argument thus marked has control properties by itself. In contrast, in the case of experiencer verbs like *gefallen*, the higher argument (*dem Lehrer* 'the teacher'; [-hr, +lr] by default) is marked with the feature [+hr]; here, reference to a higher argument invites the inference that the argument thus marked is somehow affected. Either argument is thus specified by the features [+hr,+lr], and so is assigned dative case. While the assignment of features is lexical, the assignment of dative case is purely structural (Wunderlich, 1997). Children seem to make characteristic case and word order mistakes with these verbs until they have mastered dative case marking in German; these errors receive a straightforward explanation by the feature assignment analysis proposed by Wunderlich (Sonja Eisenbeiß, personal communication).

(29) *sprühen* 'spray'

λP λy λx   (SPRAY (x, y) & Q(y))

[+DIR] | |

         acc   nom

(30) a.   Hans sprühte Farbe an die Wand. 'Hans sprayed paint onto the wall'

     b.   Hans besprühte die Wand mit Farbe. 'Hans *be*-sprayed the wall with paint'

SPRAY (x, y) in the P-A structure of the verb *spray* is a two-place predicate constant that denotes an activity of *x* by which some liquid *y* becomes spatially dispersed.The predicate conjoins with Q(y), as indicated by the conjunction symbol & in (29). The presence of this conjunction in the P-A structure of a verb like *spray* affects the way in which arguments are assigned to syntactic functions. In terms of its logical properties, a predicate conjunction is symmetrical. But recall that P-A structure is strictly binary: Predicates combine with their arguments one at a time. Therefore, the conjunction of predicates in a P-A structure can proceed only *asymetrically*. For the representation in (29), this implies that Q(y) is the internal argument of the conjunction, while SPRAY (x,y) is its external argument — this means that Q(y) is more deeply embedded in the SF of *sprühen* than SPRAY (x,y).

So what does Q(y) mean? Q(y) is a one-place predicate variable, which means that it must be realized by a suitable (lexical) predicate independently of the verb. The symbol +DIR in the verb's thematic structure indicates that Q must be realized by a directional prepositional phrase. The internal argument of this phrase is not represented in the argument structure of the verb itself; it shows up only if we zoom in on the argument structure of the preposition, as given in (31a) for the preposition *an* 'at'.[14] This is one of the differences between the representation in (29) and the representations proposed for the lexical entries of locative verbs by other authors (e.g., Rappaport & Levin, 1988; Pinker, 1989; Randall, 1992).

(31) *an* [+DIR] λz λu   [BECOME (LOC (u, AT* (z)))]

     'onto' |

                     acc

Why does the internal argument of the preposition, *z*, not show up directly in

---

14. I will not explicate the specific semantic structure of *an* but simply represent it by the symbol AT*; see Herweg (1988) and Wunderlich & Kaufmann (1990) for more specific representations. Wunderlich (1991) assumes two different lexical entries for prepositions that, like *an*, can denote both static and directional location; the directional entry contains the predicate BECOME.

the lexical entry of the verb? The reason is that in Wunderlich's analysis, the verb does not take a *preposition* as an argument but a *prepositional phrase*. As shown in (31), prepositions are two-place predicates denoting relations between two entities. Thus, they take two arguments: an internal argument, which is the relatum or reference object, and an external argument, which is the theme. In a prepositional phrase like *onto the wall*, the two-place preposition has already been applied to its internal argument, so in the argument structure of a verb like *sprühen*, which takes a prepositional phrase as one of its arguments, the prepositional phrase appears as a *one-place* predicate that now needs to be applied to its external argument. For example, in (29), $Q(y)$ specifies that an entity attains the property of being located in a particular region. (In the substructure of the prepositional predicate for the sentence in (30a), this region is further specified as the AN-region of z, the wall.)

Things are different for *be*-verbs, which have incorporated a preposition. Recall that this incorporation involves functional composition — i.e., the combination of a verbal and a prepositional predicate (known as 'functions' in Categorial Grammar) to form a complex predicate. Importantly, it is a (two-place) *preposition* that is incorporated, not a (one-place) *prepositional phrase* in which the preposition has already been applied to its internal argument. Only after the incorporation has taken place will the new, complex predicate be applied to the arguments of its original component predicates.

The mechanism of preposition incorporation is the same for all verbs that take the goal as direct object. In the case of verbs like *umsegeln* 'around-sail', the effect of this mechanism is morphologically fully transparent: The prepositional prefix *um-* corresponds to the preposition *um*, an independent lexical item. In the case of *be*-verbs, the effect is less transparent — the prefix *be-* is a bound morphem that can occur only in combination with a verb. Historically, *be-* is the deaccented variant of the preposition *bei* 'at', which supports Wunderlich's claim that *be*-verbs result from preposition incorporation. (Almost all prefixes in German have been derived from prepositions or adverbs; see Stiebels, 1991, for a summary of historical analyses of German prefixes.) According to the Preposition Incorporation account of the locative alternation presented here, preposition incorporation also derives the goal-object structure of locative verbs in English; its effect, however, shows up in the morphology of the derived verbs only in a few, no longer productive cases, for example, *bedaub, bedeck*, and *bedraggle*. To explain the goal-object structure of verbs like *spray*, then, the Preposition Incorporation account has to assume that prepositions may be incorporated without changing the morphological structure of the derived verb. Whether _all_ languages use preposition incorporation to derive the goal-object structure of locative verbs is an empirical question.

But let us turn back to German. (32) gives the argument structure of the prefix _be-_, which differs from that of a preposition like _an_ only in that it is specified as a bound morphem.

(32) _be_ $\lambda z \, \lambda u$ BECOME (LOC (u, AT* (z)))
     [+DIR]
     [+BOUND]

Like _auf_ and _an_, _be-_ has both a directional and a static variant. The directional variant, shown in (32), is always selected for incorporation into transitive verbs that, like _sprühen_ 'spray', describe the transfer of an entity to a location. This means that the object NP of verbs like _besprühen_ '_be_-spray' will be interpreted as the goal. The static variant, which lacks the predicate BECOME, is selected by intransitive motion verbs like _reiten_ 'ride', which contain MOVE. This means that the object NP of verbs like _bereiten_ '_be_-ride' refers not to a goal but to the location where the motion takes place.

A locative verb that has incorporated _be-_ now has to express two internal arguments syntactically: the internal argument z (the goal) of the preposition and the internal argument y of the verb (the theme). The former becomes the direct object of the _be-_verb. This is because the incorporated preposition changes the ranking of arguments in the P-A structure of the locative verb: λz in the thematic structure of the _be-_verb takes precedence over λy because in the verb's P-A structure, z is ranked lower in the argument hierarchy than y. This is shown in (33) for _besprühen_ '_be_-spray'.

(33) _besprühen_ '_be_-spray'
     $\lambda z \, \lambda y \, \lambda x \, \lambda s$ [SPRAY (x,y) & BECOME (LOC(y, AT*(z)))]

In (33), AT* is more deeply embedded than SPRAY, BECOME, and LOC, so its internal argument z is the lowest argument of the verb. This means that λz will be marked with the features [+hr] (there is a higher role) and [-lr] (there is no lower role, z itself occupies the lowest role). These features are compatible only with the feature specification of the accusative case, [+hr] (see Section 3.2.1), which means that λz will be realized as the direct object of the verb.

The WITH-*phrase in the goal-object structure*

As shown in (33), *be*-verbs derived from transitive verbs take three arguments, the goal (z), the agent (x), and the theme (y). Why then is the theme not expressed by a complement in the dative case, by virtue of the features [+hr,+lr]? This is because the theme is excluded from structural linking — it does not L-COMMAND the lowest argument (Wunderlich, 1997):[15]

(34) **L-command**
   α L-commands β iff the node γ, which either directly dominates α or dominates α via a chain of nodes type-identical to γ, also dominates β.

(35) **Restriction on structural linking**
   An argument is structural only if it is either the lowest argument or if each of its occurrences L-commands the lowest argument.

L-command is similar to c-command in syntactic structures (Reinhart, 1981; see Haegeman, 1991, for an overview) in that it defines structural dependencies between nodes in a tree diagram; unlike c-command, the nodes it is defined over are specified in terms of their LOGICAL TYPES, not in terms of syntactic categories.

Logical types relevant to be-*verbs.* A number of different logical types are involved in the representation in (33), with each predicate constant in the verb's semantic form introducing its own logical type. The two-place predicate SPRAY denotes a relationship between two entities, the agent and the theme. Its logical type is therefore <e<e,t>>, where e stands for 'entity' or 'individual', and t for 'proposition' or 'truth-valued expression'. Given this logical type, the predicate combines first with an expression of type e, the one given in the outer brackets (which corresponds to the first occurrence of *y* in the tree shown below). This yields the simpler logical type <e,t>. The predicate then combines with e in the inner brackets, yielding t, an expression that can be assigned a truth-value. BECOME is a one-place predicate of the type <t,t>: It takes a proposition P and yields the proposition BECOME (P), expressing the change into the state in which P holds. SPRAY and BECOME are conjoined by &, which is of type <t<t,t>>, since it combines two propositions to yield another proposition. Next comes the two-place predicate LOC, which

---

15. L-command and the restriction on structural arguments also account for other linking phenomena, e.g., for resultative constructions like *Er trank den Weinkeller leer* 'He drank the wine cellar empty' (Wunderlich, 1997).

denotes that an object (e in the inner brackets) has the property of being located in a particular region (e in the outer brackets), and so is of type <e,<e,t>>. The region itself is introduced by AT*, which, in terms of its logical properties, is a functor on individuals that yields a region, and so is of type <e,e>.

On the basis of these logical types, we can now establish the tree diagram in (36). The tree shows the structural dependencies between the various logical types holding for this representation, thereby revealing which arguments L-command other arguments.

(36)

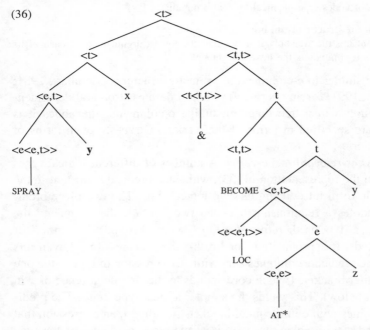

As shown in (36), *y* in the left-hand side of the tree (typed in bold letters for ease of reference) does not L-command the verb's lowest argument, *z,* shown in the right-hand side of the tree. It does not L-command *z* because it is dominated by a node of a different logical type — <e,t> — than the remaining nodes dominating *y.* According to the definition of L-command and the restriction on structural linking, this means that *y* cannot L-command anything except SPRAY.

The restriction on structural linking states that the lowest argument will always be expressed in a structural position. The restriction also ensures that the highest argument always L-commands the lowest argument and so will always be expressed in a structural position (Wunderlich, 1997). It is the middle argument that sometimes may not end up in a structural position (where it would be assigned dative case in a language like German). This is the case for the theme in the goal-object construction: It does not L-command the goal in each of its occurrences, and so it cannot be assigned dative case. Since it cannot be expressed as a structural argument and be assigned dative case, it must instead be linked by an oblique marker, which is the preposition *mit* in German and *with* in English.

The Presupposition of Indivisibility

Recall that the concept of hierarchical ranking explains why z, the goal, becomes the direct object of the *be*-verb. In an earlier chapter (cf. 2.5), I pointed out that making the goal the direct object is associated with a difference in interpretation. When the theme is the direct object, as in (37a), the state of the goal is irrelevant; if it is a container, it might or might not be full, and if it is a surface, it might or might not be completely covered. In contrast, when the goal is the direct object, as in (37b), the goal is usually interpreted holistically: The container is understood to be filled, and the surface to be completely covered (Anderson, 1971).

(37) a. She hung her pictures of Johnny Depp on the wall.
     b. She hung the wall with her pictures of Johnny Depp.

To explain the different interpretations, Wunderlich invokes the PRESUPPOSITION OF INDIVISIBILITY, a principle of predication proposed by Löbner (1990, 1996):[16]

(38) **Presupposition of Indivisibility**
Whenever a predicate is applied to one of its arguments, it is true or false of the argument as a whole. (Löbner, 1996, p. 18)

The principle explains why some sentences may be neither true nor false, or, put differently, why they may introduce truth-value gaps. For example, the

---

16. In Löbner (1990), the principle is called the Homogeneity Presupposition, which is also the term used by Wunderlich (1992). In more recent work, Wunderlich also uses the term Presupposition of Indivisibility (Brinkmann & Wunderlich, 1996).

sentence *The flag is blue* is neither true nor false when predicated of the Swedish flag (Löbner, 1996, p. 18). According to Löbner, truth-value gaps arise whenever the Presupposition of Indivisibility is not fulfilled.

Because of this presupposition, a sentence like *The flag is blue* will, without evidence to the contrary, be taken to describe a flag that is completely blue (or one whose non-blue spots are irrelevant; see Löbner, 1996, for a discussion of the types of predicate that allow speakers to adopt a pragmatic definition of indivisibility). Cooperative speakers will therefore qualify their utterances whenever the presupposition is not fulfilled, for example, by adding that the flag is only *partly* blue. (Allowing speakers to qualify their utterances in this sense can thus be considered the main function of quantifiers; cf. Löbner, 1990, 1996.)

Importantly, the Presupposition of Indivisibility is relevant only with respect to instances of *direct* predication; that is, x must be a direct argument of a predicate P (as *the flag* is with respect to *blue*). Recall that in the theme-object structure, another predicate — a preposition — intervenes between the verb and the locative argument. This preposition introduces its own semantics, so the Presupposition of Indivisibility no longer holds for the relationship between the verb and the locative argument. We can now see how the principle explains the holistic interpretation accompanying goal-object constructions.

In a sentence like *She hung her pictures of Johnny Depp on the wall,* *hang* predicates directly of the agent argument *she* and the theme argument *her pictures of Johnny Depp,* so these must be indivisible with respect to *hang*. This means that the sentence is true only if all of the pictures are being hung. The degree to which the whole wall is being covered does not influence the truth conditions of the sentence: Since *the wall* is separated from the verb by a preposition, the Presupposition of Indivisibility does not apply (for the relation between *hang* and *the wall*). In contrast, when *the wall* is the direct object of the verb, it has to be indivisible with respect to *hang*: *She hung the wall with her pictures of Johnny Depp* is true only if there are pictures all over the wall.

Drawing on Löbner's Presupposition of Indivisibility, Wunderlich proposes two satisfaction criteria that specify what must be the case in order for the sentences in (37a) and (37b), respectively, to be true. The criteria are shown in (39a) and (39b).

(39) a. For all y: y is a picture of Johnny Depp $\Rightarrow$ y is on the wall
     b. For all z: z is a subregion of the wall $\Rightarrow$ there is a y: y is a picture of
                                                            Johnny Depp and y is located in z

These satisfaction criteria define two perspectives on the event of hanging, one in terms of the pictures being hung on the wall and the other in terms of the subregions of the wall that must have pictures on them. The Presupposition of Indivisibility and the satisfaction criteria thus account for the holistic interpretation of the goal and for the change in perspective that is associated with the alternation: When the theme is the direct object, the sentence tells us about what happens to the pictures, whereas when the goal is the direct object, the sentence tells us about the fate of the wall.

Advantages of the Preposition Incorporation Account over the Change of State Account

Two concepts are central to the Preposition Incorporation account presented in the preceding sections: the ranking of arguments, which explains why the goal becomes the direct object when the preposition is incorporated, and the Presupposition of Indivisibility, which explains the semantic effects of this argument structure change. Together, these concepts provide a true alternative to the Change of State account proposed by Pinker (1989) and Gropen et al. (1991a,b) (cf. 2.5).

Let us first consider how either account explains the shift in perspective associated with the goal-object form of a verb. The proponents of the Change of State account argue that the shift follows from the different semantic representations attributed to the verbs in its two variants, as shown in (40):

(40) a. She hung her pictures of Johnny Depp on the wall: x (CAUSE y (to GO-TO z))
     b. She hung the wall with her pictures of Johnny Depp: x (CAUSE z (to CHANGE
                                                              STATE) (by means of x
                                                              (CAUSE y (to GO-TO z))))

Recall further that the perspective focussing on the wall (40b) is, accordingly, characterized as being caused or brought about by means of the perspective focussing on the pictures (40a). But as Wunderlich (1992) has pointed out, it makes no sense to assume that one perspective causes another perspective, since perspectives represent mutually exclusive choices of how to conceptualize an event. This problem does not arise when, following Wunderlich, we attribute the perspective shift to the Presupposition of Indivisibility.

The present account also avoids problems associated with the Object Affectedness Linking Rule. For convenience, the rule is repeated in (41):

(41) **Object Affectedness Linking Rule**
An argument is encodable as the direct object of a verb if its referent is specified as affected in a specific way in the semantic representation of the verb. (Gropen et al., 1991a, p. 118)

One problem associated with this rule is the claim that for the goal to become the direct object of the verb, it must be the theme of a Change of State predication — but a change of state is not always involved in goal-object constructions (as shown by the grammaticality of constructions like *die Wand mit Steinen bewerfen* '*be*-throw the wall with stones'). Goal-object sentences also do not pass standard tests for showing completive aspect, which they should if the goal were specified as undergoing a change of state. But there is yet another, even more basic problem: Why do we need a linking rule specifically designed for linking affected arguments to the direct object position in the first place? In Wunderlich's account, the direct object has no special semantic significance: Unless otherwise indicated, the lowest argument will end up automatically as direct object. In the case of a verb that has incorporated a directional preposition, this argument will be the goal. To qualify as direct object, then, the goal does not have to be 'affected'.

In summary, we do not have to stipulate a specific relationship between affected arguments and the position of direct object. When a verb incorporates a directional preposition, the goal automatically becomes direct object due to its change in rank in the verb's P-A-structure, and once it is direct object, the holistic interpretation follows automatically from the Presupposition of Indivisibility. Two concepts central to Wunderlich's account — the ranking of arguments and the Presupposition of Indivisibility — thus obviate the need for the Object Affectedness Linking Rule.

Chapter 4

The Nonindividuation Hypothesis

The Preposition Incorporation account of the locative alternation shows that we do not need the Object Affectedness Linking Rule to explain why the locative argument may become the direct object of a verb. But what happens to the theme of a transitive locative verb when it is no longer expressed in object position? Answering this question is the goal of this chapter. I will argue that in order for a transitive verb to take its goal as direct object, the quantificational properties of its theme must be irrelevant. The existence of the theme may then be presupposed, and so the theme does not need to be expressed syntactically. If the theme need not be expressed syntactically, the object position is available for the goal. A theme whose quantificational properties are irrelevant may be interpreted by speakers as nonindividuated, i.e., as an unbounded amount of stuff or objects. I will refer to the claim that a verb must allow speakers to interpret the theme as nonindividuated in order to take its goal as direct object as the Nonindividuation Hypothesis.

The Nonindividuation Hypothesis is a proposal about the representation of the locative alternation in the adult grammar. But it also has implications for a theory of the acquisition of the alternation. According to the Nonindividuation Hypothesis, the major requirement for using a transitive locative verb in the goal-object construction is the ability to deindividuate the verb's theme, i.e., to treat a bounded amount of stuff or objects as though it were unbounded. No deindividuation is needed for verbs like *spray*, which denote only the motion of substances. But deindividuation is necessary for verbs like *load*, which may describe the motion of both substances and bounded objects. If the Nonindividuation Hypothesis is correct, children should acquire the goal-object construction for verbs like *spray* earlier than for verbs like *load*. The hypothesis also implies a constraint on which verbs may participate in the alternation, i.e., only those whose theme may be interpreted as nonindividuated when not specified. Once children have learnt that a given verb does not meet the condition, they may infer that it does not participate in the locative alternation.

In the following, I will first explain what the Nonindividuation Hypothesis means for the representation of the alternation in the adult grammar (Section 4.1), and then turn to what the hypothesis predicts about the acquisition of the alternation (4.2).

4.1 What Happens to the Theme in the Goal-Object Form?

Both the Preposition Incorporation account and the Change of State account of the locative alternation are mainly concerned with explaining how the locative argument becomes the direct object of the verb. But what about the theme? After all, when a transitive verb like *spray* takes its goal as direct object, the theme undergoes a dramatic change in its syntactic expression: It is no longer the direct object of the verb but instead can only be expressed in an optional *with*-phrase.

The role of the theme in goal-object constructions has often been seen as problematic. Fraser (1971), for example, points out that the goal-object form sounds strange when the *with*-phrase contains a singular NP, while the theme-object form is not restricted in this way:

(1)   a.   He jammed a pencil into the jar.
      b.   ? He jammed the jar with a pencil.

Fraser assumed that (1b) violates some selectional restriction that is missing from (1a), and concluded that the two forms have different underlying structures (in this he argued against Hall, 1965, according to whom (1b) was derived from (1a); see also Chapter 2). Fillmore (1977, 1978) treated the *with*-phrase as equivalent to instrumental *with*-phrases as in *load the wagon **with a shovel***: Both represent entities that 'move with respect to something else' but are not 'brought into perspective' (Fillmore, 1978, p. 78). But Kefer (1980) argued that the two types of *with*-phrase behave differently in a number of respects, and so should not be considered members of the same category. Recent approaches share this view (Rappaport & Levin, 1985, 1988; Baker, 1988, 1992; Wunderlich, 1987, 1992; Hoekstra & Mulder, 1990; Gropen et al., 1991a,b; Booij, 1992). Whether the *with*-phrase is an argument or an adjunct is also a matter of debate: In Wunderlich's Preposition Incorporation analysis the theme remains an argument of the verb, but other authors take the optionality of the phrase as (one piece of) evidence that it is an adjunct (see, for example, Booij, 1992, and Hoekstra & Mulder, 1990).

The *with*-phrase is striking for still another reason: It has a strong tendency to contain a bare plural (e.g., *boxes*) or a mass term (e.g., *hay*) (Dowty, 1991; Schwartz-Norman, 1976; Fillmore, 1978; Hopper & Thompson, 1980; Wunderlich, 1987; Rappaport & Levin, 1988). The tendency toward bare plurals and mass terms is clearly reflected in the examples linguists use to discuss the alternation. To examine this phenomenon more closely, I analyzed a total of 193 examples taken from 13 articles on the locative alternation (Anderson, 1971; Schwartz-Norman, 1976; Fillmore, 1978; Rappaport & Levin, 1985, 1988; Levin & Rappaport Hovav, 1991; Wunderlich, 1987; Hoekstra & Mulder, 1990; Dowty, 1991; Gropen et al., 1991a,b; Booij, 1992; Randall, 1992).

To see whether themes are specified by bare plurals and mass terms (bare theme NPs) primarily when the goal is the direct object, or whether this is common to *both* theme- and goal-object sentences, I first searched for examples in which one or the other form of the verb is presented in isolation. The reason for looking at unpaired sentences is that when authors present theme- and goal-object sentences as a pair, they presumably will tend to keep them as semantically similar as possible so as to showcase the effects of the alternation on syntax. I found that when the goal-object construction is presented in isolation, 85% (29 of 34 examples) have a *with*-phrase containing a bare theme NP (i.e., a bare plural or a mass term). This differs markedly from the proportion of bare theme NPs when the theme-object construction is presented in isolation — only 37 percent (10 of 27).

Although the figure of 37% for bare theme NPs in theme-object constructions is much lower than the 85% in goal-object constructions, there is reason to think that even this figure is artificially elevated by the desire of authors talking about the locative alternation to illustrate the two constructions with similar examples. To get an estimate of how often bare theme NPs appear in theme-object sentences when the locative alternation is *not* the topic of the study, I also looked at examples from articles that deal with properties of locative expressions other than those that are relevant for the alternation. I included in this analysis a total of 69 examples from 8 studies (Neumann, 1987; Herweg, 1988; Wunderlich & Herweg, 1991; Levin, 1993, Chapter 5; Rappaport Hovav & Levin, 1992; Maienborn, 1992, 1994; Wunderlich &

Kaufmann, 1990). For these theme-object constructions, the percentage of bare theme NPs drops to 13 percent!

But the strongest piece of evidence that bare theme NPs are a specific characteristic of goal-object constructions is provided, after all, by examples in which the theme- and goal-object form are presented as a pair. For these sentences, we might expect that bare theme NPs will appear equally often in both constructions, but this is not the case: The theme is still much more likely to be a bare NP in the goal-object construction than in the theme-object construction: 71% to 55% (47 versus 36 of 66 examples). That is, in 17% of these examples (11 of 66), the *with*-NP in the goal-object construction is a bare NP, whereas the theme NP in its theme-object counterpart in fact has a determiner, as illustrated in (2).

(2) He loaded *the hay* on the wagon.
     He loaded the wagon with *hay*.

The results of these three analyses are summarized in Table 1. The first column shows the examples in which only the goal-object form of an alternating verb was presented, the second column shows the examples in which only the theme-object form of an alternating verb was given, the third and fourth columns show the number of examples in which both forms were presented as a pair, and the fifth column shows theme-object constructions used to demonstrate properties of locative expressions other than whether they participate in the locative alternation.

Why do so many *with*-phrases contain a bare plural or mass term? One plausible answer might be that NPs like these contribute toward the holistic interpretation of the goal associated with the goal-object form (Anderson,

Table 1: Frequency of different types of theme NPs used by linguists to exemplify the locative alternation (columns 1-4) or properties of locative expressions not relevant for the alternation (column 5).

	goal-object	*theme-object*	*goal-object*	*& theme-object*	*theme-object*
	constructions non-paired		*constructions paired*		*constructions not used to discuss the locative alternation*
Bare plurals	85%	37%	71%	55%	13%
& mass terms	29	10	47	36	9
Other	5	17	19	30	60
Total	34	27	66	66	69

1971; cf. 2.5 and 3.2.2) — a wagon, for example, is harder to interpret holistically if it is loaded with a single box than if it is loaded with several boxes. However, the desire of authors to be consistent with the holistic interpretation cannot explain why they used **bare** *with*-NPs — the goal can, after all, also be interpreted holistically when the *with*-NP is definite or quantified, as in *with the boxes* and *with 20 bales of hay*. Since definite and quantified *with*-NPs can contribute toward the holistic interpretation just as well as bare NPs, the holistic interpretation also cannot explain why the determiner has *disappeared* in the goal-object form in 17% of the examples in which the theme- and goal-object forms were presented as a pair. Clearly, the holistic interpretation is not sufficient to explain why so many *with*-phrases in goal-object constructions contain a bare plural or a mass term. A more satisfying answer might be found in examining what bare plurals and mass terms have in common: These NPs do not INDIVIDUATE their referents.

'Individuation' means that the referent of a noun phrase is treated as a countable entity. A countable entity is typically a bounded object, i.e., an object with a certain gestalt such as a stone. Bounded objects are typically named by count nouns. When we conceive of a referent as nonindividuated, we treat it as though it could not be counted, i.e., we make no specific assumptions about its quantificational properties. This is how we usually conceive of unbounded entities like substances. Unbounded entities are typically named by mass nouns like *paint* and *mud*. But bounded objects may also be conceived of as nonindividuated, e.g., when there are several of them and their number is ignored. When bounded objects are conceived of as nonindividuated, they are referred to with bare plurals of count nouns, e.g., *stones* and *boxes*. Conversely, unbounded entities may also be conceived of as countable. In this case, they are individuated with 'unitizers', as in *a can of paint* or *a kilo of mud* (see Carlson, 1980; Wierzbicka, 1985; Krifka, 1986, 1989a,b; Talmy, 1985; Pelletier & Schubert, 1989; Jackendoff, 1991; Croft, 1993; Ojeda, 1993, among others, for analyses of our means for individuating entities).

The fact that bare *with*-NPs are apparently so frequent in goal-object constructions suggests that the theme in these sentences is typically conceived of as nonindividuated. Why should this be so? One reason might be that speakers are aware of the different satisfaction criteria that underlie theme- and goal-object sentences (Wunderlich, 1992; cf. 3.2.2). When a speaker conceives of an event in which, e.g, John is loading beets on a wagon in terms of the wagon, he assumes that the action ends when the wagon is full, and so will use the goal-object form of *load*. He then probably does not care about how many beets were loaded since their number is irrelevant for determining the end of the action; accordingly, he will specify the beets with a bare plural, and so say *John is loading the wagon with beets*.

This is certainly a plausible account for why the theme is so often conceived of as nonindividuated in goal-object constructions. But I do not think that it is the correct one. I will argue that the nonindividuation of the theme is a direct consequence of the change in the argument structure of the verb: That is, in order for a transitive verb to take its goal as direct object, the meaning of the verb must be such that it allows the quantificational properties of the theme to be irrelevant. This is necessary in order for speakers to simply presuppose the existence of the theme. The *with*-phrase is so often a bare plural or mass term because the quantificational properties of the theme NP are irrelevant anyway when the goal is the direct object. Being able to disregard the theme's quantificational properties is necessary for using the verb in the goal-object form. Once a speaker has acquired the goal-object argument structure of a verb, he may, when using the verb in this argument structure, provide additional information about the theme by using a *with*-phrase; he may then also be more specific about how much stuff or how many objects are involved in the event he is describing by using a definite *with*-NP like *with the beets* or a quantified *with*-NP like *with ten bales of hay*.

In the following, I discuss this claim and its implications for the characterization of the locative alternation in the adult grammar. I first show why the quantificational properties of a verb's theme must be irrelevant in order for the object NP to be interpreted as the goal. I then show that in order for speakers to be able to consider the theme's quantificational properties irrelevant, the verb must have specific semantic properties. Finally, I examine examples like those in the second row of Table 1, in which the *with*-NP was *not* a bare plural or mass term.

4.1.1 *Why Must the Quantificational Properties of the Theme Be Irrelevant for the Object NP to Be Interpreted as the Goal?*

Why must the quantificational properties of the theme be irrelevant for the object NP to be interpreted as the goal? This is because if speakers can use the verbs without having to make specific assumptions about the amount of stuff or objects involved, they may simply presuppose the existence of the theme. In *John loaded the wagon*, for example, the theme is not mentioned at all. Its omission is possible because *load* allows us to assume that when the theme is not mentioned, its quantificational properties are irrelevant. We may therefore assume that the theme is nonindividuated and so may simply presuppose that something loadable was involved in the event. Since we may assume that John has loaded something on the wagon, we do not need further information about the theme, so the theme does not have to be specified. And this means that the NP in object position can be interpreted as the goal when the preposition has been incorporated.

A theme whose quantificational properties are irrelevant may be conceived of as nonindividuated, i.e., as an unbounded amount of stuff or objects. This allows us to ignore exactly *which* theme entity was involved in an event of loading (for example) and to simply treat whatever it was as something loadable. The reason for this is the link that exists between the individuation of an entity and its possible identification (Löbner, 1990): Only an individuated entity can be identified as a *particular* entity, i.e., as an entity whose actual identity the speaker believes to know.

Since identification presupposes individuation, nonindividuation precludes it. That is, we only have to conceive of an entity as nonindividuated in order to disregard its actual identity. An entity whose identity is unknown or irrelevant cannot or need not be distinguished from other entities of the same type. A verb like *load* allows us to conceive of its theme as nonindividuated when it is not specified. By conceiving of the theme as nonindividuated, we may consider the actual identity of what is being loaded as irrelevant. We therefore do not need to distinguish it from other loadable entities and so may simply presuppose that it was something loadable. That is, verbs like *load* allow us to derive information about their themes on the basis of the verbs themselves.

If the theme's quantificational properties must indeed be irrelevant in the goal-object structure, why could we not conceive of the theme of a verb like *pull* in this way, thereby allowing the verb to alternate? To communicate, for example, that there is a supermarket employee 'pulling shopping carts all over the parking lot', we could simply ignore the specific amount of carts, get rid of the theme argument in object position, and make *the parking lot* the direct object of the verb, as in **Douglas pulled the parking lot*. Why is this sentence ungrammatical? This is because the quantificational properties of the theme of verbs like *pull* can be considered irrelevant only if we explicitly refer to it with a bare plural or mass noun, as in *Douglas pulled **shopping carts** onto the parking lot*; but the verbs do not allow us to construe the theme in this way when it is not specified. Nor is it sufficient to specify the theme of *pull* in a *with*-phrase (as in **Douglas pulled the parking lot with shopping carts*). *With*-phrases in goal-object constructions are always optional, so we cannot rely on the *with*-phrase to render the theme's quantificational properties irrelevant — for a verb to alternate, the verb must allow us to treat its theme in this way *regardless* of whether it is combined with a *with*-phrase. A transitive locative verb allows us to disregard the theme's quantificational properties when not specified only if it takes an INCREMENTAL THEME: This is true for *spray* and *load*, but not for *pull*.

4.1.2 *Incremental Themes*

The claim that verbs that participate in the locative alternation must specify an incremental theme was first made by Dowty (1991). An argument is an incremental theme if it is *gradually involved* in the action described by the verb. For example, if John is eating a sausage, then the longer he eats, the shorter the sausage gets. The gradual involvement of the sausage in the action of eating has an important implication: The length of the sausage sets an upper limit to how long the eating may continue. That is, the amount of sausage is systematically related to the temporal properties of the action denoted by the verb. An entity may be gradually involved because it is used up bit by bit in the action denoted by the verb, as in *eat a sausage*, because it undergoes a change of state, as in *cut a sausage*, or because it is effected, as in *build a house*. The gradual involvement of the theme may sometimes be fairly abstract: In *John read the book*, the book need not show any traces of the action, but it is still an incremental theme because the longer John continues reading, the less there remains to be read.[1]

Dowty's notion of incremental theme is closely related to — and partly based on — Krifka's (1986, 1989a,b) analysis of the interdependency be-

---

1. Dowty's (1991) notion of incremental theme differs from Gropen et al.'s (1991a,b) notion of affected theme in that it excludes certain cases that Gropen et al. would classify as affected. For example, Gropen et al. would consider *the cart* in *push the cart onto the parking lot* as affected because it changes location, but *the cart* is not an incremental theme, for reasons that will become clear below.

tween nominal reference and the temporal constitution of a sentence (first observed by Verkuyl, 1971; see also Tenny, 1987, 1989, 1992, and van Hout, 1994, 1996). Krifka captures this interdependency by proposing that certain verbs involve a HOMOMORPHISM between the quantificational properties of one of their arguments and the temporal structure of the situation specified by the verb. A homomorphism is a structure-preserving function between, for example, objects and situations. If *eat* is used to describe a temporally bounded event, the structure that is preserved by the homomorphism is the *part-of* relation: If x' (e.g., a slice of the sausage) is a part of X (the whole sausage), and if a predicate like *eat* maps X onto the event E (the eating of the whole sausage), then it must also map x' onto an event e' (the eating of one slice) which is part of E. Put differently, if X is an incremental theme, then parts of X will be related to parts of the event described by the verb.

When there is a homomorphism between objects and situations, the aspectual reading of the verb and the status — individuated or not — of the theme are *interdependent*: When the theme is interpreted as nonindividuated, the verb will automatically be construed as specifying a temporally un-bounded process, and, conversely, when the verb is interpreted as specifying a temporally unbounded process, the theme will automatically be construed as nonindividuated. Recall that the aspectual properties of a sentence can be diagnosed by using temporal adverbials (cf. Section 2.5): If a sentence combines with a durational adverbial like *for hours*, it denotes a (temporally unbounded) process, and if it combines with a frame adverbial like *within an hour*, it denotes a (temporally bounded) event. A sentence like *The tourist ate sausages* combines only with durational adverbials, not with frame adverbi-als, as shown in (3a), so we can conclude that it specifies a process. This is because the bare plural *sausages* refers to an unbounded amount of sausage, so we cannot determine the endpoint of eating. In contrast, *The tourist ate two sausages* combines only with frame adverbials, not with durational adverbi-als, as shown in (3b), so we can conclude that it specifies an event. Since the NP *two sausages* refers to a bounded amount of sausage, we can infer that the eating will end when both sausages are eaten up. Thus, an incremental theme is a major determinant of the aspect of the sentence.[2]

---

2. See also Dowty (1979), Tenny (1987, 1989, 1992), Grimshaw (1990), Jackendoff (1990), Van Valin (1990), Verkuyl (1993), and van Hout (1996) for analyses of the relationship between the aspectual properties of verbs and their argument structure.

(3) a.   The tourist ate sausages for 10 minutes/*within 10 minutes.[3]
    b.   The tourist ate two sausages *for 10 minutes/within 10 minutes.

Now, notice that *spray* and *load*, two verbs that alternate, take an incremental theme: When the theme is specified in object position by a bare mass term like *water* or a bare plural like *boxes*, the verbs denote processes, as shown in (4a), and when the theme is specified by a quantified object NP like *3 liters of water* or *3 boxes*, the verbs denote events, as shown in (4b):

(4) a.   He sprayed water on the lawn for hours/*within an hour.
         He loaded hay/boxes on the wagon for hours/*within an hour.
    b.   He sprayed 3 liters of water on the wall *for hours/within an hour.
         He loaded 3 bundles of hay/3 boxes on the wagon *for hours/within an hour.[4]

Unlike *spray* and *load*, *pull* — a nonalternator — does not take an incremental theme, as can also be shown by combining the verb with temporal adverbials (see also Dowty, 1991, on *push*). The quantificational properties of the object NP of *pull* do not influence the temporal properties of the situation denoted by the verb, as shown in (5a). A definite object NP yields an event reading only in the presence of a directional PP like *onto the parking lot*, as shown in (5b).

(5) a.   Douglas pulled shopping carts for hours/*within an hour.
         Douglas pulled two shopping carts for hours/*within an hour.
    b.   Douglas pulled two shopping carts onto the parking lot *for hours/within an hour.

So far, we have established that alternating verbs like *spray* and *load* take an incremental theme and that nonalternating verbs like *pull* do not. We can now see why the theme must be incremental in order to be construed as nonindividuated when not specified and so be omissable: Only an incremental theme can be construed as nonindividuated when the verb is given a process

---

3. There are two special interpretations that render a sentence like *He ate sausages within 10 minutes* acceptable. On the first, the sentence may be understood as specifying the beginning of the eating, as in *Within 10 minutes, he had started to eat sausages*. On the second, the sentence may be taken to mean that within 10 minutes, some activity of eating sausages had taken place at all. In general, when I classify examples as ungrammatical on grounds that they are combined with a frame adverbial, these interpretations will be disregarded.

4. A sentence like *He loaded 3 boxes on the wagon for an hour* is acceptable if we interpret it iteratively, i.e., as meaning that the boxes were loaded and taken off again, and reloaded, etc., for a period of one hour. Thus, reinterpretations of otherwise ungrammatical sentences are possible for both durational and frame adverbials (cf. 2.5 and Footnote 5). When I classify a sentence as ungrammatical on grounds that it is combined with a particular temporal adverbial, reinterpretations like these are disregarded.

reading. When the theme is not incremental, however, a process reading of the verb does not result in an interpretation of the theme as nonindividuated and so will not obviate the need to express the theme syntactically.

Let us see *why* a process reading of a verb like *load* brings about the nonindividuation of the theme. *Load* specifies a homomorphism between objects and situations. This means that the parts of the entity whose motion is at issue — for example, *the hay* in *John loaded the hay on the truck* — correspond to parts of the event to which the verb refers. Phrased informally, one might say *the longer, the more*: The longer I keep loading, the more hay I will have loaded. Notice that for each subunit of time that we can truthfully say represents an instance of loading, a different portion of hay will be loaded onto the truck — i.e., the portions of hay being loaded keep changing. On a process reading of *load*, as in *John loaded hay on the wagon for hours*, we conceive of the action as though it had no endpoint. Since the hay is gradually involved in the action, we assume that as long as the action lasts, there is at least some hay being loaded — i.e., we conceive of the theme of *load* as nonindividuated.

Verbs like *pull*, in contrast, do not express a homomorphism between objects and events but instead a homomorphism between *sublocations* and events — those sublocations that constitute the path along which the object is moved. These verbs might be characterized by the slogan *the longer, the farther*: The longer Douglas keeps pulling a shopping cart, the farther he will have pulled it. This time, the theme *remains identical throughout the event*, but its location changes: For each subunit of time that we can truthfully say represents an instance of pulling a shopping cart, there will be a different location along which the object is pulled. Giving a process reading to *pull* has no influence on our interpretation of how many objects are pulled; it only makes us unable to determine the length of the path. The process reading of *pull*, then, unlike that of *load*, does not allow us to assume that the theme is nonindividuated.

Let me now put forward what I will call the Nonindividuation Hypothesis. The hypothesis claims that there is a specific relationship between the omissability of an object of transitive locative verbs and the semantic properties of the corresponding argument:

(6) **The Nonindividuation Hypothesis**
The direct object of a transitive locative verb may be omitted only when the quantificational properties of the corresponding argument are irrelevant; the argument may then be existentially bound.

According to this hypothesis, in order for a transitive locative verb to take its goal as direct object, the quantificational properties of the theme must be irrelevant: The verb must allow speakers to assume that the theme is nonindividuated when it is not specified. The theme then does not need to be expressed syntactically, so the object position is available for the goal. To participate in the locative alternation, a transitive verb must take an incremental theme, since only a verb with an incremental theme offers speakers a way to conceive of the theme as nonindividuated when not specified: All they have to do is turn the verb into a process predicate.

The proposal does not imply that the theme has disappeared completely from the verb's argument structure — instead, it remains a semantic argument of the verb. I base this assumption on the fact that goal-object sentences derived from transitive locative verbs always imply the existence of the theme. An alternative criterion for argumenthood is the obligatoriness of a phrase. This criterion has been taken by many authors as evidence that the (optional) *with*-phrase is an adjunct (Hoekstra & Mulder, 1990; Booij, 1992, among others). The Nonindividuation Hypothesis leaves open whether the *with*-phrase is the direct expression of the theme as a semantic argument and so should be given syntactic argument status or whether it is an adjunct modifying the information about the theme entailed by the verb. Since the Preposition Incorporation account of the locative alternation treats the *with*-phrase as a syntactic argument, I will adopt this classification.

As the preceding discussion has shown, the Nonindividuation Hypothesis explains why certain verbs do not participate in the locative alternation, i.e., those that do not take an incremental theme. Taking an incremental theme is thus one condition that transitive locative verbs have to meet in order to participate in the locative alternation, in German and in all languages that allow this change in argument structure. This means that children only have to learn that the theme of verbs like *pull* and *push* is not incremental in order to infer that the verbs do not participate in the alternation. To preview the arguments to be made in Chapter 6 about nonalternating verbs in German, incremental themehood is but one condition locative verbs have to meet. Many nonalternating verbs do not alternate simply because they fail to take an incremental theme. However, some verbs that *do* take an incremental theme do not alternate for independent reasons.

4.1.3 *Optional Object Deletion: Independent Evidence for the Nonindividuation Hypothesis*

Independent evidence that there is a close relationship between an incremental theme's omission from object position and its construal as nonindividuated comes from the phenomenon of optional object deletion in another kind of construction, as illustrated in (7). The only verbs that can undergo optional object deletion are those that allow us to conceive of the omitted themes as nonindividuated.

(7) *John ate/wrote/read.*

Recall that *eat* takes an incremental theme (cf. 4.1.2). The same holds for *read* and *write*. If the verbs are combined with a definite NP like *the article*, the sentence will be temporally bounded, as shown in (8a), but if the verbs are combined with a bare plural like *articles*, the sentence will be temporally unbounded, as shown in (8b):

(8) a. The student read/wrote the article *for an hour/within an hour.[5]
     b. The student read/wrote articles for an hour/*within an hour.

What do we infer about the theme of *read* or *write* when it is omitted? That it involves an individuated portion of reading or writing material, or a nonindividuated amount? Evidence for the latter interpretation has been provided by Mittwoch (1982), who argues that omitting the theme goes paired with a process interpretation, and hence with the interpretation of the theme as nonindividuated, as shown through the patterning with time adverbials in (9a). That is, the sentences show the same aspectual behavior as when the verbs are combined with NPs that do not individuate their referents, i.e., bare plurals or mass terms, as shown in (9b).[6]

(9) a. The student read/wrote for an hour/*within an hour.
     b. The student read/wrote articles for an hour/*within an hour.

The aspectual behavior of *John read/wrote* shows, then, that when an incremental theme is not specified, it is interpreted as nonindividuated. But what do

---

5. I ignore here the possible reinterpretation of *read/write the article for an hour* as meaning that the student kept on reading/writing the article but did not finish it. See Croft (1993) and Krifka (1989a) for analyses of these reinterpretations.

6. Notice that *John ate within five minutes* is acceptable, and so seems to be counterevidence to the claim that the omission of the theme goes paired with a process reading of the verb. See Footnote 8 for discussion.

we infer when a *non*incremental theme is omitted, as in *Douglas is pulling*? This sentence does not invite the inference that Douglas is pulling an un-bounded amount of entities; instead, it suggests that he is pulling one particular thing whose identity is known from the context. This shows that the argument is omitted for *pragmatic reasons* (which we discussed in 2.4); *Douglas is pulling* is not, then, an example of optional object deletion. Optional object deletion is possible only for verbs that take an incremental theme.

There is a clear reason why different inferences are made about these different kinds of omitted arguments. Incremental themes — unlike nonincremental themes — are major determinants of whether the action denoted by the verb is construed as temporally bounded or unbounded. If no information is available about their quantity, we cannot use this information to determine an endpoint for the action. If no other elements in the sentence provide this information, we conceive of the action as though it had no endpoint. Since the referent of the incremental theme NP is gradually in-volved in the action, we must assume that as long as the action lasts, there is some stuff or objects involved in it. In the absence of evidence for exactly how much stuff or how many objects, we do not make any specific assump-tions about the theme's quantificational properties at all, i.e., we conceive of an incremental theme as being nonindividuated.

So far, the interdependency between the quantificational properties of an incremental theme and the temporal properties of the event only explains why omitting the incremental theme of *read* yields a process reading of the verb, and why this, in turn, causes the theme to be conceived of as nonindividuated. But it does not yet show that the theme *must* be construed as nonindividuated in order to be omitted. For example, what if elements in the sentence *other* than the theme indicate that the sentence is to be seen as temporally bounded — could the theme then be omitted as well? Evidence that it may not be omitted in this case has been provided by van Hout (1994; see also Krifka, 1989a).

Drawing on evidence from Dutch and Russian, van Hout shows that nonstative verbs that take two logical arguments typically do not require the syntactic expression of the argument in object position as long as nothing in the sentence interferes with the interpretation of the sentence as temporally unbounded.[7] In contrast, when such verbs are combined with a particle or

---

7. This claim holds for only a subset of nonstative verbs with two logical arguments. Some nonstative verbs require the expression of both arguments even when they are combined with durational adverbials like *for hours* that require a process interpretation of the sentence — e.g., **He devoured for hours* is ungrammatical.

prefix that renders them temporally bounded, both arguments must be expressed syntactically; cf. the Dutch examples in (10-11) (van Hout, 1994). I also include here, as (12), an example discussed by Krifka (1989a, p. 171), which shows that the same relationship holds for German particle verbs. The examples in (13) show that when the object is omitted, the sentence combines with durational but not with frame adverbials and so must be temporally unbounded.[8]

(10) a. Ze schreef haar proefschrift. 'She wrote her thesis'
   Ze schreef. 'She wrote'
  b. Ze at de appeltaart. 'She ate the apple pie'
   Ze at. 'She ate'

(11) a. Ze schreef haar proefschrift af. 'She wrote her thesis off' ('She finished writing her thesis')
   *Ze schreef af. 'She wrote off'
  b. Ze at de appeltaart op. 'She ate the apple pie up' ('She finished eating the apple pie')
   *Ze at op. 'She ate up'

(12) a. Anna las das Buch. 'Anna read the book'
   Anna las. 'Anna read'
  b. Anna las das Buch durch. 'Anna read the book through' ('Anna finished reading the book')
   *Anna las durch. 'Anna read through'

(13) Ze schreef urenlang/*in een uur. 'She wrote for hours/*within an hour'
   Ze at urenlang/*in een uur. 'She ate for hours/*within an hour'
   Anna las stundenlang/*innerhalb von einer Stunde.
   'Anna read for hours/*within an hour'

Van Hout's analysis shows that the theme can be omitted only under the process reading. If the sentence is temporally bounded, but by some element other than the theme, such as a verb particle, the theme may not be omitted.

---

8. Sometimes, combinations of verbs and particles like those in (11-13) are acceptable — whenever we can infer a specific referent from the context. In German, for example, a sentence like *Anna aß auf* 'Anna ate up/finished eating' is somewhat acceptable (the example is taken from van Hout, 1994). It implies that Anna finished eating a particular meal and is acceptable because our conventions of eating tell us that there are particular meals at particular times of the day, and so we only need to know the time of the day to infer that Anna was having dinner, for example. This also explains why in English, the theme of *eat* may be omitted even though the event is taken to be bounded, as in *John ate within 5 minutes* — John may be having a TV dinner (cf. Footnote 6). Even a combination of *lesen* and *durch* may be acceptable sometimes. For example, if we imagine that Anna has just been handed an instruction to read, an imperative like *Lies durch* 'read through' seems fine.

According to aspectual analyses of verb argument structure proposed by Grimshaw (1990), Pustejovski (1991), Grimshaw and Vikner (1993), and van Hout (1994, 1996), the process reading of the verb is more or less directly responsible for the omissability of the theme. These authors assume that when a verb specifies a process, it has a less complex event structure than when it specifies a temporally bounded event, because it then does not specify a transition (e.g., *Anna is reading*, which is unbounded, does not involve a transition from reading to not reading). Since processes do not involve a transition, they can be characterized sufficiently by a single argument, as in *Anna las* 'Anna read'; transitions, in contrast, require the expression of at least two arguments, as in *Anna las das Buch durch* 'Anna finished reading the book', in order to identify the state of affairs that follows the transition.

However, the process reading of a verb cannot be directly responsible for the omissability of the object NP. *Douglas is pulling*, for example, also specifies a process, but it is acceptable only when the omitted object can be immediately inferred from the context. According to the Nonindividuation Hypothesis, the process reading of a verb allows the omission of the object NP only when the theme is incremental since the process reading is only the necessary *means* for omitting the theme. It allows us to ignore, for a sentence like *Anna was reading,* how much Anna was reading, so we may presume that it is irrelevant *what* she was reading. In contrast, when a sentence is temporally bounded, the existence of the theme may no longer be simply presupposed.

Let me summarize the arguments I have made so far. An analysis of examples used by linguists to discuss the locative alternation has shown that the *with*-phrase in goal-object constructions has a strong tendency to be a bare plural or mass term. I have argued that this tendency reflects the fact that the quantificational properties of the theme are irrelevant in the goal-object argument structure of the verb. They must be irrelevant since the verb then allows speakers to conceive of the theme as nonindividuated when it is not specified and to thereby ignore the actual identity of the theme. This in turn allows them to presuppose the theme's existence on the basis of the verb being used. The theme then does not have to be expressed syntactically, so the object position is available for the goal. A verb allows speakers to treat the quantificational properties of an unspecified theme as irrelevant only if it takes an incremental theme, since only such a verb offers speakers a way to construe the theme as nonindividuated when the theme is not specified: by turning the verb into a process predicate.

4.1.4 *Run-Up Activities: How to Integrate Process Predicates into Temporally Bounded Events*

The Nonindividuation Hypothesis states that in order for verbs like *spray* and *load* to take their goal as direct object, they must be turned into process predicates. At first sight, this appears to clash with the facts: Not all goal-object constructions specify a process — for example, *John loaded the wagon within an hour* is perfectly acceptable. How does the Nonindividuation Hypothesis account for these examples?

A sentence like *John loaded the wagon within an hour* is temporally bounded because it asserts that the wagon changes from not being full to being full, i.e., it asserts that the wagon undergoes a transition or change from one state to another. But this transition does not take place abruptly — instead, it is the result of a process during which John was engaged in loading the wagon bit by bit by putting some stuff or objects on it. Transitions that are the result of a process have been called RUN-UP activities (Croft, 1993). According to the Nonindividuation Hypothesis, goal-object sentences that are temporally bounded are run-up activities: They denote a process that leads to a transition.

But why can we not interpret a sentence like **Anna las durch* 'Anna finished reading' as a run-up activity, thereby allowing the theme to be construed as nonindividuated, and so be omissable? This is because in *Anna las durch*, there is no _new_ object NP whose referent defines the end of the process. The boundedness of the sentence therefore *depends* on the theme's being individuated, so its omission is ungrammatical. If there is a new object NP whose referent defines the end of the process, then the boundedness of the sentence does not depend on the individuation of the theme, and the construction is grammatical.

To appreciate this, consider the resultative constructions in (14). In these sentences, *lesen* 'read', *essen* 'eat', and *schreiben* 'write' are combined with a new object NP. The sentences specify a run-up activity in which the end of the process is determined by the referent of the new object NP and so does not depend on the construal of the omitted theme as individuated (see Simpson, 1983; Levin & Rappaport Hovav, 1991; Carrier & Randall, 1992; Kaufmann, 1995, among others, for analyses of resultative constructions).

(14) Anna las die ganze Nacht durch. 'Anna read the whole night through'
      Anna aß ihren Teller auf. 'Anna ate her plate empty' (lit.: 'Anna ate her plate up')
      Anna schrieb ihr Tintenfaß leer. 'Anna wrote her ink pot empty'

A sentence like *Anna aß ihren Teller auf* does not specify what Anna had to eat in order to empty her plate. Since nothing is specified, we will take the sentence to mean that she ate some edible stuff or objects. But since the to-be-eaten amount is not specified in any way, the sentence could also characterize a situation in which she ate, e.g., only a single peanut — that is, a portion of food so small that it can be consumed all at once, without taking the time we usually associate with processes. However, since there is a new direct object that determines the end of the process, the amount of food being eaten is irrelevant. Even if Anna ate only a single peanut to empty her plate, a speaker would have to conceive of *essen* as a process predicate in order to render the quantificational properties of the peanut irrelevant and characterize the action as *den Teller aufessen*. Since it is conceptually difficult and pragmatically odd to ignore the quantificational properties of a single peanut (i.e., to conceive of it as though it could not be counted), a construction like *Anna aß ihren Teller auf* is unlikely to be used in such a situation, although it would be grammatical. Importantly, even if *Anna aß ihren Teller auf* involves the eating of only a single peanut, the sentence still specifies a run-up activity, since its temporal boundedness is defined by the emptiness of the referent of the new object NP, the plate, and not by the consumption of an unspecified peanut.

In goal-object constructions, a locative verb is, by definition, combined with a new object NP. When these constructions are temporally bounded, they specify a run-up activity — a process leading to a transition — because the end of the action is defined in terms of the goal and not in terms of the theme (see also Wunderlich, 1992, who proposes that theme- and goal-object constructions have different satisfaction criteria; cf. 3.2.2). The boundedness of the process does not provide counterevidence to the claim that the theme can be construed as nonindividuated in these constructions because the end of the action does not depend on the individuation of the theme but is defined instead in terms of the goal. Put differently, the theme's quantificational properties are rendered irrelevant in goal-object constructions (and in resultative constructions like those in (14)) by turning the verb into a predicate that specifies a process leading to a transition and whose endpoint is not defined in terms of the theme.

Let us now discuss examples that contain definite or quantified *with*-NPs like *with the hay* or *with the boxes*. The goal-object form of a verb like *load* requires that the theme's quantificational properties be irrelevant, which is achieved by turning the base verb into a predicate that describes a process or a process leading to a transition not defined in terms of the theme. When speakers use the goal-object form of a verb, they may specify the theme more closely by using a *with*-phrase. In doing so, they can also specify how much stuff or how many objects change location — i.e., they may use a definite or quantified *with*-NP. That is, a sentence like *John loaded the wagon with ten boxes* specifies a run-up activity that ends when the wagon is full; the *with*-phrase simply informs us that ten boxes sufficed for loading the wagon. Notice that the end of the process does not depend on the theme's being individuated, since the endpoint is determined in terms of the goal, and not the theme. The same reasoning can be applied to *with*-NPs that refer to a *single* object, as in *John loaded the wagon with **a box***. According to the Nonindividuation Hypothesis, these sentences are often questionable because it is conceptually difficult and pragmatically odd to ignore the quantificational properties of a single object.

4.2 Implications of the Nonindividuation Hypothesis for the Acquisition of the Locative Alternation

4.2.1 *Learning How to Change the Argument Structure of Alternating Verbs*

The Nonindividuation Hypothesis predicts that a necessary step in acquiring the alternation is to conceive of a verb's theme appropriately: Children must be able to consider the theme's quantificational properties as irrelevant. Acquiring the goal-object form of a verb will be particularly difficult if it means that a theme that is typically individuated in the theme-object form must be treated as though its quantificational properties were irrelevant.

Verbs differ in whether this reconceptualisation is needed. Some verbs — for example, *spray* — denote only the motion of substances. As unbounded entities, substances are commonly conceived of as nonindividuated to begin with. Thus, the theme of *spray* does not have to be reconceptualized in order for the object NP to be interpreted as the goal — its quantificational properties already *are* irrelevant. But reconceptualizing the theme is needed for verbs like *load*, which may denote the motion of both substances and bounded objects. If the Nonindividuation Hypothesis is correct, children should acquire the goal-object construction for verbs like *spray* earlier than for verbs like *load*.

To make it clear why the goal-object form of *spray* should be acquired earlier than that of *load*, it is not sufficient to distinguish the verbs only in terms of the selectional restrictions on their themes. We must also take into account how easily the verb can be used to describe a process, or a process leading to a transition, since, as I have argued, a process reading of the verb is essential for the goal-object argument structure.

Verbs like *spray*, which denote only the motion of substances, always describe processes or run-up activities.[9] This is because their themes do not provide a criterion for determining the endpoint of the action: Substances do not come in natural units, and so do not, by themselves, allow us to conceive of the action in terms of temporal units. The temporal units can be established only by some additional means, e.g., by unitizing the theme, as in *He sprayed a liter of water onto the roses*. But even then a process is included as a component of the event — the spraying continues until a liter of water has been sprayed. In contrast, verbs like *load*, which denote the motion of both substances and bounded objects, do not necessarily describe processes leading to a transition — they can denote the motion of a single bounded object, which provides a clear criterion for determining the endpoint of the action. In *John loaded a box on the wagon*, for example, *load* only specifies a single event of loading, and no process is involved.

That spraying, but not loading, always involves a process is also reflected in our interpretations of sentences in which the verbs are used to describe temporally unbounded events. Cf. (15):

(15) a.   John sprayed water on the roses for half an hour.
     b.   John loaded hay/boxes on the wagon for half an hour.

While (15a) is understood as describing the continuous application of water, (15b) is interpreted as describing a series of subevents of putting hay or boxes on the wagon — i.e., (15b) is interpreted *iteratively*. The iterative interpreta-

---

9. By 'substance', I mean either homogeneous stuff like water or mud, or multiple objects like peas. Thus, when I speak of 'verbs like *spray*' and 'verbs that denote motion only of substances' in the following, I also refer to verbs like German *schütten* 'pour', which can denote the motion of bounded objects as long as the objects can be construed as though they were a substance. (That *schütten* requires such a construal of its theme is reflected in the fact that it cannot describe the motion of a single bounded object — cf. *John schüttete die Erbsen/*die Erbse in die Schüssel* 'John poured the peas/*the pea into the bowl'.)

tion of *load* in (15b) indicates that *load* is basically TELIC, whereas the absence of iterativity in (15a) suggests that *spray* is basically ATELIC.[10]

The terms 'telic' and 'atelic' are closely related to the terms 'temporally bounded' and 'temporally unbounded', respectively, and they are often used interchangeably. Following a proposal by Croft (1993), I will use the term '(a)telic' for the inherent aspectual properties of verbs, and 'temporally (un)bounded' for the temporal properties of sentences. A telic verb describes an event that has a natural endpoint. Whether a sentence is temporally bounded or unbounded — i.e., describes a bounded event or an unbounded process — depends not only on the verb's inherent aspectual properties but also on a number of other factors, for example, the quantificational properties of the object NP (cf. 4.1.2) and the presence of particles (cf. 4.1.3). This means that a verb's inherent aspectual properties may or may not correspond to the temporal properties of the sentences that include it. But the *intrinsic* aspectual properties of verbs like *spray*, but not *load*, correspond to the interpretation of the verb as specifying a process (that does or does not lead to a transition) that is needed for using the verb in goal-object constructions.

The different ways in which a process interpretation can be obtained from sentences containing *spray* and *load* can be made explicit by using a representational format proposed by Pustejovsky (1991), as shown in (16). (This is a simplified version of Pustejovski's notational system: P simply refers to process, and e_t to a telic event):

(16) a.   *spray* paint   b.   *load* hay/boxes
       on the wall   on the truck
       for 5 minutes   for 5 minutes

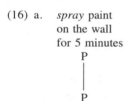
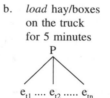

10. There are verbs that, like *spray*, are subcategorized for substances, but that describe discrete rather than continuous motion. This might suggest that they are telic, just like *load*. An example is *daub* — cf. *He daubed (the) paint onto the wall*. But *daub* is in fact atelic, like *spray* and *schütten* — sentences containing it are commonly interpreted as describing a process. For example, the most natural interpretation of *John daubed (the) paint on the wall* is to assume that John daubed repeatedly for an indefinite time (process) or until the paint was gone (run-up event), and not just once. The physical properties of a substance like paint — i.e., the absence of natural units — is responsible for this interpretation. A process interpretation is ruled out only if we use a unitizer like *a handful of (paint)*: *John daubed a handful of paint on the wall* means that he daubs only once (a more explicit discussion of the linguistic means to 'unitize' substances, and how they differ from the means to refer to bounded objects, is provided by Krifka, 1989a,b).

Notice that the process predicate for *load* is more complex than that for *spray* (regardless of whether the theme is *hay* or *boxes*). This suggests that it is more difficult to construe *load* as a process than *spray*, because doing so requires the speaker to override the verb's inherent telicity and envision several instances of telic events strung together to form a larger unbounded event.

Is it true that all verbs behave either like *spray* or like *load*? Or are the representations in (16) appropriate only for these verbs? That verbs like *spray* are always atelic seems uncontroversial: Their themes do not, by themselves, provide a criterion for determining the endpoint of the action, so the verbs cannot describe events that have natural endpoints, i.e., are telic. But it is less clear whether verbs that, like *load*, can describe the motion of either bounded or unbounded objects are always telic, and so, when they are turned into process predicates, have the more complex structure shown in (16b). But all verbs that I have found that can undergo the locative alternation in English or German are either like *spray* or like *load*. In what follows, I will therefore distinguish between two kinds of motion verbs, mass verbs and count verbs. These are defined as follows:

(17) Definition MASS VERB: *The referent of the theme NP must be a substance (or objects that are construed as a substance), and the verb is atelic.*

(18) Definition COUNT VERB: *The referent of the theme NP can be either a substance or one or more bounded objects, and the verb is telic.*

If my analysis of motion verbs is correct, goal-object constructions should be easier for mass verbs than for count verbs for two reasons. First, mass verbs denote the motion only of substances or of objects that are construed as substances, so the themes of these verbs are nonindividuated to begin with. Count verbs, in contrast, can denote the motion of both substances and (singular) bounded objects, and so their themes will often have to be deindividuated. Second, mass verbs are atelic and so they are already process predicates. But count verbs can describe a process, or a run-up activity, only if they are interpreted as describing a series of subevents — and this interpretation yields a more complex process predicate than if no such iteration of subevents is required. The Nonindividuation Hypothesis predicts, then, that children should find the goal-object construction easier, and so acquire it earlier, for mass verbs than for count verbs.

I have tested the prediction that children acquire the goal-object construction earlier for mass verbs than for count verbs in two experiments, a production experiment, presented in Chapter 5, and a comprehension experiment, presented in Chapter 7.

4.2.2 *How does the Nonindividuation Hypothesis Solve the No Negative Evidence Problem?*

So far we have been concerned only with what children have to learn in order to change the argument structure of the verbs that do participate in the locative alternation. But to be credited with full knowledge of the alternation, children must also be able to identify — without the help of negative evidence — those verbs that do not alternate. How does the Nonindividuation Hypothesis contribute to a solution to this problem?

Most basically, the hypothesis accounts for how children determine that verbs that do not take an incremental theme, such as *pull*, do not alternate. Once learners have understood the basic machinery of the locative alternation, they will automatically know that these verbs cannot take their goal as direct object. Children should make errors with a verb like *pull* only if they erroneously believe that it does take an incremental theme — most likely, because they do not yet know its meaning. The constraint that a verb must take an incremental theme in order to participate in the locative alternation should hold for all languages employing this change in argument structure, enabling children to identify the corresponding nonalternating verbs. But a language may have verbs that do not alternate for other reasons. Verbs that do not participate in the locative alternation in German — either because they do not take an incremental theme or for some other reason — will be discussed in detail in Chapter 6.

4.2.3 *How Do Children Learn that a Verb Takes an Incremental Theme?*

If the Nonindividuation Hypothesis is correct, then in order to acquire the locative alternation and to tell which verbs participate in it, children must know whether a verb takes an incremental theme. Incremental themehood depends on the meaning of the verb, so children may infer that a verb takes an incremental theme once they know the verb's meaning. How then do they learn the meaning of verbs?

In attempting to answer the question as to how children acquire the meaning of verbs, and of lexical items more generally, we are faced with what is known as the induction problem in research on language acquisition (a problem first pointed out by Quine, 1960). The situations referred to by verbs (or, more generally, the entities referred to by words) may always be characterized in infinitely many different ways. This implies that children, in trying to derive the possible meaning of a verb, must somehow be constrained to perceive situations in only a limited set of ways, so as to come up with a finite and possibly small set of hypotheses about what the verb may mean. Approaches to the acquisition of verb meaning differ in the assumptions they make about the type of constraints that underlie children's hypotheses about verb meaning.

According to what I will refer to as the observational approach, children acquire the meaning of verbs mainly by registering the relevant properties of the situations the verbs refer to. Various proposals have been put forward within this approach, again differing mainly in the constraints on hypothesis-formation they propose children to be equipped with (cf. Pinker, 1984, 1989; Slobin, 1985, 1995, among others). An alternative approach to the acquisition of verb semantics is the Syntactic Bootstrapping account proposed by Gleitman and her colleagues (Landau & Gleitman, 1985; Gleitman, 1990; Naigles, 1990; Fisher, Gleitman, & Gleitman, 1991, Naigles, Gleitman, & Gleitman, 1992, among others. See also Grimshaw, 1994, and Pinker, 1994, for a critical evaluation of the account). Proponents of this account argue against observational accounts on grounds that registering the relevant situational properties is insufficient for determining verb meaning. First, one and the same situation may be described by more than one verb; for example, a situation in which one person hands an object to another person may be described as either *giving* or *receiving*. Thus, merely observing that an object passes from one person to another will not help children to figure out the difference between *give* and *receive*. Second, parents often use verbs even though the corresponding perceptual correlates are not present, so there is likewise no way for children to figure out the verb's meaning on the basis of observing the relevant situational properties. Since observation is insufficient, so it is argued, children must draw on alternative sources of information for deriving the semantics of verbs. According to the Syntactic Bootstrapping account, these alternative sources of information are the various syntactic frames children hear a verb being used in. The syntactic frames of a verb provide this information because they are abstract surface reflexes of the verb's meaning. Exploiting this information is proposed to be a necessary means for narrowing down the semantic properties of the verb.

Section 4.1 has shown that certain argument structure alternations are available only for verbs taking an incremental theme. Thus, locative verbs that take an incremental theme may participate in the locative alternation; these and other verbs taking an incremental theme may appear in resultative constructions like *Anna ate her plate empty*, and they may be used without any object NP at all, as in *Anna was eating*. This suggests that children may use the appearance of a verb in these constructions as evidence that the verb takes an incremental theme, in line with the claims put forward by proponents of the Syntactic Bootstrapping account. I will therefore discuss whether the Syntactic Bootstrapping account provides an answer to the question as to how children infer that a verb takes an incremental theme. To preview the results of the discussion, I will conclude that it does not. To infer that a verb takes an incremental theme, children must first rely on observing the relevant properties of the situation.

Let us first look at the characteristic way in which incremental theme verbs alternate between a process and an event reading. Recall that a verb like *eat* describes a process when its object NP refers to an unbounded amount of stuff or objects, and an event when its object NP refers to a bounded amount of stuff or objects. Recall further that this correlation exists because verbs taking an incremental theme denote a homomorphism between objects and events. The correlation between type of object NP and type of situation may suggest that children infer that some verbs denote a homomorphism between objects and events because whenever an unbounded amount of time is specified (for example, by frame adverbials and verb inflection like *-ing* in English), the object NP refers to an unbounded amount of stuff or objects, whereas when a bounded amount of time is specified, the object NP is also bounded (see Brown, 1973; Weist, Wysocka, Witkowska-Stadnik, Buczowska, & Konieczna, 1984; Slobin, 1985; Bickerton, 1981; Cziko, 1989; Rispoli, 1990; Behrens, 1993; Anderson & Shirai, 1994, among others, for evidence that children are able to distinguish between process and event readings from very early on). While this reasoning may seem plausible at first sight, it cannot in fact be correct. The parallelism between type of object NP and type of situation as such provides no information about the *gradual* involvement of the theme. The object NP informs us only as to whether its referent is conceived of as bounded, and inflectional marking and temporal adverbials (for example) inform us only as to whether the situation is conceived of as temporally bounded. That is, in both cases we are only informed about the presence or absence of an endpoint, but not about what happens to *parts* of a single referent over the course of the situation. I do not see how the gradual involvement of the theme could be inferred on this basis.

Could the various syntactic frames incremental theme verbs may appear in provide a clue as to the status of the theme? That is, are the syntactic frames associated with the locative alternation, optional object deletion, and resultative constructions like *Anna aß den Teller auf* 'Anna ate her plate empty' sufficiently informative? Common to these constructions is that the theme is no longer expressed in object position and so must be omissable; this might be taken as evidence that it must be an incremental theme. But again, I believe the answer is no. First, it is unclear why the omissability of the theme as such would suggest that it is incremental. Second, the syntactic properties of a construction like *Anna aß den Teller auf* is less informative than it may appear at first sight. To see why, we must keep in mind that information about the lexical content of the noun phrases in a sentence — e.g., whether the object NP refers to food or to containers of food — plays no role in the proposed process of syntactic bootstrapping (Pinker, 1994). Relevant to syntactic bootstrapping is only the information that verbs like *eat* may appear in the syntactic frame [subject-NP verb object-NP adjective/particle]. The problem now is that this frame may be used both for resultative constructions like *Anna aß den Teller auf*, in which the theme NP is omitted, and for resultative constructions like *Anna aß ihr Butterbrot auf* 'Anna ate her sandwich up', in which it is preserved. (In the presence of an adjective, we may not even arrive at a resultative reading; a sentence like *Er bügelte seine Hemden trocken* 'He ironed his shirts dry' may either mean that he ironed his shirts until they were dry or as soon as they were dry.) Thus, the syntactic frame as such does not tell us whether the theme is actually omitted. The same holds for the syntactic frames associated with the locative alternation. The frame [subject-NP verb object-NP (*with*-NP)] could also contain the verb's theme NP in object position, as in *They sprayed the paint with spray cans*.

Even if there is no object NP at all, as in *John was eating*, the resulting intransitive frame cannot be critical to inferring that the theme has been omitted and so must be incremental. First, the object NP may also be omitted in the case of nonincremental theme verbs, provided the context allows speakers to clearly identify the intended referent, as in *The Cubs won* (Rispoli, 1992, p. 583; see also Chapter 2, Footnote 9 and 11). Second, causativizable verbs like *break* and *roll* may likewise appear in transitive and intransitive syntactic frames. Since the learning procedures proposed in the Syntactic Bootstrapping account do not draw on information provided by the content of a noun phrase, the intransitive frames of *break* and *roll*, in which the theme is expressed in subject position, are indistinguishable from those of *eat* and *drink*, in which it is omitted. In sum, I do not see how Syntactic Bootstrapping could account for how children determine that verbs like *eat* and *load* take an incremental theme. First contact with the concept of incremental themes thus has to be made by observing the relevant properties of the situation the verb refers to.

Chapter 5

The Production Experiment: Testing the Nonindividuation Hypothesis

In this chapter, I present the main experiment that I conducted to test the Nonindividuation Hypothesis. The experiment tested the predictions derived from the Nonindividuation Hypothesis against the predictions of Gropen et al.'s (1991a,b) and Lebeaux's (1988) Affectedness hypotheses (cf. Chapter 2). The goal of the experiment was to test which verbs children would use most frequently with the goal as direct object under circumstances designed to elicit this argument structure. The verbs used to test the predictions were both mass verbs and count verbs that do or do not specify their goal as affected.

5.1 Theoretical Predictions

The Nonindividuation Hypothesis states that for a transitive verb to take its goal as direct object, the quantificational properties of its theme must be construed as irrelevant; to this end, the verb must be turned into a predicate that specifies a process or a process leading to a transition. Transitive motion verbs that participate in the alternation differ both in the type of incremental theme they take and in their temporal properties. Mass verbs denote the motion only of substances and are atelic. Count verbs can denote the motion of both substances and bounded objects and are telic. Turning a verb into a process predicate will be more difficult for count verbs than for mass verbs, since for count verbs this requires interpreting the verb as describing an iteration of subevents. The Nonindividuation Hypothesis predicts, then, that productive knowledge of the goal-object form is acquired later for count verbs than for mass verbs.

I assume that affectedness does not play a role in children's acquisition of the alternation for two reasons: First, in German, motion verbs may alternate even when they do not specify affectedness, and second, the Preposition Incorporation account of the locative alternation explains the locative alternation without positing that the goal must be specified as affected. Therefore, I predict that children learning German acquire productive knowledge of the goal-object form earlier for mass verbs than for count verbs, regardless of whether the verbs specify that their goal is affected.

Gropen (1989) and Gropen et al.'s (1991a,b) Affectedness Hypothesis predicts that a content verb will alternate only if it specifies the affectedness of the goal in its base argument structure, i.e., if it specifies a particular endstate of the goal. This prediction is challenged by verbs like *werfen* 'throw', which alternate even though they do not specify a change of state of the goal (as determined, for example, on the basis of their combination with temporal adverbials). According to the logic of Gropen et al.'s hypothesis, children could acquire the goal-object form of verbs like *werfen* in two ways: They could erroneously assume that the base forms of the verbs do specify affectedness, and derive the goal-object form productively, or, on encountering the *be*-forms of these verbs in the input, they could reinterpret the meanings of the verbs in terms of affectedness (because the Object Affectedness Linking Rule will be applied backwards to predict a verb's meaning from the syntactic arrangement of its arguments). Either way, the Affectedness Hypothesis predicts that even in a language like German, in which the locative alternation does not depend on affectedness, children will initially use the goal-object form of verbs of motion only if they assume that the verb specifies the affectedness of the goal.

In evaluating Gropen et al.'s Affectedness Hypothesis, I also discussed Lebeaux's (1988) theory of affectedness, pointing out that his theory can account for why verbs may alternate in German even though they do not specify their goal to be affected. I interpret Lebeaux's theory to predict that speakers will restrict the goal-object form to verbs specifying an affected goal only if their language does not mark the derived argument structure morphologically. If the goal-object form *is* morphologically marked, they will also be willing to use the goal-object form for verbs that do not specify an affected goal. Regardless of marking, children acquiring every language would initially rely on affectedness in producing a goal-object form of a verb. If they later discover that goal-object forms are morphologically marked, they will also extend the form to verbs that do not specify affectedness. Like Gropen et al.'s hypothesis, then, Lebeaux's hypothesis predicts that children will acquire the goal-object form earlier for verbs that specify an affected goal than for verbs that do not.

In 5.3, these theoretical predictions will be reformulated as more specific hypotheses about the outcomes of the tasks I used. I will now turn to the experimental operationalization and testing of these predictions.

5.2 The Experiment

5.2.1 *Subjects and Overview of the Experiment*

The experiment consisted of a pretest, which assessed the subjects' understanding of the verbs to be used in the main task, followed about two weeks later by the main task, in which subjects were shown a series of video films depicting actions that were instances of the verbs and asked to describe them to a listener.

Eighty-six native speakers of German participated in the study: 20 children (6 boys, 14 girls) aged 6;4 to 7;6 (mean 7;01); 22 children (14 boys, 8 girls) aged 7;7 to 8;5 (mean 8;01); 17 children (7 boys, 10 girls) aged 8;6 to 10;0 (mean 8;11);[1] 13 students attending Realschule (which corresponds to the A-levels of high school) (mean age 17) and 14 students studying psychology at the University of Heidelberg (mean age 25). The university students participated only in the main experiment. The students were paid for their participation. The children and the high school students lived in Kleve, a town in Northwest Germany; the university students came from various parts of Germany.[2]

---

1. The elementary school children who participated in the experiment were somewhat older than what is usually considered to be a relevant age range in studies of language acquisition. In Appendix 2, I explain my reasons for assuming that this age range would be critical.

2. I did not obtain information about whether the subjects were bilingual and/or spoke the local dialect in addition to High German. If differences in their linguistic background had influenced their behavior in the experiment, this would have increased the variance in the group, thus making it more difficult to obtain any systematic effect. To the extent that a systematic effect was obtained (cf. 5.4), then, differences in the subjects' linguistic background may be considered irrelevant.

5.2.2 *The Pretest: Assessing Children's Knowledge of the Meaning of the Verbs Included in the Main Task*

In this section, I describe the criteria I used for selecting verbs as stimuli, the verbs that were chosen, and the pretest that assessed children's interpretation of the verbs.

Criteria for Selecting the Verbs

The independent variable in the experiment was the type of verb used to elicit goal-object constructions. The verbs had to be transitive verbs of motion that participate in the locative alternation. To test the Nonindividuation Hypothesis, I needed mass verbs and count verbs, and to test the Affectedness hypotheses, I needed verbs that, in their base forms, do or do not specify that the goal is affected. Taken together, these criteria define four different types of verbs, which I will call +AFF and -AFF mass verbs, and +AFF and -AFF count verbs. Table 1 shows the verbs that were selected to represent each type.

Table 1. Verbs chosen to represent the four different types of verbs needed in the experiment

| | GOAL | |
THEME	+aff	-aff
mass verbs	*schmieren* 'smear'	*gießen* 'pour'
	spritzen 'spray'	*rieseln* 'sprinkle'
count verbs	*packen* 'pack'	*werfen* 'throw'
	laden 'load'	*ballern* 'smash'[3]

All these verbs undergo the locative alternation in German. While the categorization of verbs as mass versus count is probably uncontroversial, the distinction with respect to affectedness may not be obvious. I used the following two criteria to classify and select verbs: 1) I classified a verb as +AFF if its *be*-form specified a *specific* effect on the goal (cf. Gropen et al. 1991a,b), and as -AFF if its *be*-form could be used felicitously in at least some contexts in which the theme does *not end up* on the goal or leave any visible trace; 2) from among

---

3. The meaning of *ballern* 'smash' could be described as 'throw carelessly but with impact', as in *bang/smash tennis balls against the garage door*; *rieseln*, which can be used both intransitively and transitively, means something like 'drizzle/sprinkle'.

candidate verbs, I selected +AFF verbs with English translation equivalents that alternate, and -AFF verbs with English counterparts that do not alternate. This criterion was chosen because English is the language on which Gropen et al.'s account is based. Since these authors assume that affectedness is a necessary condition for a verb to alternate, they must assume that an alternating verb in English specifies affectedness, so its translation equivalent in other languages is also likely to specify affectedness. Conversely, a verb that does not alternate is likely not to specify affectedness, so its counterpart in other languages is not likely to specify affectedness either. By taking into account whether the English translation equivalent of a verb alternates, I wanted to ensure that my operationalization of affectedness would jibe as much as possible with Gropen et al.'s definition of affectedness.

Recall that *laden* (a +AFF count verb) has been characterized as a container verb (cf. 3.1): The base form of the verb can be used when the goal object is a truck or similar object. The goal objects used in the present study (cf. Table 5 below) were toy trailers, so subjects could simply use the base form of *laden* (e.g., *Er lädt den Anhänger* 'He's loading the trailer'). Nevertheless, *laden* may also be used as a regular *be*-verb. Similarly, the other +AFF count verb, *packen*, may sometimes take a goal without being prefixed (e.g., *den Koffer packen* 'pack the suitcase'), but, unlike *laden*, *packen* must (according to my intuition) be prefixed with *be*- when the goal NP refers to a trailer. (*Packen* differs from *laden* in that it necessarily involves the use of one's hands, whereas *laden* may also involve the use, for example, of a crane. As we will see below, this difference was exploited in the experiment.) These properties of the +AFF count verbs chosen may make it easier for subjects to use the verbs in the required *be*-forms (or, in the case of *laden*, in the grammatical unprefixed goal-object form). But, if so, this facilitation would work in favor of the Affectedness hypotheses and against my Nonindividuation Hypothesis. It therefore seemed legitimate to include these items as stimuli.

A factor that may influence subjects' willingness to use a particular *be*-verb is how often the base verb and the corresponding *be*-form are used in everyday speech. To obtain the needed frequency information to control for this factor, I used the CELEX database (Baayen, Piepenbrock, & van Rijn, 1993; Burnage, 1990). The German database of CELEX is based on the Mannheim-corpus (see Baayen et al., 1993, for a description of this corpus); it contains 6,000,000 items, most from written texts representing a variety of

discourse types (e.g., literature, newspapers, science, etc.). Frequency information about the verbs included in the study and about their *be*-forms is given
in Table 2.

Table 2. *Frequency of usage of the verbs included in the study and of their correspond-
          ing* BE-*forms based on the CELEX corpus (per 6,000,000 items)*

	Base Verbs		*be*-Verbs	
+AFF	*schmieren* 'smear'	18	*beschmieren* '*be*-smear'	10
mass:	*spritzen* 'spray'	10	*bespritzen* '*be*-spray'	8
-AFF	*gießen* 'pour'	65	*begießen* '*be*-pour'	7
mass:	*rieseln* 'sprinkle'	10	*berieseln* '*be*-sprinkle'	2
+AFF	*packen* 'pack'	188	*bepacken* '*be*-pack'	4
count:	*laden* 'load'	269	*beladen* '*be*-load'	23
-AFF	*werfen* 'throw'	902	*bewerfen* '*be*-throw'	18
count:	*ballern* 'smash'	0	*beballern* '*be*-smash'	0

The +AFF count verbs *packen* and *laden* and the -AFF count verb *werfen* are
considerably more frequent than the remaining verbs. The frequent usage of
packen and *laden* is unproblematic: If subjects are more willing to use
bepacken and *beladen* on grounds that they are more familiar with the verbs'
base forms, then this facilitation would work in favor of the Affectedness
hypotheses, and against the Nonindividuation Hypothesis. The frequency of
werfen is also unproblematic since it works equally against both the Affectedness hypotheses and the Nonindividuation Hypothesis. The table shows that
the *be*-forms of all verbs are infrequent. This is encouraging, since it suggests
that children will not be willing to use some *be*-verbs more often than others
only because they have observed them more often in the input.

To determine how children interpreted the verbs used as stimuli in the
experiment, I conducted a pretest about two weeks before the main task. The
next section describes this pretest.

The Design of the Pretest

To test the predictions of the Nonindividuation Hypothesis and the Affectedness hypotheses, we must study the linguistic behavior of subjects who know
that the mass verbs included in the study are restricted to denoting the motion
of substances, and who know whether or not a given test verb in its base form
specifies that the goal is affected.

The pretest did not assess whether children knew the restrictions on the themes of the mass verbs included in the study. I assumed that children know the restrictions on the themes of common mass verbs before they acquire the locative alternation. Many mass and count verbs in German are simple, everyday verbs that are used frequently and are likely to be acquired very early, so I decided not to test children's knowledge of this difference. There are certain risks involved in presupposing that children know the difference between mass and count verbs. Some subjects might not know that there is a difference at all, and so treat all verbs alike. This would be reflected in the results, in that mass *be*-verbs would not be used significantly more often than count *be*-verbs. In this case, I would be forced to repeat the experiment with a prior screening task to identify subjects that do know the difference between mass and count verbs. The other risk is that children might treat some mass verbs as count-verbs and vice versa. Again, this would make it difficult to find any systematic pattern in their responses, and I would have to repeat the experiment with a prior screening task. If their responses *are* systematic, these corrections will not be necessary.

While it seems safe to presuppose that children know the sortal restrictions on everyday verbs of transfer before they acquire the locative alternation, it *is* important to determine whether they know whether a verb specifies affectedness of the goal. After all, the Affectedness hypotheses predict that children are more likely to use the goal-object form if they assume that the verb specifies an affected goal, or even only then.

The test that I used to determine whether children attribute affectedness to the verbs under study was based on the test developed by Gropen (1989) to assess children's interpretation and use of locative verbs (see also Gropen et al., 1991a, and the description of their experiments in 2.5). The basic idea of the test is to present children with a picture showing an event that has both the prototypical manner and endstate associated with a particular verb, and then to present them with pictures in which these two properties are separated so as to test which property they find most essential. While Gropen used the test both for assessing subjects' interpretation of verbs and for eliciting theme- and goal-object forms of the verbs tested, I used it only for testing the interpretation of verbs. I adopted Gropen's method to make our tests of verb interpretation maximally comparable. But the method has some disadvantages for my purposes. Most importantly, verb interpretation is assessed somewhat differently depending on whether or not the verb specifies affectedness of the goal (see Gropen, 1989, for discussion). My reasons for assessing verb knowledge in two different ways are discussed in Appendix 3.

For both +AFF and -AFF verbs, the test required subjects to choose which of two pictures, which differed in manner and/or endstate, best represents the meaning of the verb. For each verb, two sets of pictures were developed, each set depicting a different scenario as a candidate instance of the verb. The sets testing the +AFF verbs each contained 5 line drawings per scenario, and the sets testing the -AFF verbs each contained 3 drawings per scenario. (The two kinds of sets contained different numbers of pictures because of the way in which knowledge of the +AFF and the -AFF verbs was assessed, as explained below.) Thus, a total of 64 line drawings was created, 10 for each of the +AFF verbs and 6 for each of the -AFF verbs.

Each drawing was composed of two 15cm x 20cm panels, much like a comic strip, with the first depicting the manner in which a theme changed location during the course of the action, and the second depicting the endstate of the goal, which had or had not changed state as a result of the action. (Notice that the term *drawing*, as it is used here, always refers to a *pair* of panels).

The first drawing of a scenario was the introductory drawing — it served to introduce a given verb but did not yet test how the subject interpreted it. As the experimenter, I showed this introductory drawing to the child and named the action depicted so as to establish a common frame of reference. Figure 1 shows the two-panel introductory drawing for one of the scenarios for *rieseln* 'sprinkle', a -AFF mass verb. *Rieseln* specifies a particular manner of motion, i.e., that a fine-grained substance is made to move slowly downwards, but it specifies no particular endstate of the goal. As shown in Figure 1, the first panel (manner) of the introductory drawing depicts a girl and a boy who are sprinkling sand onto the belly of a man lying on the beach; the second panel (endstate) shows the sand piling up on the man's belly.

*Figure 1. Introductory drawing for the scenario SPRINKLE/SAND ON BELLY, testing children's knowledge of the -AFF mass verb **rieseln** 'sprinkle'.*

Figures 2 and 3 (presented together to the child) show the drawings that actually tested the child's interpretation of the verb. The two drawings tested whether the child was *biased* toward assuming that *rieseln* specifies an endstate of the goal object. A *bias* (Gropen's 1989 term) toward an endstate interpretation means that a child erroneously assumes that a verb specifies a particular endstate of the goal, and that she takes this endstate to be *more* important than any manner the verb might also denote. The manner panel in Figure 2 is identical to that of the introductory drawing (depicting the two children sprinkling sand onto the man's belly). The endstate panel differs from that of the introductory drawing; it shows the sand piling up next to the man rather than accumulating on his belly. This figure is an acceptable instance of *rieseln* since *rieseln* specifies a particular manner of motion but no particular endstate. Figure 3 reverses what is retained from the introductory drawing: The manner panel depicts the children pouring sand out of a bucket onto the man's belly, and the endstate panel, as in the introductory drawing, shows the sand piling up on the belly.[4]

A subject who knows that *rieseln* specifies manner but not endstate should choose Figure 2 over Figure 3 as the better example of *rieseln*. Conversely, a subject who is biased toward an endstate interpretation of *rieseln* should choose Figure 3 instead of Figure 2. Appendix 4 describes the drawings used in testing the -AFF verbs, organized by scenario.

The picture sets for the +AFF verbs differed from those just described with respect to both the introductory picture and the drawings the child had to decide on. For these verbs, both a characteristic manner *and* a characteristic endstate are important. A bias test for assessing children's knowledge of the verbs is not appropriate since it assesses which aspect of a verb's meaning a child takes to be more important, but for the +AFF verbs, manner and endstate are equally important. Therefore, the drawings for testing children's knowledge of the +AFF verbs were designed so as to test the child's *sensitivity* to each aspect of a verb's meaning separately (Gropen, 1989). A child who is *sensitive* to an endstate specification of a verb obviously knows something about the typical endstates associated with the verb. This need not imply, however, that she takes endstate to be *more* important than a potential manner aspect of the verb, as the bias test attempts to determine. The idea underlying the sensitivity test is to treat a verb

---

4. This action is an instance of *schütten* 'pour'. It differs from *gießen* 'pour', the other -AFF verb, in that it is not restricted to denoting the motion of liquids. I will use 'pour2' to translate *schütten*.

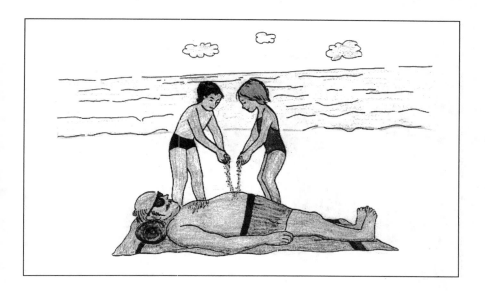

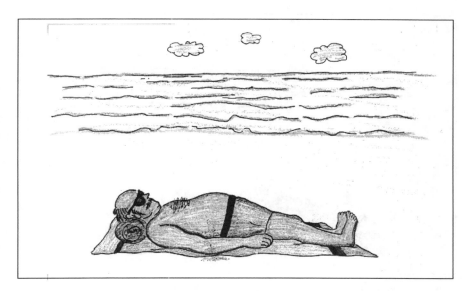

Figure 2. Test drawing SPRINKLE/SAND NEXT TO BELLY for the -AFF mass verb **rieseln** *'sprinkle', assessing whether children were **biased** toward assuming that **rieseln** specifies an endstate of the goal object (presented together with Figure 3).*

Figure 3.   *Test drawing* POURING2/SAND ON BELLY *for the* -AFF *mass verb* **rieseln** *'sprinkle',
assessing whether children were **biased** toward assuming that **rieseln** specifies
an endstate of the goal object (presented together with Figure 2).*

as though it were two different verbs, one specifying only manner and the other only endstate, and to test each aspect separately. (Each aspect was tested by two drawings; this explains why more pictures were needed for assessing knowledge of the +AFF verbs than the -AFF verbs.)

Take, for example, the verb *schmieren* 'smear', a +AFF mass verb. Like its English counterpart, *schmieren* specifies that a semi-liquid substance is applied to a surface (Pinker, 1989, p. 126); typically, the substance is applied by hand with no intermediate instruments, and ends up unevenly distributed over the surface. Testing whether a child is sensitive to the endstate specified by *schmieren* involves having him choose between a very good representation of the endstate (for example, some paint spread out over a surface) and a very bad one (for example, a figure painted on the surface). If he picks the good endstate representation twice (for both scenarios of *schmieren*), we can conclude that he takes this endstate to be typical of actions denoted by the verb, and so he is likely to know that *schmieren* specifies a specific endstate of the goal.

As in the bias test, each drawing consisted of a manner and an endstate panel. Consider, for example, Figure 4, which depicts the introductory drawing of one of the scenarios for *schmieren*. The manner panel depicts a somewhat imperfect instance of the manner of motion typically associated with *schmieren*: The boy uses a 'brush' to apply paint, and so might also be said to brush the paint onto the paper (*streichen* 'streak/brush' in German). The endstate panel also represents an imperfect instance of a typical endstate associated with *schmieren*: The few dots on the paper do not really disfigure or deface the paper as is typical of an object affected by *schmieren*.

The introductory drawing showed imperfect instances of *schmieren* so that the test drawings could provide either better or worse instances of the verb, thus testing whether the child would consistently choose the better representation. The manner aspect of a verb's meaning was tested with two drawings, each containing the same endstate panel as the introductory drawing but different manner panels. Similarly, the endstate aspect was tested by showing the same manner panel as in the introductory drawing but two different endstate panels.

Figure 5 shows the two panels testing the child's sensitivity to the manner aspect of *schmieren*. The first manner panel shows a typical instance of the verb: The boy spreads the paint over the paper with his hands. The second manner panel shows the boy drawing on the paper. The endstate

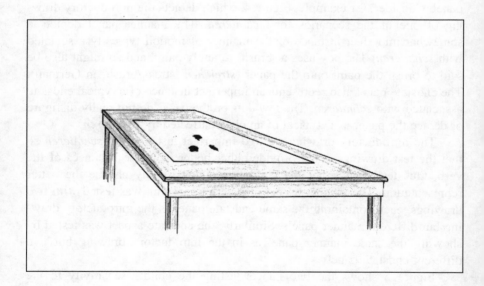

Figure 4.   Introductory drawing BRUSH/FEW DOTS ON PAPER, testing children's knowledge
            of the +AFF mass verb **schmieren** 'smear'. (The drawing shows an imperfect
            instance of both the manner and the endstate associated with **schmieren**.)

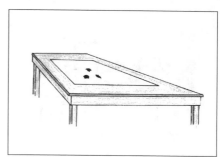

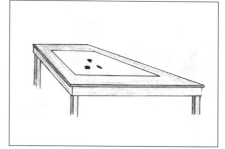

Figure 5. Test drawing SMEAR/FEW DOTS ON PAPER *and* DRAW/FEW DOTS ON PAPER *for the* +AFF *mass verb* **schmieren** *'smear', assessing whether children were **sensitive** toward the particular manner associated with **schmieren**. (The drawings were presented together to the child.)*

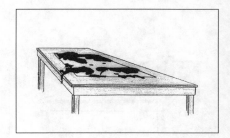

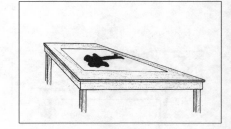

*Figure 6. Test drawing BRUSH/PAINT ALL OVER PAPER and BRUSH/TREE ON PAPER for the +AFF mass verb **schmieren** 'smear', assessing whether children were **sensitive** toward the particular endstate associated with **schmieren**. (The drawings were presented together to the child.)*

panels for each of these manner panels are identical to that of the introductory drawing. A child who is sensitive to the manner aspect of the verb should select the former drawing. Figure 6 shows the panels testing endstate sensitivity: The first endstate panel shows a typical result of smearing, i.e., paint all over the paper, and the second depicts a tree painted on the paper, i.e., not a probable result of smearing. Children who know that *schmieren* specifies a particular endstate should choose the first of these drawings over the second. The drawings that were used to test the +AFF verbs are also described in Appendix 4.

Order of presentation. Verbs were tested one at a time in two blocks, one comprising the +AFF verbs and the other the -AFF verbs. The purpose of blocking was to allow children to become familiar with the arrangements of drawings for a given type of verb. Within a block, mass verbs alternated with count verbs. The order of blocks and the order of mass and count verbs within a block was counterbalanced across subjects, yielding four different orders of presentation. The order of scenarios per verb was counterbalanced as well.

Warm-up drawings. Before the subjects were asked to select the drawings that best represented their interpretation of the verbs, they were introduced to the format of the task with two warm-up drawings (recall that *'drawing'* always refers to a pair of panels). The first drawing depicted a boy at the hairdresser's. In the first panel his hair was very long, and the second panel it was neatly cut. The first panel of the second warm-up drawing showed a boy and a girl shaking a tree full of red apples, and the second panel showed the tree with the apples lying on the ground. The warm-up drawings were used to ensure that subjects understood that the drawings depicted two situations that were causally related to each other. In addition, I included a filler item, *reißen* 'tear' to prevent subjects from distinguishing experimental from filler items in the main task (i.e., from homing in on exactly that subset of items that had been tested in the pretest). *Reißen* served as a filler item in both the pretest and the main task (cf. below).

Procedure

The subjects were tested individually in a separate room of their school.[5] As the experimenter, I sat next to the subject and introduced each scenario by

---

5. As noted in 5.2.1, the university students did not participate in the pretest. With few exceptions, the high school students had agreed with my judgments of the pictures of the pretest, so I felt that it was safe to assume that university students would do so as well.

showing the introductory drawing and first naming the person(s) and objects depicted in the manner panel, and then in the endstate panel. I then said, e.g., for the introductory drawing shown in Figure 4, 'Now, look at the first picture. When the child does this (pointing to the manner panel), it ends up like that (pointing to the second panel). This is smearing.' (*Das ist Schmieren.*) After the introductory drawing was removed, the two test drawings were shown simultaneously. (Recall that the +AFF verbs, of which *schmieren* is an example, involved a total of *four* test drawings. That is, for these verbs, the test sequence involved first showing the two test drawings for the manner aspect (for example), followed immediately by the two test drawings for the endstate aspect.) One drawing was put on the table in front of the child, while the other was held up slightly slanted, right above the one on the table. (Across subjects, each drawing was equally often put on the table and held up slanted.) This allowed the child to easily inspect and compare the two drawings. He (she) was then asked: *Welches von diesen Bildern ist Schmieren?* 'Which of these drawings is smearing?', and encouraged to make a choice. Notice that in the absence of contextual information, the question is ambiguous, in that *Bild* may refer either to one of the four panels or — as intended — to one of the two drawings. In the beginning I therefore added *Ist dies hier Schmieren, oder ist dies hier Schmieren?* 'Is this smearing, or is this smearing?', while pointing back and forth between the two panels of one drawing during the first part of the question, and between the panels of the second drawing during the second part of the question. When I had the impression that the child understood how *Bild* should be interpreted, I skipped this additional question. The answers were recorded on a prepared response sheet.

Results of the Pretest

Scoring. Responses to the pretest were scored according to whether the chosen endstate picture was consistent or inconsistent with the meaning of the verb. In the case of the sensitivity tests (which tested whether children were sensitive to the typical endstates associated with the +AFF verbs *schmieren*, *spritzen*, *laden*, and *packen*), the criterion of consistency was whether the endstate panel of the chosen drawing provided a good or a bad match to my own native speaker intuitions (which were largely confirmed by those of the high school students; cf. Table 3). In the case of the bias tests (which tested whether subjects took endstate to be more important than manner for the -AFF verbs *gießen, rieseln, werfen,* and *ballern*), responses were classified as consistent with the meaning of the verb if the chosen drawing preserved the manner of the original drawing.

The results for both +AFF and -AFF verbs are given in Table 3. For the +AFF verbs, the figures to the left and right of the slash show how many subjects selected the wrong endstate drawing for *at least one* of the verb's two scenarios, and for *both* (e.g., *brushing/tree on paper* instead of *brushing/dots all over paper* for the verb *schmieren* 'smear'); the same figures are also given as percentages. For the -AFF verbs, the figures show how many subjects selected an endstate drawing instead of a manner picture at least once, or both times (e.g., *pouring2(schütten)/sand on belly* instead of *sprinkling/sand next to belly* for *rieseln* 'sprinkle').

Table 3. Number of subjects per age group who selected the wrong drawing in the pretest at least once/both times.

VERB	AGE 6;4-7;6 (n=20)		7;7-8;5 (n=22)		8;6-10;0 (n=17)		mean age=17 (n=13)	
+AFF verbs		%		%		%		%
schmieren	1/10	5/10	1/0	5/0	2/0	12/0	0/0	0/0
spritzen	9/3	45/15	11/4	50/18	10/4	59/24	1/0	8/0
laden	4/2	20/10	4/1	18/5	4/1	24/6	3/0	23/0
packen	7/1	35/5	10/0	46/0	4/1	24/6	2/0	15/0
−AFF verbs		%		%		%		%
gießen	3/1	15/5	2/0	9/0	1/0	6/0	0/0	0/0
rieseln	7/5	35/25	6/3	27/14	2/1	12/6	0/0	0/0
werfen	1/0	5/0	1/0	5/0	0/0	0/0	1/0	8/0
ballern	7/2	35/10	4/2	18/9	3/3	18/18	1/1	8/8

As shown in Table 3, the high school students (henceforth 'adults') seldom selected the wrong drawing, and only one did so twice for the same verb (*ballern*). In general, then, they agreed with my interpretation of the verbs. For the children, one of the verbs of each type was consistently more difficult than the other: *spritzen* versus *schmieren, packen* versus *laden, rieseln* versus *gießen,* and *ballern* versus *werfen.* Except for *spritzen,* the tendency to select a wrong picture decreases with age, which suggests that the data reflect a true developmental effect of coming to grips with the meanings of the verbs.

Why was *spritzen* difficult for even the older children? Possibly, the drawings were misleading. For both scenarios, children had to decide between drawings in which a girl was pouring2 water from a bucket vs. spraying water with a hose or water pistol. The drawings with the buckets should have been rejected. In all the drawings, the stream of water coming out of the container or instrument was emphasized by thin black lines; perhaps children misinterpreted the black lines on the (incorrect) bucket-drawings as splashes, and so thought that these drawings also represented instances of *spritzen*.

The data from the pretest were used in two different ways. One analysis considered a subject's responses for a verb in the main task only if she had selected the correct pictures for both scenarios for that verb in the pretest. In a second main task analysis, the child's responses in the pretest determined whether a particular verb was classified as +AFF or -AFF for that child. For example, if the child selected the drawing depicting *pouring2/sand on belly* instead of *drizzling/sand next to belly* for the -AFF verb *rieseln*, thus showing that she considered the endstate of the goal more important than the manner of the action, *rieseln* was treated as a +AFF verb for that child. Conversely, if she selected the drawing showing *holding box by string/single box on trailer* instead of *holding box by string/trailer full of boxes* for the verb *packen*, the verb was reclassified as -AFF for that child. In discussing the results of the main task in 5.4, I will refer to this analysis as the RECLASSIFICATION ANALYSIS.

5.2.3 *The Main Task: Assessing Children's Use of* BE-*Verbs*

Motivating the Design of the Task

The dependent variable was the children's use of *be*-verbs in the main task. What is a good way to elicit *be*-verbs? In other words, how can we motivate subjects to use a verb of transfer in its goal-object form rather than in its theme-object form?

My goal was to provide a setting in which the use of *be*-verbs is a natural and felicitous means for communicating a particular state of affairs. From the perspective of communicative purposes, goal-object forms provide a means for communicating relevant information about a goal while downplaying information about the theme. 'Relevant information' is understood here in the sense of Grice (1975) as information that is not yet shared between a speaker and a listener and that the speaker wants to share.

One way of getting children to use a goal-object construction is to explicitly ask them about the goal. For example, Gropen (1989) showed children pictures in which a woman was filling a pitcher with water. The children were asked to describe, by using the verb *fill*, what the woman was doing to the pitcher. A natural response to this query is to say *She's filling it with water*, thus expressing the goal as the direct object of the verb. I initially intended to use Gropen's method for eliciting *be*-verbs so as to make Gropen's study and mine maximally comparable. However, in a pilot study conducted with several 5 year-olds and adults, I found that both children and adults used *be*-verbs only occasionally. I attributed the failure to elicit *be*-verbs to two aspects of the task. First, the task requires subjects to use a particular verb; for example, I asked subjects to tell me, by using the verb *schmieren* 'smear', what happened in the pictures. This elicits the use of a goal-object form only if subjects take *beschmieren* as the same verb as *schmieren* — an inference that might require a rather abstract metalinguistic evaluation. Second, Gropen's task prompted children only twice per verb (once for each scenario), and I hoped to be luckier at eliciting *be*-verbs by having them specify the same action repeatedly.

A task in which an action has to be specified repeatedly had the additional advantage of allowing me to manipulate which information would be new to a listener and thus relevant: If the actions involve different goals but identical themes, then information about the goal will be new and so will have to be specified. This should invite subjects to use the goal-object form instead of the theme-object form of the verbs. Of course, information about the action must be new as well, since otherwise the action need not be specified either and no verb need be used at all.

The actions and the themes and goals they involved had to have a number of specific physical properties. First, the actions had to be describable by the stimulus verbs, and second, because of the topological restrictions on *be*-verbs, the goals could not be containers. The goals should also be readily namable by children. The themes of the mass verbs had to be substances, while those of the count verbs had to be conceivable as nonindividuated, i.e., they could not be a single object.

In addition to the physical properties of the individual goals and themes, the relations to be established between them also had to be of a particular kind, since the action had to either affect the goal or not. As a rough rule of thumb, an action can be said to affect a goal if the theme stays on the goal after the action is completed. Conversely, an action can be said not to affect the goal if the theme does not stay on the goal and leaves no visible traces.

What is the best way to show the actions to the children? If the actions were acted out in front of the child, they would likely be too complex to be performed in an identical way each time. Pictures are also unsatisfying because they capture neither the dynamics of the actions nor the required properties of the theme-goal relation. In contrast, showing subjects a video-tape of the actions allows us to both capture the dynamics of the actions and standardize what has to be described. Therefore, I decided to videotape the actions.

The Design of the Main Task: Eliciting BE-Verbs

The goal of the main task was to test which verbs children would use most frequently with the goal as direct object under circumstances designed to elicit this argument structure. The subjects were shown a series of video films depicting actions of spraying, smearing, etc., which they were asked to describe to a listener seated behind the TV-monitor (see below). The series consisted of 10 separate sets of films (4 experimental, 2 filler, and 4 warm-up sets). Each experimental set was centered around three goal objects, which differed only in color, and two different actions, which could be described by one or the other of the two verbs of a given verb type (cf. Table 4). The actions were carried out by two boys, either alone or together.[6]

For a given set, the child had to describe 5 different scenes in a row. (I used 5 scenes so as to maximize the number of responses obtained from each child without making the task too boring. I will comment on this measure below.) One of the sets is illustrated in Table 4 (note that the table contains summaries of the scenes, not sentences produced or evaluated by the child).

Table 4. Example of a set of scenes to be described by the child

---

1) A boy smearing some semi-liquid stuff onto a green bottle.
2) The boy spraying some liquid onto a yellow bottle.
3) The boy smearing some semi-liquid stuff onto a red bottle.
4) The boy smearing some semi-liquid stuff onto a yellow bottle.
5) The boy spraying some liquid onto a green bottle.

---

6. I am grateful to Johannes and Fabian Ehrich for participating as the actors in the films.

The five successive scenes of a given set differed in either the action, the goal object, or both (the theme objects were similar or identical), and these differences presented new information to be conveyed to the listener. The action pairs, goals, and themes for the four experimental sets are listed in Table 5.

Table 5. Action pairs, goals, and themes in the elicitation task

ACTIONS	GOALS	THEMES
smearing/spraying +AFF/mass	**bottles**	brown semi-liquid/liquid stuff
pouring/sprinkling -AFF/mass	**cones**	water/poppy seeds
packing/loading +AFF/count	**toy wagons**	small brown boxes
throwing/banging -AFF/count	**walls**	colored balls

To ensure that the child focussed on the goal and used only the relevant verbs to describe the actions, each set of films started with one scene that introduced the goal objects and two subsequent scenes each of which introduced one of the pairs of actions. During these introductory scenes, the experimenter, who sat next to the child, named the goal objects and described the actions with an infinitive without mentioning the theme or goal argument, e.g., *Das ist Schmieren* 'This is to smear (smearing)'. The introductory scenes were repeated twice as still pictures; the first repetition was again described by the experimenter and the second by the child. Some children were already able to describe the first repetition; the experimenter then did not describe any repetition scenes and skipped the second repetition. The scenes introducing the actions (as opposed to the goal objects) showed a goal object only if this was unavoidable for depicting the action (i.e., for *schmieren* 'smear', *laden* 'load', and *packen* 'pack').

The scenes lasted 6 seconds, except for the repetition scenes described by the experimenter, which lasted only 3 seconds. The introductory scenes and the experimental scenes were preceded by a six-second pause showing a grey screen. Shortly before a new scene began, the screen showed a warning signal, a white circle appearing in the middle of the screen for about 625 msec. After the warning signal, an additional grey screen of about 460 msec appeared before the next scene started. (All pause pictures showed a grey screen; they differed only in length and in whether they contained a warning signal). The repetition scenes (both the ones described by the experimenter and those described by the child) were preceded by a 625 msec pause picture, which did not contain a warning signal. The pause picture appearing before the first experimental scene lasted 8 seconds, and again contained the warning signal. The pause pictures appearing between different sets of films (e.g., between the *schmieren/spritzen* and the *laden/packen* sequences) lasted 5 seconds and contained no warning signal.

There were 8 different orders of presentation, with 4 different orders of experimental sets of films and 2 orders of actions per set. Thus, each experimental set appeared about equally often as the first, second, third, or fourth experimental set, and each kind of action within a set (e.g., *smearing* versus *spraying*) appeared about equally often as the first or second action of that set. Unfortunately, the films were unbalanced in one respect: Of the 5 experimental scenes within a set, one verb of a particular type was always shown three times, whereas the other was only shown twice. Although in retrospect, this was an unnecessary imbalance in the presentation of the stimuli, it does not interfere with analysis, nor will it influence the results, since the imbalance affects all verb types in the same way.

The *filler sets* always appeared after the first and third experimental sets. The first filler set showed a boy either cutting or tearing a sheet of paper in two, and the second set showed the same boy using a straw to either drink Coca Cola out of a glass or blow bubbles on the liquid's surface. The objects to be specified in the filler sets were the sheet of paper and the straw, respectively.

The set of experimental and filler sets was preceded by four warm-up sets to familiarize subjects with the task. The first two warm-up sets contained only a single type of action, whereas the last two warm-up sets alternated, like the remaining films, between two types of action. In this way, the children could first become familiar with the task of specifying different objects before they had to specify two types of actions and different types of objects. The warm-up sets differed from the experimental and filler sets in that they contained fewer scenes to be described by the child. The first two warm-up sets contained 3 scenes, and the last two sets contained 4 scenes.

The second and fourth warm-up sets were designed to elicit *be*-verbs. The second set showed a boy spilling some brown liquid onto a tablecloth (the target object), and the three actions to be described in this set each involved a different tablecloth. The action was introduced as *kleckern* 'spill/make a mess'. *Kleckern* is an intransitive verb that alternates, and the actions could be specified with *bekleckern*. The fourth set showed the same boy either scribbling or drawing on a sheet of paper. The actions were introduced as *kritzeln* 'scribble' and *malen* 'draw/paint', respectively. *Kritzeln* is an intransitive verb, *malen* is optionally transitive. Both verbs have a *be*-verb counterpart, *bekritzeln* and *bemalen*, and it was hoped that the children would use these verbs to refer to the actions. *Kleckern, kritzeln*, and *malen* were chosen because they do not require the expression of the theme as direct object in their base forms, so I thought that children would find it easy to use their *be*-forms and also that the verbs would not interfere with the transitive verbs of the main task. The actions and objects shown in the warm-up sets are summarized in Table 6.

Table 6. Actions and objects used in the warm-up sets in the elicitation task

VERBS/ACTIONS	OBJECTS
1) *aufblasen* 'blow up'	balloon
2) *kleckern* 'spill'	tablecloth
3) *anzünden/auspusten* 'light/blow out'	candle
4) *malen/kritzeln* 'paint/scribble'	sheet of paper

Procedure

All subjects were tested individually in a separate room. The task was introduced to the subject as a game between him (her) and another person, who was in fact the experimenter's collaborator.[7] (No collaborator was present in the sessions with the university students; with these subjects, I conducted the task by myself.) The subject was told that he (she) had to describe the actions shown on the TV-monitor so that his (her) partner would know which action and which object were involved in a given scene. The partner would then use the information given to her by the child in order to select, for each of the main scenes in a set, a picture showing the action, and pair it with a card of the same color as the object involved in the action. The collaborator had in front of her a slanted board (about 100cm x 30cm) with

---

7. I am grateful to Frauke Hellwig for acting as my collaborator in these sessions.

two rows of hooks for attaching the action pictures and the colored cards. The action pictures for a set were to be hung next to each other in the top row, with the colored cards representing the objects beneath them — e.g., for an action of loading a red trailer, a red card was to be hung beneath the picture depicting loading. The pictures and cards were lying in front of the collaborator and were shown to the child when the experimenter introduced him (her) to the game. After the game had been explained, the experimenter and the child sat down next to each other in front of the monitor, opposite the collaborator, who could not see the screen. The child was told not to worry that the game would be too difficult because there would be enough time to learn how to do it. The responses of the subjects were tape-recorded.

5.3 Experimental Hypotheses

In this section, the theoretical predictions formulated in Section 5.1 are reformulated as more specific hypotheses about the outcomes of the tasks I used. The Nonindividuation Hypothesis states that children acquire the goal-object forms available in their language earlier for mass verbs than for count verbs. The most common goal-object form in German involves *be*-prefixation, but goal-object forms may also have a separable or inseparable prefix instead of *be*- (e.g., *über-* 'over-'; cf. Chapter 3), or may be unprefixed. I predict, then, that in the experiment, younger children will use a *be*-prefixed or other goal-object form more often when the action has to be specified by a mass verb than by a count verb. Older children and adults will also use count verbs in these goal-object forms.

Gropen et al.'s theory of affectedness predicts that children are more likely to use goal-object forms for verbs that they think specify an affected goal. As explained in 5.1, I assume that Gropen et al. would predict that German-speaking children, when faced with evidence that verbs like *werfen* 'throw' alternate, will reinterpret them as specifying the affectedness of the goal, even if they have previously classified them as not specifying affectedness. Thus, Gropen et al.'s theory predicts that children will use a *be*-prefixed or other goal-object form more often when the action has to be specified by a verb that they think is +AFF than by a verb that they think is -AFF.

According to my adaptation of Lebeaux's theory of Affectedness to the problem at hand, once children have correctly determined the role of the prefix *be-*, they should be able to produce a *be*-prefixed goal-object form even of verbs that do not specify their goal as affected. But learning the role of these prefixes may take time. Hence, Lebeaux's theory predicts that younger children will be more likely to use a *be*-prefixed goal-object form of a verb if the action must be specified by a +AFF verb than when it must be specified by a -AFF verb, while older children and adults will not differ in their treatment of the two kinds of verbs. Lebeaux's theory predicts that subjects of all ages should use an *unprefixed* goal-object form of a verb only when they think that the verb specifies an affected goal.

The null hypothesis, against which the above hypotheses will be tested, is that the type of verb is not a determinant of how often a goal-object form of a verb is produced — i.e., that children are not sensitive to verb-specific properties in acquiring the locative alternation. There will be no systematic differences among verbs in how often they are prefixed with *be-* or paired with a goal-object form without prefixation.

5.4 Results

Scoring. The subjects' responses were classified into one of three categories. Since I was interested only in whether subjects expressed the goal as direct object, I did not distinguish between grammatical and ungrammatical constructions in the scoring; I will comment later on the consequences of this scoring procedure. The categories were as follows:

(1) BE-VERB **responses**
The goal is the direct object *and* the verb is prefixed with *be-* (e.g., *Die Jungen bewerfen die blaue Wand* 'The boys *be*-throw the blue wall').

(2) DIR.OBJ. **responses**
The goal was made the direct object by some other means. Subjects employed several other (grammatical and ungrammatical) means for making the goal the direct object: resultative constructions (e.g., *Er schmiert die grüne Flasche voll* 'He's smearing the green bottle full'); separable and inseparable prefix verbs (e.g., ?*Sie werfen die rote Wand an* 'They are throwing the red wall at'; ?*Er verspritzt die grüne Flasche* 'He's *ver*-spraying the green bottle'); or simply the base verb plus goal as direct object (*Er lädt den gelben Wagen* 'He's loading the yellow wagon'; *Er rieselt den blauen Kegel* 'He is sprinkling the blue cone').

(3) PREP.OBJ. **responses**

The goal is not the direct object. Goals that were not the direct object were usually expressed with a directional PP (e.g., *Sie werfen an die rote Wand$_{acc}$* 'They throw at the red wall') but sometimes also with a stative PP (e.g., **Der Junge gießt auf'm blauen Kegel$_{dat}$* 'The boy pours on the blue cone'). Children also sometimes used the preposition *mit* to introduce the goal (e.g., *Er schmiert mit der roten Flasche* 'He smears with the red cone'), or simply used the infinitive and introduced the goal in a directional prepositional phrase (*Laden auf den gelben Anhänger$_{acc}$* 'To load on the yellow trailer').

Five times, the goal was not mentioned at all, either because some other object was specified (e.g., *mit der Spritze abspritzen* 'with the syringe off-spray'), or because only the infinitive was given, with no reference to either the goal or another object. These responses are excluded in the analyses.

5.4.1 *Responses per Verb*

Table 7 shows, for each verb, how often subjects used a *be*-form of a verb (BE-VERB), some other means of expressing the goal as direct object (DIR.OBJ.), or a construction in which the goal was a prepositional object (PREP.OBJ.). In this table, the responses are *not* distinguished in terms of how subjects interpreted the verbs in the pretest. The responses to the verbs of a given type differ in frequency because of the unequal number of action scenes in the main experiment (cf. 5.2.3): One verb always appeared twice in each experimental set, and the other three times.

The breakdown of response categories for the two verbs of each type is rather similar. This may to some extent reflect a set effect due to the structure of the task: The verbs of a given type always appeared in direct succession, so that if subjects had produced, e.g., *beschmieren* for the first scene in a set, they might be more likely to use *bespritzen* for the second set than if they had produced the prepositional form of *schmieren*. This set effect is not problematic for interpreting the data in Table 7, since each verb appeared about equally often as the first item in each age group. Nor will it interfere with statistical analyses comparing responses to the different verb types, since if there were such an effect, it would presumably affect all verb types in the same way. The similarity in response patterns for verbs of the same type shows that frequency of usage of the base verbs did not influence responses. Recall, for example, that the CELEX database lists 902 instances of *werfen*,

Table 7. Responses of different types per verb in the elicitation task. (Percentages are given in brackets.)

VERB	AGE				
	6;4 - 7;6 (N=20)	7;7 - 8;5 (N=22)	8;6 - 10;0 (N=17)	17 (N=13)	25 (N=14)
+AFF, MASS					
schmieren					
be-verb	11 (18.3%)	15 (22.7%)	26 (51%)	27 (69.2%)	30 (71.4%)
dir.obj.	28 (46.7%)	37 (56.1%)	18 (35.3%)	4 (10.3%)	6 (14.3%)
prep.obj.	21 (35%)	14 (21.2%)	7 (13.7%)	8 (20.5%)	6 (14.3%)
spritzen					
be-verb	10 (25%)	12 (27.3%)	19 (55.9%)	20 (77%)	13 (46.4%)
dir.obj.	19 (47.4%)	27 (61.45%)	13 (38.2%)	0 (0%)	2 (7.1%)
prep.obj.	11 (27.5%)	5 (11.4%)	2 (5.9%)	6 (23.1%)	13 (46.4%)
+AFF, COUNT					
laden					
be-verb	0 (0%)	5 (7.6%)	10 (19.6%)	17 (43.6%)	26 (62%)
dir.obj.	12 (20%)	27 (31.8%)	10 (19.6%)	12 (30.8%)	3 (7.1%)
prep.obj.	48 (80%)	40 (60.6%)	31 (60.8%)	10 (25.6%)	13 (31%)
packen					
be-verb	0 (0%)	6 (13.64%)	4 (14.7%)	14 (53.8%)	16 (57.1%)
dir.obj.	8 (20%)	14 (31.8%)	9 (26.5%)	5 (19.2%)	4 (14.3%)
prep.obj.	32 (80%)	24 (54.5%)	20 (58.8%)	7 (26.9%)	8 (28.6%)
−AFF, MASS					
gießen					
be-verb	13 (21.7%)	15 (22.7%)	23 (45.1%)	15 (38.5%)	18 (42.9%)
dir.obj.	28 (46.7%)	20 (30.3%)	5 (9.8%)	0 (0%)	0 (0%)
prep.obj.	19 (31.7%)	31 (47%)	23 (45.1%)	24 (61.5%)	24 (57.1%)
rieseln					
be-verb	8 (20%)	8 (18.2%)	12 (35.3%)	10 (38.5%)	7 (25%)
dir.obj.	18 (45%)	15 (34.1%)	5 (14.7%)	0 (0%)	0 (0%)
prep.obj.	14 (35%)	21 (47.7%)	17 (50%)	16 (61.5%)	21 (75%)
−AFF, COUNT					
werfen					
be-verb	3 (5%)	6 (9.1%)	11 (21.6%)	8 (20.5%)	3 (7.1%)
dir.obj.	11 (18.3%)	3 (4.5%)	2 (3.9%)	0 (0%)	0 (0%)
prep.obj.	46 (76.7%)	57 (86.4%)	38 (74.5%)	31 (79.5%)	39 (92.9%)
ballern					
be-verb	2 (5%)	2 (4.5%)	5 (14.7%)	4 (15.4%)	3 (7.1%)
dir.obj.	8 (20%)	4 (9.1%)	3 (8.8%)	0 (0%)	0 (0%)
prep.obj.	30 (75%)	38 (86.4%)	26 (76.5%)	22 (84.6%)	26 (92.9%)

but no instances of *ballern* — but the proportion of different types of responses to the verbs hardly differs.

Adults occasionally expressed the goal as direct object without prefixing
the verb with *be-*. Interestingly, they never used such a construction for the
-AFF verbs; if these verbs were used in a goal-object form, they were consistently prefixed with *be-*. This seems to support Lebeaux's claim that an
argument in object position must be specified by the verb as affected unless
the verb is morphologically marked.

5.4.2 *Comparison of Responses to Verbs of Different Types*

Recall that results from the pretest were applied to the analysis of subjects'
main task responses in two ways: One type of analysis used only those
responses to verbs that subjects correctly understood as +AFF or -AFF in the
pretest, and the other used all the responses, but reclassified the verbs on the
basis of how each subject actually understood them in the pretest. This
distinction was cross-cut by another for a total of four separate analyses: First,
main task BE-VERB responses were compared with OTHER responses (i.e., DIR.
OBJ. and PREP.OBJ. responses), and second, GOAL-OBJECT (GOAL=D.O.) responses, regardless of whether the verb was prefixed with by *be-* (these
included both BE-VERB and DIR.OBJ. responses), were compared with OTHER
responses (i.e., PREP.OBJ. responses). Figures 7-10 show the data displayed in
these four ways.

Figures 7 and 8 show that adults produced *be*-verb responses almost
exclusively in connection with verbs that were +AFF, but they were also
influenced by the count/mass distinction: They gave more *be*-verb responses
for -AFF mass verbs than -AFF count verbs. It seems to be difficult for children
to prefix the verb: *Be*-verbs figured in no more than 30% of all responses in
the two youngest age groups, and only the oldest children were systematically
able to prefix with *be-* across verbs. Affectedness was not at all relevant to the
willingness of the youngest children to use a *be*-verb, but the count/mass
distinction was: Although *be*-verb forms were infrequent overall in this age
group, there were more for the mass verbs than for the count verbs (about
20% for the former, and only about 4% for the latter). The two youngest
groups produced almost no *be*-forms of the count verbs, and the '*be*-verb
spurt' of the oldest children is less pronounced for the count than for the mass
verbs. These findings hold regardless of whether we use only responses to

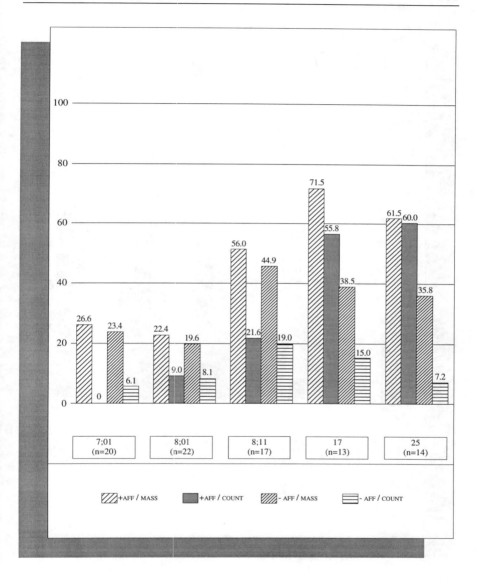

Figure 7. Proportion of BE-VERB responses for verbs of different types. (Based only on subjects' BE-VERB responses containing verbs that they had interpreted correctly as affected/non-affected on the pretest.)

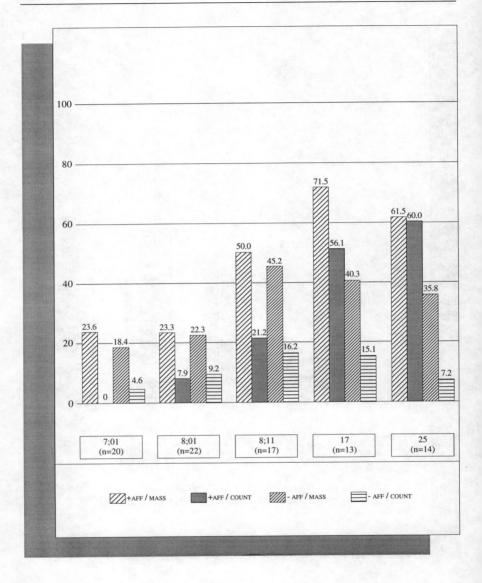

Figure 8.   *Proportion of* BE-VERB *responses for verbs of different types. (Based on all* BE-VERB *responses, with verbs classified as affected/non-affected on the basis of each subject's interpretation on the pretest.)*

verbs that the children correctly understood as +AFF or -AFF (Figure 7) or reclassify the verbs according to the children's own understanding (Figure 8).

Figures 9 and 10 show the responses in which the goal was the direct object regardless of *be*-prefixation (GOAL=D.O.). Again, affectedness is important for the adults but not for the children. The youngest children were not at all influenced by affectedness but they were by the count/mass distinction: They gave GOAL=D.O. responses about 60% of the time for mass verbs but less than 30% for count verbs. The mid-age and oldest children were also more likely to give a GOAL=D.O. response for mass than for count verbs, but they also show a development toward the adult pattern, with more GOAL=D.O. responses for the +AFF than for the -AFF verbs.

Let us now turn to an analysis that allows us to account for the factors determining the responses in a more principled way. As is often true in experiments on language acquisition, we are dealing with frequency data (e.g., how often was the *be*-form used for a particular verb?), and not with measurements (e.g., how quickly did a subject respond?). Thus, an analysis of variance is not the best choice for analysing the contributions of the within-subject factors COUNT/MASS and AFFECTEDNESS and the between-subjects factor AGE. Nor can a traditional chi-square analysis be applied, because it is incompatible with repeated observations of the same subject, and cannot be used to study the effects of several variables and their interactions — i.e., it cannot be applied to a multidimensional contingency table like the one we are dealing with. A technique devised to deal with multidimensional contingency tables is LOGLINEAR ANALYSIS, which is an advanced chi-square method (see, for example, Rietveld & van Hout, 1993). I therefore subjected the data initially to a loglinear analysis.[8]

---

8. Loglinear analysis has in common with traditional chi-square analysis that it is based on the assumption that the observations are independent of each other, so technically, it should not be applied to repeated observations of the same subject. But opinions as to whether loglinear analysis can be used for data of this sort vary. One way to deal with repeated observations is to treat the repetition as a factor itself so as to calculate its effect on the overall distribution of the data. This was not done in the present study because it turned out that loglinear analysis could not be successfully applied for independent reasons (cf. below).

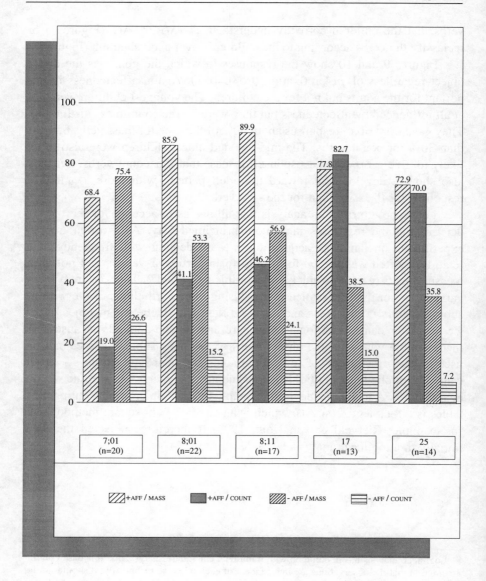

Figure 9. *Proportion of GOAL=D.O. responses for verbs of different types. (Based only
on subjects' GOAL=D.O. responses containing verbs that they had interpreted
correctly as affected/non-affected on the pretest.)*

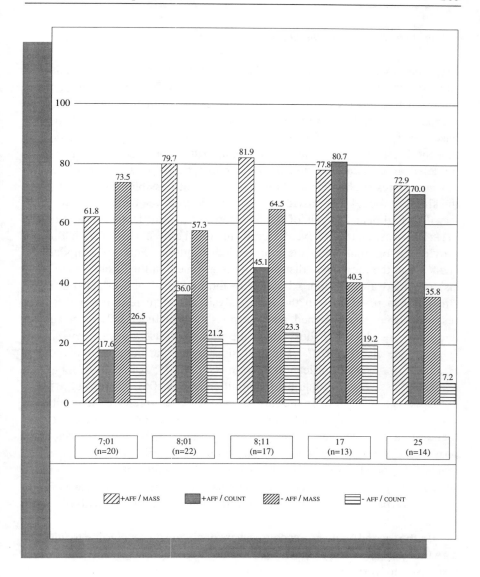

Figure 10. Proportion of GOAL=D.O. responses for verbs of different types. (Based on all GOAL=D.O. responses, with verbs classified as affected/non-affected on the basis of each subject's interpretation on the pretest.)

A *Loglinear Analysis of the Data*

Loglinear analysis is a procedure that specifies and compares different possible MODELS (hypotheses) about the observed data. Each model predicts the observed frequencies by means of a number of parameters linked with the independent variables and their interaction. In this it is similar to ANOVA-based analyses. The difference between ANOVA and loglinear analysis is that the logarithm of the ratio of *be-* and OTHER (for example) responses is modeled as a linear function of the parameters. As in standard regression design, the researcher has to explore the range of possible models and select the simplest model that provides an acceptable fit to the data.

The loglinear analysis of the data showed that all factors (COUNT/MASS, AFFECTEDNESS, and AGE) were significant (cf. below). However, it did not provide an optimal fit to the empirical distribution: For every model, the chance that the theoretical distribution (determined on the basis of the analysis) provided a good approximation to the empirical one turned out to be smaller than p. < .001. In the first analysis, BE-VERB response and OTHER responses were distinguished, and a response was included only if the subject had correctly classified the verb in the pretest (*BE-VERB/OTHER: correct responses*; see also Figure 7). The analysis showed that the effects of COUNT/MASS and AGE were significant (COUNT/MASS: p. < .04; AGE: p. < .02), but that AFFECTEDNESS was only marginally significant (p. < .06). Therefore, AFFECTEDNESS was not included in the further analysis so as to reduce the number of variables, and the only variables now considered were COUNT/MASS, AGE, and their interaction. However, the probability that the theoretical distribution provided a good approximation to the observed distribution was again less than .001, for chi^2 (5) = 18.28, so the model could not be considered a sufficiently good representation of the data. The same lack of fit was found with the verbs reclassified in terms of affectedness (Figure 8) (with p < .001, for chi^2 (4) = 17.03).

In the second analysis, responses were distinguished according to whether a goal-object form or a prepositional form was used, based on only the correct responses to verbs in the pretest (*DIR.OBJ./PREP.OBJ.: correct responses*; cf. Figure 9). The analyses showed that the factors COUNT/MASS, AFFECTEDNESS, AGE, and the interaction between AGE and AFFECTEDNESS were significant (COUNT/MASS: p. < .03, AFFECTEDNESS: p.< .03, AGE: p.< .05, interaction between AGE and AFFECTEDNESS: p.< .04) (no other interactions were included). For this analysis, the chance that the theoretical distribution corresponded to the empirical one was also very low (p. < .001, for chi^2 (9) = 37.30). As before, the analysis based on the reclassified verbs (Figure 10) also did not provide a sufficient fit to the empirical distribution (p < .001, for chi^2 (9) = 42.52).

In sum, loglinear analysis shows that the factors COUNT/MASS and AFFECT-EDNESS both influenced the subjects' willingness to use a *be*-verb or, more inclusively, a goal-object construction, and indicates that COUNT/MASS is more important than AFFECTEDNESS. But why did the reduced models not fit the observed data well enough? Reducing the saturated model may fail for various reasons — for example, because there are too many cells with zero frequencies or too few observations per cell, or because the assumption of a linear relationship between the factors is simply false, or because none of the factors should in fact be excluded. This last reason may account for why the present analyses did not provide an optimal fit: For example, even though affectedness was in fact marginally significant, it had to be excluded in the first analysis in order to reduce the number of variables.

Since loglinear analysis did not yield a satisfactory solution, I subjected the data to a TREE-BASED MODELING PROCEDURE (Breiman, Friedman, Olshen, & Stone, 1984; Clark & Pregibon, 1992), which is a relatively new technique for uncovering structure in data.

A Tree-based Modeling Analysis of the Data

Tree-based modeling is an exploratory technique for uncovering structure in data. Unlike standard statistical analyses, it does not try to answer the question whether a particular null hypothesis should be rejected (i.e., it does not follow the Neyman-Pearson paradigm of statistical analysis); this means that the results of tree-based modeling are not expressed in terms of significance levels. Instead, decisions as to which factors are important for explaining the data are based on CROSS-VALIDATION, a concept that will be explained below.

The goal of a tree-based modeling procedure is to classify the response types (the use of a *be*-verb versus some other construction in this case) on the basis of the independent variables (AFFECTEDNESS, COUNT/MASS, and AGE). The resulting classification is represented in the form of a tree with several binary branches or subtrees. Each binary split represents a distinction made in the data according to a predictor variable (e.g., +/-AFFECTEDNESS). The tree shows how many binary distinctions must be made in order to capture the classificational structure in the data.

For example, if the factor AFFECTEDNESS is the best predictor of response type, it will partition the data into two initial sets that differ maximally in their relative proportion of *be*-forms versus OTHER responses. Each of the two subsets will then be split into two further subsets on the basis of the factor that again maximizes the differences in the relative proportion of *be-* versus OTHER responses, e.g., the factor COUNT/MASS. In this way, tree-based modeling successively splits the data set into increasingly smaller subsets that differ maximally with respect to the dependent variable.

A subset (or 'node') is classified according to the dominant response type it contains, e.g., the node governing responses to the +AFF mass verb stimuli might be classified as a *be*-verb response node. If a node were completely homogeneous, it would contain only responses of the same type. But nodes are almost never completely homogeneous. This means that the responses of the nondominant type falling under a node are misclassified. If a *be*-response node contains 20 *be*-responses and 5 OTHER responses, the misclassification rate for that node is 5/25, or 20 percent. In an optimal tree, the overall misclassification rate is minimized.

But the goal of minimizing the misclassification rate must be weighed against another goal: to minimize the number of factors needed to account for the data. The algorithm for building an optimal tree starts out by building an overly large tree with the maximal possible number of terminal nodes, or leaves. Such a tree will lead to the lowest possible number of misclassifications, since the rate of misclassification decreases with each additional factor. For some data sets, the reduction of misclassification may continue *ad absurdum*, leading to terminal nodes that contain only a single observation. While such a tree has a misclassification rate of zero, it is not informative, since it includes many factors that are of no systematic importance. The optimal tree is thus one that is as small as can be achieved while still keeping the number of misclassifications to an acceptable minimum.

To obtain such a tree, we must evaluate its complexity against its misclassification rate. This is achieved by MINIMAL COST-COMPLEXITY PRUNING: The maximal tree is pruned by systematically snipping off branches. A branch may be cut off if the disadvantage of pruning — the increase in misclassifications — does not outweigh the advantage of having a less complex, more explanatory tree. This produces a unique sequence of trees of decreasing complexity, of which the first is the maximal tree and the last only the root node.

If we build such a sequence of trees on the basis of the data set as a whole, we cannot determine which of the (successively smaller) trees should be selected — this is because the sequence of trees is fully determined by the data used to establish the tree. Going beyond the data set as a whole, there are two ways to determine which of the trees is optimal. One is to collect new data and classify them according to each of the trees in the sequence. The tree that yields the lowest misclassification rate should then be selected. The other is to use the method of cross-validation. This method consists of repeatedly building the sequence of trees on the basis of a subset of the observations, e.g., 90%, and using the remaining 10% to test which of the trees is the best one. The tree in the sequence that yields the lowest number of misclassifications — i.e., that most accurately predicts whether a *be*-verb response or a OTHER response is observed — is the optimal tree.

In ten-fold cross-validation, the complete data set is split ten times into two sets of 90% versus 10% of the data. Each 90% set is then used to build a tree sequence, with the corresponding 10% used to test which tree in the sequence yields the lowest number of misclassifications. Each time, a different 10% of the data is used to compute the misclassification rate. In this way, each item in the data set is used exactly once in the procedure of testing which tree yields the lowest misclassification rate. Averaging over the resulting ten sequences of trees, we can now determine which tree size yields the lowest number of misclassifications. This tree size will then be adopted in selecting the optimal tree size from the sequence of trees constructed for the complete data set.

The data from the experiment were subjected to a tree-based analysis. The trees shown below are based on the three (pre-determined) classification factors COUNT/MASS (2 levels), AFFECTEDNESS (2 levels), and AGE (5 levels); the response factors for each tree have two levels, BE-VERB versus OTHER, or GOAL=D.O. versus OTHER, respectively. Four classification trees were grown: Trees 1 and 2 show BE-VERB versus OTHER responses for 'only verbs correctly classified in the pretest' and 'reclassified verbs', respectively, and Trees 3 and 4 show GOAL=D.O. vs. OTHER responses for 'correctly classified verbs' and 'reclassified verbs'. Let us look at the first tree, shown in Figure 11 (BE-VERB VS. OTHER, correctly classified verbs).

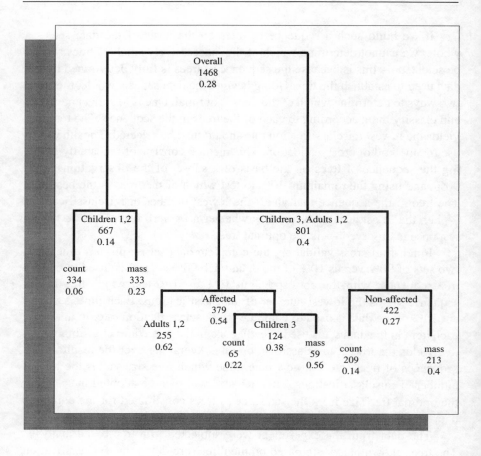

*Figure 11. Classification tree showing proportion of BE-VERB responses for verbs of
different types across all subjects. (Based only on subjects' BE-VERB responses
containing verbs that they had interpreted correctly as affected/non-affected
on the pretest.)*

The root node shows that there was a total of 1468 responses, of which 28% were *be*-verbs. The first and thus most important split is made on the basis of age: Children from the two youngest age groups (Child1 and Child2 groups) behaved differently from the older children (Child3) and both groups of adults (Adult1 and Adult2). This difference is also reflected in Figures 7 and 8, where a large increase in *be*-verbs is shown for the Child3 group.

For the Child1 and Child2 groups, only a single additional split is required: the distinction between mass verbs and count verbs. These children were more likely to produce a *be*-form for mass verbs (23%) than for count verbs (6%). In contrast, they were not influenced by the distinction between +AFF and -AFF verbs.

The Child3, Adult1, and Adult2 groups differ from the Child1 and Child2 groups in two ways: Their response patterns require two additional splits instead of one, and the first distinction must be made in terms of affectedness. For the +AFF verbs, two more distinctions are required, one for age, separating adults from the children, and one for mass versus count verbs, the latter being relevant only for the children. For the +AFF verbs, adults were not influenced by whether a verb was a mass or a count verb, whereas the subjects in the Child3 group *were* sensitive to this difference, producing more *be*-forms for the mass verbs (56%) than for the count verbs (22%). For the -AFF verbs, the distinction between mass and count plays a role for *both* adults and the Child3 group: Across all three groups, -AFF mass verbs elicited *be*-forms more often (40%) than -AFF count verbs (14%).

The second tree, shown in Figure 12, also compares *be*-verb responses with the remaining responses, but it is based on a subject-by-subject reclassification of the verbs on the basis of the subject's behavior in the pretest. Both trees make the same number of splits and, more importantly, the splits are made in the same order. This suggests that overall, subjects' use of *be*-forms was not influenced by whether they had classified the verb correctly in terms of affectedness.

The third and fourth tree, shown in Figure 13 and 14, take a different perspective on the responses: They show the conditions under which subjects were most likely to express the goal as direct object (as opposed to using a prepositional construction), regardless of whether they prefixed the verb with *be-*. These trees are more complex, and, unlike the previous trees, they differ depending on whether they are based only on responses to verbs that subjects had correctly classified in the pretest (Figure 13) or on all responses (Figure 14).

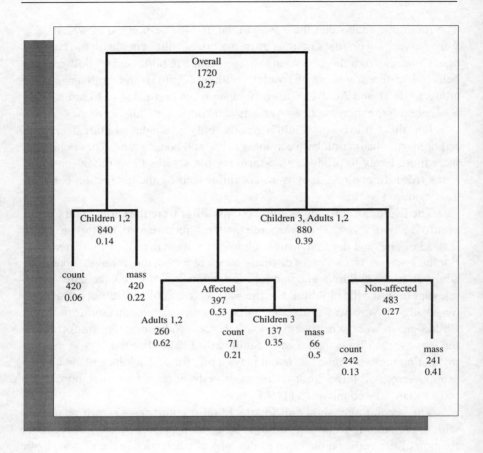

Figure 12. Classification tree showing proportion of BE-VERB responses for verbs of different types across all subjects. (Based on all BE-VERB responses, with verbs classified as affected/non-affected on the basis of each subject's interpretation of the verb on the pretest.)

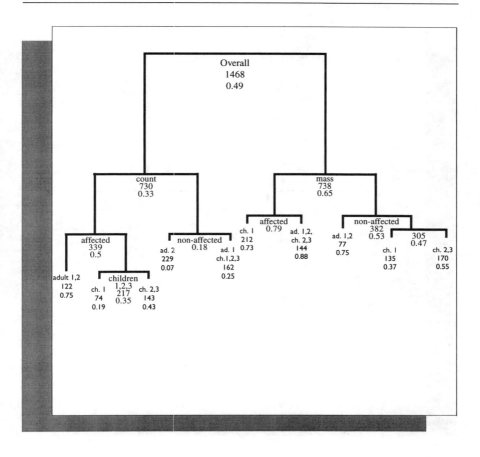

Figure 13. Classification tree showing proportion of GOAL=D.O. responses for verbs of different types across all subjects. (Based only on subjects' GOAL=D.O. responses containing verbs that they had interpreted correctly as affected/non-affected on the pretest.)

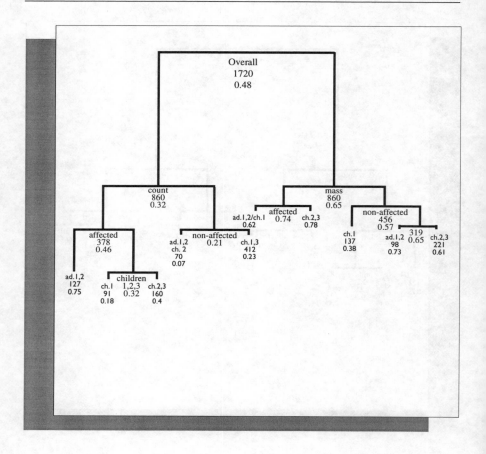

Figure 14. Classification tree showing proportion of GOAL=D.O. responses for verbs of different types across all subjects. (Based on all GOAL=D.O. responses, with verbs classified as affected/non-affected on the basis of each subject's interpretation of the verb on the pretest.)

According to these trees, the distinction between mass and count verbs is even more important than age and, again, more important than affectedness: Across all age groups, subjects were more likely to express the goal as direct object when the verb was a mass verb (65%) than when it was a count verb (32% and 33%).

Before turning to the role of age in Tree 13 and 14, let me first comment on another commonality between them. In both trees, the +AFF count verbs and the -AFF mass verbs require one more split than the -AFF count verbs and the +AFF mass verbs. The Child1 group produced fewer goal-object constructions for the +AFF count verbs, and more for the -AFF mass verbs, than the older children and both groups of adults. The trees are somewhat surprising with respect to the role of age. The third tree, based only on verbs that were correctly classified in the pretest (cf. Figure 13), shows that for the -AFF count verbs, the Adult1 group behaved similar to the children, expressing the goal as direct object 25% of the time, whereas the Adult2 group did so only 7% of the time. The fourth tree, which is based on all the responses (cf. Figure 14), shows that the two adult groups and the Child2 group produced fewer GOAL=D.O. responses for the -AFF count verbs (7%) than the Child1 and Child3 groups (23%). Moreover, for the +AFF mass verbs, the two groups of adults behaved similarly to the youngest children, producing fewer GOAL=D.O. responses (62%) than the two older groups of children (78%).

These counterintuitive results can to some extent be explained by looking at the responses to the individual verbs shown in Table 7. Overall, there seems to be one major pattern of development: Prepositional constructions come before grammatical goal-object constructions and true *be*-forms. Exactly which construction predominates depends on the age of the subject and the type of verb. This pattern interacts with a second, more minor, tendency to treat the two verbs representing a given verb type differently. This second tendency surfaces only late, after the construction as such seems to have been mastered for the verb type in question. Let us now look at the individual trees.

The split for the -AFF count verbs in the third tree (cf. Figure 13) seems to result from the Adult2 group's using *bewerfen* and *beballern* only infrequently, unlike the Adult1 and Child3 groups. This made the Adult1 and Child3 subjects group together with the Child2 subjects, whose GOAL=D.O. constructions include *bewerfen* and several ungrammatical constructions for *ballern*, and also with the Child1 subjects, who used ungrammatical GOAL=D.O. constructions for both verbs.

Turning now to the fourth tree (cf. Figure 14), notice that the tree shows that for the +AFF mass verbs, Adult1 and Adult2 subjects group together with the Child1 subjects in producing fewer GOAL=D.O. responses than the Child2 and Child3 subjects. This is because adults almost exclusively used *be*-verbs and not unprefixed goal-object constructions *and* because the Adult2 subjects used *bespritzen* less often than *beschmieren*. In contrast, the Child2 and Child3 subjects used both *be*-prefixed and unprefixed forms for all +AFF mass verbs about equally often (the Child2 subjects using predominantly unprefixed forms, and the Child3 subjects predominantly *be*-verbs). The Child1 subjects produced fewer *be*-verbs and fewer unprefixed forms than the Child2 and Child3 subjects; therefore, they group together with the adults, who disliked unprefixed goal-object constructions and also tended to avoid *bespritzen*.

Finally, the split for the -AFF count verbs in the fourth tree must be explained. The tree shows a contrast between both the Child2 and adult groups and between the Child1 and Child3 groups. Neither group of adults used unprefixed goal-object constructions, and the Adult2 subjects hardly ever used a *be*-prefixed goal-object form for the verbs of this type. The Child3 group produced somewhat more *be*-forms for *werfen* and *ballern* than did the Adult2 group, and the Child1 group produced no *be*-verbs but often used unprefixed goal-object forms (which were often ungrammatical). The Child2 subjects did neither — their response pattern was like that of the adults, who preferred PREP.OBJ. constructions for these verbs.

5.5 Discussion

The main experiment discussed in this chapter tested three hypotheses about the acquisition of the locative alternation: The Nonindividuation Hypothesis proposed in Chapter 4 of this thesis, and Gropen et al.'s and Lebeaux's somewhat different versions of hypothesis that affectedness is a major determinant of a speaker's willingness to use a goal-object form. Before analyzing what the results imply for these hypotheses, I will discuss potential problems with the tasks I used.

5.5.1 Potential Problems with the Tasks

The purpose of the pretest was to assess subjects' interpretations of the stimulus verbs. Recall that for the -AFF verbs, the test assessed whether the subjects were *biased* toward a manner or an endstate interpretation of the verbs, i.e., whether they assumed that manner is more important than endstate or vice versa. For the +AFF verbs, it assessed whether they were *sensitive* to these aspects of the verb meaning, i.e., whether they knew the typical endstate and/or manner associated with these verbs. Both ways of assessing subjects' interpretations of verb meanings are somewhat problematic (in Appendix 3, I explain why I used two different tests for assessing verb meaning).

As noted, the sensitivity test (for the +AFF verbs) assesses only what children take to be a typical endstate associated with a verb; it does not test whether they take this endstate aspect to be *essential* (Gropen, 1989). Strictly speaking, their correct choice of pictures may just reflect their world knowledge of typical effects of, e.g., smearing, but not what they take the *meaning* of the verb to be. However, I think it is reasonably safe to conclude that a subject who consistently prefers the correct endstate drawing does know that endstate is important for the verb. The bias test has a different shortcoming. Most of the children and the younger adults were (correctly) biased toward a manner interpretation (recall that the pretest was not given to the older adults). However, this manner bias does not necessarily mean that the subjects thought these verbs specify nothing at all about the endstate of the goal — it only means that they in any event considered manner more important (see also Gropen, 1989). The main experiment might, then, have underestimated the role of affectedness, since children might in fact have mistakenly thought that the -AFF verbs specified affectedness, and used the goal-object constructions only because of this.

Several arguments can be made against this possibility. First, previous research has suggested that children are more likely to assume that an endstate verb describes a particular manner than that a manner verb specifies a particular endstate. Gentner (1978) compared children's knowledge of the verb *mix*, which she suggests specifies a particular endstate (a greater increase in homogeneity) but no particular manner of motion, with their knowledge of the verbs *beat, stir*, and *shake*, which require a particular manner of motion but are noncommittal about the resulting state. Children between the ages of 5 and 9, and adults, were asked whether a particular event could be described appropriately by one of these verbs. The relevant events consisted of a beating, stirring, or shaking motion performed on either salt and water, which can be mixed, or cream, which cannot be mixed because it is already homogeneous. Ninety-seven percent of the 5- to 7-year-olds and 93% of the 7- to 9-year-olds accepted the manner verbs *stir, shake*, and *beat* for the appropriate events. In contrast, only 48% of the 5- to 7-year-olds accepted *mix* on those trials where the substances were indeed mixable, and they also accepted it on 46% of the trials where it was not (but see Behrends, 1990, who has presented counterevidence to Gentner's results).

Gropen et al.'s (1991a) study also shows that children are more likely to misinterpret an endstate verb as specifying a particular manner of motion than to misinterpret a manner verb as specifying a particular endstate. For example, in their first experiment, only 3 of the 32 children of the two youngest age groups (2;6-4;5) were biased toward an endstate interpretation of the manner verbs used in the study (*pour* and *dump*), and the oldest children — who were about two years younger than the youngest subjects in the present experiment — showed no endstate bias for these verbs. In contrast, many children of all age groups misinterpreted the endstate verbs (*fill* and *empty*) as specifying a particular manner of motion instead of an endstate. Thus, the results of Gropen et al. (1991a) support Gentner's (1978) finding that in general, children are not likely to misinterpret manner verbs in terms of an endstate specification.

The responses to the +AFF verbs in my own experiment also speak against the possibility that the present experiment underestimates the role of affectedness. If affectedness had had a great deal of influence on the children's responses, we would expect that the +AFF count verbs *packen* and *laden* (as correctly interpreted on the pretest) would have elicited about as many goal-object responses as the +AFF mass verbs *schmieren* and *spritzen*, but they did not — they patterned just like the -AFF count verbs *werfen* and *ballern*. In sum, it is unlikely that the children used goal-object constructions as often for the -AFF mass verbs as for the +AFF mass verbs because they really thought that these were +AFF verbs as well, even though this was not detected by the pretest.

Assuming, then, that the pretest was valid, we must still ask whether affectedness was successfully operationalized in the main experiment. That is, did the film sets really distinguish actions that affected the goal object from those that did not? In particular, the scenes showing water being poured over a cone might suggest that the action affected the cone because it got wet. And when poppy seeds were sprinkled over the cone, subjects might not have realized that no poppy seeds stayed on the cone. If these actions were interpreted as affecting the goal object, children might have been more likely to use goal-object constructions for the -AFF mass verbs *gießen* 'pour' and *rieseln* 'sprinkle' than for the -AFF count verbs *werfen* 'throw' and *ballern* 'smash', not because they were mass verbs, as posited by the Nonindividuation Hypothesis, but because they mistakenly thought that these verbs, but not the +AFF count verbs specified an affected object. This critique is weakened by the fact that the adult subjects did not use goal-object constructions to describe these scenes, which suggests that the scenes depicting actions of pouring and sprinkling were effective in conveying that the goal object was not affected.

In sum, there are good reasons for assuming that, in general, both the pretest and the main task tested what they were designed to test, i.e., subjects' interpretation of the verbs and their readiness to use goal-object constructions to describe actions that did or did not affect a goal object.

5.5.2 *Implications of the Results for the Hypotheses under Investigation*

The Nonindividuation Hypothesis is clearly supported by both the BE-VERB and the GOAL=D.O. analyses of the data. Mass verbs elicited more BE-VERB responses than did count verbs for the children of the two youngest age groups, and more GOAL=D.O. constructions for subjects of all age groups. While affectedness of the goal was the main determinant of whether the oldest children and the adults used a *be*-verb, the difference between mass and count verbs continued to exert some influence. For the oldest children, this difference showed up in their use of *be*-verbs regardless of affectedness, and for the adults only for the -AFF verbs. One factor, the count-mass verb distinction thus gradually comes to be dominated by another factor, affectedness.

The two Affectedness hypotheses are not supported by the data. First, affectedness did not influence the younger children's willingness to use a *be*-verb at all, although it *did* influence adults' likelihood of exercising their syntactic knowledge of *be*-prefixation. This pattern of results refutes Lebeaux's theory of acquisition most dramatically, since this theory predicts exactly the opposite: that children, but not adults, will restrict their use of *be*-

prefixation to verbs that specify an affected goal. Recall that Lebeaux hypothesized that a child first uses the thematic specification of arguments to determine their syntactic position, but later abandons this criterion for alternations that she realizes are morphologically marked. The present findings are all the more surprising, since Lebeaux's theory of affectedness had seemed especially promising because — unlike Gropen et al.'s hypothesis — it could account for why -AFF verbs alternate at all in German.

The results also go counter to Gropen et al.'s Affectedness Hypothesis. The children of the two youngest age groups consistently ignored affectedness: They were just as likely to make the goal the direct object of the verb (with or without prefixing the verb with *be-*) when the goal was *not* specified as affected as when it was. Gropen et al. cannot explain how children succeed in making a nonaffected goal the direct object: According to their account of the locative alternation, only an affected goal can be linked to that position.

Affectedness does play a role in the locative alternation, but only, it seems, *after* the structural properties of *be*-prefixation have been mastered. In consequence, in order to explain the acquisition of the alternation, we need an analysis of the alternation that does not draw on affectedness to explain how a verb can take its goal as direct object. The Preposition Incorporation account developed by Wunderlich (1992) obviates the need for postulating the Object Affectedness Linking Rule, and, consistent with this, the results of the present experiment show that children are unlikely to acquire the locative alternation on the basis of this linking rule.

The results strongly support the Nonindividuation Hypothesis. According to this hypothesis, for a transitive verb to take its goal as direct object, the quantificational properties of its theme must be irrelevant and the verb must describe a process (or a process leading to a transition). For count verbs, this requires deindividuating the theme and construing the verb as describing a series of subevents strung together to form one temporally unbounded event. The results of the experiment show that this hypothesis correctly predicts that children find it harder to use a count verb in the goal-object construction than a mass verb. But adults' responses suggest that it is not sufficient to learn *how* to deindividuate the theme and make the verb describe a process: One must also learn *when* to do so. A reason for doing so, from the adult point of view, is when the goal is affected.

Chapter 6

Restrictions on *be*-Prefixation

As I have mentioned in the introduction, there are restrictions on *be*-prefix-ation in German: Some locative verbs may not be prefixed with *be*- and take their locative argument as direct object, and some may do so only with specific additional contextual information. For ease of reference, I will refer to all these verbs as nonalternating verbs (or, interchangeably, as verbs that do not alternate or do not participate in the locative alternation). In this chapter, I will try to account for why these verbs do not alternate. In doing so, I will also discuss why some of the verbs are acceptable as *be*-verbs under certain contextual conditions.

The search for nonalternating verbs presupposes a particular theoretical stance on what the alternation is. I will start out, then, by motivating my search for these verbs (cf. 6.1). I then present all the nonalternating verbs that I have identified, categorizing them according to some salient syntactic and/or semantic criteria (cf. 6.2). To explain how children solve the No Negative Evidence problem posed by the locative alternation, all these verbs must be taken into account. A prerequisite for an explanation is to understand what children need to know in order to determine whether a verb may take its goal as direct object, so I try, whenever possible, to explain why a certain restriction holds (cf. 6.3). If there does not seem to be a principled reason for a verb not to alternate, I at least try to describe what it is that distinguishes this verb from those that do participate in the alternation. On the basis of this analysis, I then make proposals about how children can determine that certain verbs do not alternate.

6.1 What Kinds of Restrictions Must be Taken into Account?

In traditional analyses of the locative alternation, the theme-object form of the verb was considered to be basic, and the goal-object form to be derived. For example, in the transformational analysis proposed by Hall (1965), the goal-object form was derived by transformations from the theme-object form. If the goal-object form is taken to be derived, the search for restrictions will focus only on the theme-object verbs, and the leading research problem will be to characterize the verbs that cannot be used in the goal-object argument structure.

A different position is taken by Pinker (1989) and his collaborators (Gropen et al., 1991a,b) (and is also implied by the notions *content* and *container verbs* (Schwartz-Norman, 1976) on which he draws; cf. also Rappaport & Levin, 1985, 1988). According to Pinker, the alternation may go either way: The theme-object form is basic for some verbs, like *smear* and *spray*, and the goal-object form for others, like *load* and *stuff*. Either argument structure may be the input to the bidirectional broad range rule that mediates between the two syntactic frames related by the alternation. On this view, two kinds of restrictions must be accounted for: why some verbs are confined to the theme-object form and others to the goal-object form.

In line with the traditional view, and unlike Pinker, I assume that only the goal-object form is derived, and so will concentrate only on why certain theme-object verbs cannot take their goal as direct object. My main reason for taking this position is that I assume, following Wunderlich (1992), that *be*-prefixed verbs like *beschmieren* '*be*-smear', and the goal-object forms of English verbs like *smear*, result from the verbs' incorporation of a preposition. This conception is supported by the direction of morphological marking in languages like German and Dutch: The verb is marked only in the goal-object construction. The satisfaction criteria for both argument structures proposed by Wunderlich (1992; cf. 3.2) are also based on the idea that the theme-object form is basic. According to the Preposition Incorporation account, restrictions on container verbs like *stuff* constitute an entirely different research problem than restrictions on theme-object verbs. Since container verbs like *stopfen* 'stuff' in German are not marked morphologically in either their theme- or the goal-object form, their syntactic flexibility seems to be determined by principles other than those determining the syntactic behavior of verbs like *smear*.

6.2 Verbs that do not Participate in the Locative Alternation

My search for nonalternating verbs in German was guided by the assumption that a transitive verb is a candidate alternator if it can have the argument structure [V NP$_{theme}$ P NP$_{goal}$], and that an intransitive verb is a candidate alternator if it can have the argument structure [V P NP$_{goal}$] or [V P NP$_{location}$] (where P NP$_{location}$ is an argument of the verb). In trying to establish a list of nonalternating verbs, I have considered a variety of sources. First, I checked various lists of locative verbs in the literature (Leisi, 1953; Saile, 1984; Neumann, 1987). Second, I examined the relevant sections of the dictionary *Wörterbuch des Deutschen nach Sachgruppen geordnet*, which classifies the German lexicon according to semantic criteria. In addition, I looked for German translation equivalents of the English verbs listed by Pinker (1989, p. 126ff.). Several of the translation equivalents offered for these verbs in the dictionary were excluded because they cannot be expected to alternate for independent reasons; these include verbs that are prefixed already (e.g., *verschütten* 'spill') and combinations of verbs with other lexical elements (e.g., *mit Band versehen* (lit.: 'provide with tape') for *tape*).

Also excluded were translation equivalents derived from nouns and adjectives (e.g., denominal *stapeln*$_{theme}$ for *pile*$_{theme/goal}$ and deadjectival *ausbreiten* for *spread*). I have not considered denominal verbs, for example, because I felt that this would have required a thorough investigation of the general restrictions on denominal *be*-verbs, an investigation that is beyond the scope of this thesis. The reason for this requirement is two-fold. First, as mentioned in Section 3.1.3, German offers a productive means for deriving denominal *be*-verbs, i.e., incorporating the noun specifying the theme, as in *die Wand beschmutzen* '*be*-spot the wall' (Wunderlich, 1987). The acceptability of a denominal *be*-verb seems to critically depend on how speakers categorize the corresponding entities (e.g., piles), i.e., whether they can conceive of them as entities that can be brought to the exterior of another object. This means that the acceptability of a denominal *be*-verb depends not so much on the semantics of the base verb (if there is one) but on whether the entity in question (e.g., a pile) can be conceived of as a good theme. Thus, the question is not whether *stapeln* 'pile' can be turned into *bestapeln* '*be*-pile', but whether a pile can be conceived of as the kind of object that can be moved to the exterior of another object. Given that denominal *be*-verbs seem to be independent of potential denominal 'base' verbs, I concluded a) that the restrictions on denominal *be*-verbs are first of all a matter of object categorization, which is not the topic of this study, and b) that it would be arbitrary to restrict the analysis to those denominal base verbs that happen to be translation equivalents of the verbs discussed by Pinker (1989) and other authors. Instead, an analysis of denominal *be*-verbs should be based on research on object categorization and should include relevant *types* of objects as established on the basis of this research (cf. Biederman, 1987; Lang, 1988, 1989, among others). Even though the classification of properties, denoted by adjectives, may be less complex than that of object categorization, the same reasoning can be applied to the search for restrictions on deadjectival *be*-verbs.

The nonalternating verbs that I identified on the basis of the criteria described above were then categorized into six categories. The classification served as a first step toward understanding the syntactic restrictions on the verbs. The categories were chosen, as far as possible, on the basis of classifications of locative verbs that have already been proposed in the literature. The verbs that could not be classified in this way were categorized according to a syntactic property that could be identified independently of whether the verbs alternate — for example, whether a constituent was optional — or according to a salient semantic criterion. Both the syntactic and the semantic criteria are to some extent subjective, being dependent on my intuition about the relevant distinctive property of the verbs in question. But the classification is fairly straightforward.

Some speakers accept some of the verbs to be described below under certain contextual conditions. I will discuss this limited acceptability when discussing the reasons for why verbs of a given class do not alternate (cf. 6.3). Also, some verbs described below do have a *be*-prefixed variant, but this is not productively derived. Information about these idiosyncratic *be*-verbs will be given in a COMMENT paragraph at the end of each section. (The reader who is interested in restrictions on prefix verbs in German other than those on *be*-verbs is referred to Stiebels, 1996.)

The Categories

I.   INTO Verbs

Recall that the semantics of the *be*-prefix restricts the alternation of transitive verbs to those describing transfer to the exterior of a goal object. This topological restriction excludes verbs that can only describe transfer into a container or hollow space (cf. 3.1.1; see also Pinker, 1989, p. 126ff., who distinguishes two subclasses of verbs that denote transfer of an object into a container). I will refer to these verbs as INTO VERBS, since the term CONTAINER VERBS has been used in the literature for verbs like *load*, for which the goal-object form is the basic argument structure (Schwartz-Norman, 1976; Rappaport & Levin, 1985; Pinker, 1989; see also Section 3.1.1). INTO verbs are *füllen* 'fill', *klemmen* 'pinch/squeeze', *quetschen* 'jam', *stechen* 'stick/prick', *stopfen* 'stuff', and *zwängen* 'wedge/jam'.

(1) Jo stopfte Bohnen in den Sack.

  'Jo stuffed beans into the sack'

  *Jo bestopfte den Sack mit Bohnen.
  'Jo *be*-stuffed the sack with beans'
  (but cf.: Jo stopfte den Sack mit Bohnen voll.
  'Jo stuffed the sack with beans full')

  Sue quetschte das Gepäck in den Wagen.

  'Sue jammed the luggage into the car'

  *Sue bequetschte den Wagen mit dem Gepäck.
  'Sue *be*-jammed the car with the luggage'

Comment: The only INTO verb that can participate in the alternation is *füllen* 'fill' — cf. *befüllen* '*be*-fill'. But this rather baroque coinage is not accepted by all speakers. The verbs *beklemmen* 'constrict/oppress' and *bestechen* 'bribe' exist, but do not have a locative meaning.

II.   Accompanied Motion Verbs

Verbs in this class denote a motion that is brought about by the continuous accompanying motion of an agent; the verbs have also been characterized as lacking a result component (cf. Pinker, 1989; Wunderlich, 1992). The category includes the verbs *schieben* 'push', *schleppen* 'schlepp', *tragen* 'carry', and *ziehen* 'pull'. Their behavior is illustrated in (2):

(2) Er schob Schnee auf den Bürgersteig.

  'He pushed the snow onto the sidewalk'

  Sie schleppten die Kübel auf den Balkon.

  'They schlepped the pots onto the balcony'

  *Er beschob den Bürgersteig mit Schnee.
  'He *be*-pushed the sidewalk with snow'

  *Sie beschleppten den Balkon mit den Kübeln.
  'They *be*-schlepped the balcony with the pots'

A similar class of verbs has been proposed by Pinker (1989) in his discussion of the dative alternation. He characterizes them as verbs that describe a continuous imparting of force. His class includes *lift* and *lower*, whose translation equivalents in German, *heben* and *senken*, I have classified not as accompanied motion verbs but as directional verbs (cf. Category III below).

Comment: *Ziehen* 'pull' does have both a *be*-prefix form and a P-prefix form, *beziehen* and *überziehen*. *Beziehen* is used in contexts like 'pull the sheets over a bed' and 'cover the tennis court with artificial lawn'; *beziehen* is also used with nonlocative meanings, as in *eine Zeitschrift beziehen* 'to subscribe to a journal'. *Überziehen* is more general and means 'cover'. When used as locative verbs, both *beziehen* and *überziehen* name actions in which the theme is extended by being pulled, and they require that the theme be applied to the goal bit by bit. In contrast, actions that are more typically associated with the verb, which involve the displacement of an object, may not be referred to by either *beziehen* or *überziehen*, as shown in example (3), discussed earlier in Chapter 4:

(3) Er zog die Einkaufswagen auf den   *Er bezog den Parkplatz mit den
     Parkplatz.   Einkaufswagen.
     'He pulled the shopping carts onto the   'He *be*-pulled the parking lot with
     parking lot'   the shopping carts'

III. Directional Verbs

These verbs inherently denote direction, which may be oriented either upward, downward, or deictically (i.e., to or away from a place that must be contextually determined) (see Gruber, 1965; Fillmore, 1973; Clark, 1974; Miller & Johnson-Laird, 1976; Talmy, 1985; Levin & Rappaport Hovav, 1992, for analyses of these verbs). Directional verbs that denote upward or downward motion include intransitive *fallen* 'fall', *sinken* 'sink', *steigen* 'rise/climb', and *tauchen* 'dive' (cf. Example (4a)); and transitive *fällen* 'fell', *heben* 'lift', *hieven* 'heave', *senken* 'lower', and *tauchen* 'dip' (cf. (4b)). *Fällen, senken,* and *tauchen* are the causative forms of *fallen, sinken,* and *tauchen* (see also Category VI below). The deictic verbs of motion include intransitive *kommen* 'come' and *gehen* 'go' (cf. (5a)) and transitive *bringen* 'bring' and *holen* 'get/fetch' (cf. (5b)).

(4) a. Die Begonien fielen auf die Straße.
    'The begonias fell onto the street'
   b. Er hob die Taschen auf den Tisch.
    'He lifted the bags onto the table'

      *Die Begonien befielen die Straße.
      'The begonias *be*-fell the street'
      *Er behob den Tisch mit den Taschen.
      'He *be*-lifted the table with the bags'

(5) a. Das Kind kam ins Haus.
    'The child came into the house'

      *Das Kind bekam das Haus.
      'The child *be*-came the house'
      (grammatical only on the reading
      'The child received/inherited the
      house')

   b. Ted brachte die Post ins Haus.
    'Ted brought the mail into the house'

      *Ted bebrachte das Haus mit der Post.
      'Ted *be*-brought the house with the
      mail'

Comment: *Gehen* 'go' and *steigen* 'rise/climb' alternate when they can be interpreted as manner of motion verbs, similar to English 'walk' and 'climb/ clamber'. *Besteigen*, for example, can be used to refer only to the motion of an animate being who is clambering, as in (6a), but not to the upward motion of, e.g., a balloon, as shown in (6b). In the latter case, the verb can be combined only with a prepositional phrase like *in die Luft* 'into the air', which describes direction rather than the goal of the motion.

(6) a. Der Mann bestieg den Berg.
    'The man *be*-climbed the mountain'
   b. *Der Luftballon bestieg die Luft.
    'The balloon *be*-rose the air'

Kommen 'come' and *heben* 'lift' have a *be*-prefixed form, *bekommen* and *beheben*, but these verbs do not have the expected locative meaning: *bekommen* means 'receive', and *beheben* can only be used in constructions like *den Schaden beheben* 'to remove/repair the damage'.

IV. PRESS Verbs

The verbs of this class may express an internal argument either as a direct object or a prepositional phrase, as shown in (7a) for *drücken* 'press/push' (see Pinker, 1989; also Levin, 1993, for further discussion of these verbs). The verbs can also appear with two internal arguments, in which case they describe the transfer of an object to a goal, as shown in (7b). PRESS verbs include *drücken* 'press/push', *hacken* 'hack', *klopfen* 'beat/knock', *pressen* 'press', and *reiben* 'rub'. *Schlagen* 'beat' and *stoßen* 'push', in their noncausative, agentive readings (e.g., *Er schlug auf den Tisch* 'He beat on the table'), also belong to this class. These verbs have intransitive variants with a nonagentive reading, i.e., that describe uncontrolled motion (e.g., *Der Ball schlug gegen die Wand* 'The ball hit against the wall'); these intransitive verbs can be causativized, in which case they describe transfer (cf. Category VI).

(7) a. Er drückte auf den Knopf.   Er drückte den Knopf.
        'He pressed on the button'   'He pressed the button'
     b. Er drückte den Sticker auf den Knopf. *Er bedrückte den Knopf mit dem Sticker.

       'He pressed the sticker onto the button' 'He *be*-pressed the button with the sticker'

Comment: Prefixing the PRESS verbs with *be-* is marginally acceptable. But the *be*-forms are derived from those forms of the verbs that have only a single internal argument, as in (7a) (regardless of whether this is expressed as a direct object or prepositional argument), and not from the forms with two internal arguments, as in (7b). Thus, the grammatical *be*-verb shown in (8a), corresponding to (7a), specifies that an object is pressed repeatedly, but it does not specify transfer; the sentence in (8b), corresponding to (7b), is ungrammatical.

(8) a. Er bedrückte den Knopf. 'He *be*-pressed the button'
     b. *Er bedrückte den Knopf mit Sticker. 'He *be*-pressed the button with sticker'

V. STIR Verbs

STIR verbs are transitive verbs that, like the PRESS verbs, need a directional PP to denote transfer (see Levin, 1993, who terms a similar but not identical category SHAKE verbs). The verbs in this category differ semantically from the PRESS verbs in that they do not specify that a force is directed against an object. This is also reflected in their syntactic properties. When the PRESS verbs are used with a single internal argument, they can express this argument as either a direct object or a prepositional object; in contrast, the STIR verbs can express this argument only as a direct object. STIR verbs include *kneten* 'knead', *rühren* 'stir', *rütteln* 'shake/jog', and *schütteln* 'shake'. Without a PP, these verbs all specify that an entity is moved in one location; they require a PP to specify that the entity is transferred to a new location. Examples of a STIR verb without and with a PP are given in (9a-b), and the ungrammatical goal-object form is illustrated in (9c).

(9) a. Er rührte das Eiweiß.   'He stirred the eggwhite'
     b. Er rührte das Eiweiß an den Teig.   'He stirred the eggwhite into the dough'
     c. *Er berührte den Teig mit Eiweiß.   'He *be*-stirred the dough with eggwhite'

Comment: The verb *berühren* 'touch' exists, but it does not denote transfer. The *be*-forms of STIR verbs are marginally acceptable, but, like the *be*-forms of PRESS verbs, they never denote transfer, but rather that the action specified by the base verbs (when not combined with a prepositional phrase) is intensified.

VI. Causativizable Verbs

Causativizable verbs have an intransitive form in which the theme is the subject; these can be causativized, in which case they take the agent as subject and the theme as direct object (see Saile, 1984; Maienborn, 1990; Wunderlich & Kaufmann, 1990; Levin & Rappaport Hovav, 1992, among others). The class consists of two subgroups: *causativizable verbs of position* (VI.1) and *causativizable verbs of motion* (VI.2). In their intransitive form, the position verbs take a stative PP in which the NP is assigned dative case, as shown in (10), and the motion verbs take a directional PP in which the NP is assigned accusative case, as shown in (11).

(10) Das Kaugummi klebte an der Türklingel$_{dat}$ 'The chewing gum stuck on the doorbell'

(11) Die Murmeln rollten auf den Balkon$_{acc}$ 'The marbles rolled onto the balcony'

VI.1 Verbs of Position

Causativizable verbs of position with phonologically identical intransitive and causativized forms are *stecken* 'stick/pin', *hängen* 'hang', *lehnen* 'lean', *kleben* 'glue', and *pappen* 'stick'; in addition, there are the verb pairs *sitzen-setzen* 'sit-set', *stehen-stellen* 'stand-put' (lit: 'make stand'), and *liegen-legen* 'lie-lay', in which the causativized form differs phonologically from the intransitive form. (Terming *kleben* and *pappen* 'verbs of position' is somewhat misleading, since these verbs denote a kind of attachment rather than a particular position of the theme (see also 6.3); they have been included in this class because they behave syntactically like the other verbs in the class.) The intransitive forms of verbs of position do not participate in the locative alternation, as illustrated in (12a-b). In contrast, most of their causativized counterparts do (e.g., *kleben*, shown in (13)). But *lehnen* and *stellen* never alternate, as illustrated in (14a-b), and *setzen* and *stecken* alternate only under specifiable conditions (see below and 6.3).

(12) Intransitive *kleben* and *lehnen*

    a.   Das Kaugummi klebte an der Türklingel$_{dat}$

        'The chewing gum stuck on the doorbell'

        *Das Kaugummi beklebte die Türklingel$_{acc}$

        'The chewing gum *be*-stuck the doorbell'

    b.   Die Leitern lehnten an der Wand.

        'The ladders leaned against the wall'

        *Die Leitern belehnten die Wand.

        'The ladders *be*-leaned the door'

(13) Causativized *kleben*

    Hans klebte Kaugummis an die Türklingel.

    'Hans stuck chewing gum onto the doorbell'

    Hans beklebte die Türklingel mit Kaugummis.

    'Hans *be*-stuck the doorbell with chewing gum'

(14) Causativized *lehnen*

    Er lehnte die Leitern an die Wand.

    'He leaned the ladders against the wall'

    *Er belehnte die Wand mit den Leitern.

    'He *be*-leaned the wall with the ladders'

Comment: Causative *stecken* 'stick/pin' may take its goal as direct object provided the goal may be conceived of as a surface and not as a container:

(15) a.   Er steckte Abzeichen an den Hut.

        'He pinned badges onto the hat'

        Er besteckte den Hut mit Abzeichen.

        'He *be*-pinned the hat with badges'

    b.   Er steckte Blumen in die Vase.

        'He put flowers into the vase'

        *Er besteckte die Vase mit Blumen.

        'He *be*-put the vase with flowers'

Causative *setzen* 'set' may take its goal as direct object when the theme can be conceived of as a point, as in *Sie besetzte die Jacke mit falschen Perlen* 'She *be*-set the jacket with false pearls'; *besetzen* in this sentence merely specifies that the theme is attached to the goal but does not convey the positional information canonically associated with sitting (pearls and objects of similar shape cannot, after all, attain such a position); the theme can thus be conceived of as a point.

Besetzen, bestellen, and *belegen* have various idiomatic readings; for example: *besetzen* 'occupy/squat in', *bestellen* 'order/subscribe to/book', *belegen* 'occupy/reserve'. Several of these idiomatic meanings still reflect the locative meanings of the base verbs. For example, although *bestellen* is no longer used as the goal-object form of *stellen* in Modern German, *bestellen* 'order' (in a restaurant) is related to the waiter's action of putting the things ordered onto the table. The verb *belehnen* exists but it is unrelated to the positional verb *lehnen*; rather, it is derived from the noun *Lehen* 'fief/feudal tenure', and means 'invest with a fief/enfeoff'.

VI.2 Causativizable Verbs of Motion

Causativizable verbs of motion with identical intransitive and causativized forms are *fluten* 'flood', *kippen* 'tip over', *klappen* 'clap-fold', *kleckern* 'spill', *klecksen* 'blot', *kugeln* 'roll like a ball', *kullern* 'wiggle/roll like a raw egg', *prallen* 'bounce', *rieseln* 'drizzle/sprinkle', *rollen* 'roll', *schießen* 'shoot', *schlagen* 'strike/beat', *schleifen* 'slide/drag', *schleudern* 'skid-fling', *schnellen* 'jerk', *schwappen* 'slop', *schwingen* 'swing', *spritzen* 'splash', *sprühen* 'spray', *stoßen* 'push/thrust', *treiben* 'drift', *tropfen* 'drip/drop', *tröpfeln* 'trickle', and *wirbeln* 'whirl'.

In addition, there are the verb pairs *fließen-flößen* 'flow-float/pour' and *schwimmen-schwemmen* 'swim-sweep', whose causative forms have undergone a vowel shift in the stem. *Schwingen* 'swing' has both a causative form that is phonologically identical to the intransitive form and one that has undergone a change in the stem, *schwenken*. Causatives whose intransitive forms are, according to my intuition, no longer transparent are *schleppen* 'drag/schlepp' (derived from *schleifen* 'slide/drag'), *sprengen* 'sprinkle/blow up' (from *springen* 'spring') and *klemmen* (from *klimmen* 'climb'); these are not listed here. Three further causativizable verbs involving a change of location are the directional verbs *fallen* 'fall', *sinken* 'sink', and *tauchen* 'dive'. In contrast to the verbs discussed in this section, these verbs do not describe a particular manner of motion but rather a particular direction in which an entity moves (see also Levin & Rappaport Hovav, 1992, who discuss this difference between the two kinds of verbs); they have been discussed earlier under Category III.

Most of the intransitive forms of the motion verbs listed here do not participate in the locative alternation, as shown in (16). Some of them alternate only if they are prefixed with a prepositional prefix (e.g., *durch* 'through') rather than with *be-*, as shown in (17) (cf. Chapter 3). Most of the causativized forms do not alternate either, as exemplified in (18).

(16) Die Dachziegel wirbelten auf die Straße.   *Die Dachziegel bewirbelten die Straße.

      'The roofing tiles whirled onto the street'   'The roofing tiles *be*-whirled the street'

(17) Der Dachziegel schlug durch die Fensterscheibe.   Der Dachziegel durchschlug die Fensterscheibe.

      'The roofing tile hit through the windowpane'   'The roofing tile *through*-hit the window-pane'

(18) Tom wirbelte die Dachziegel auf die   *Tom bewirbelte die Straße mit den
     Straße.   Dachziegeln.
     'Tom whirled the roofing tiles onto the   'Tom *be*-whirled the street with the
     street'   roofing tiles'

However, a specifiable subgroup of these verbs does participate in the locative alternation: causativized verbs that denote the motion of substances, including *fluten* 'flood', *kleckern* 'spill', *klecksen* 'blot', *rieseln* 'drizzle', *schwappen* 'slop', *sprengen* 'sprinkle', *spritzen* 'splash', *sprühen* 'spray', *schwemmen* 'sweep', *tropfen* 'drop', and *tröpfeln* 'trickle'. Cf. (19):

(19) Das Kind spritzte Suppe auf die Tisch-   Das Kind bespritzte die Tischdecke
     decke.   mit Suppe.
     'The child splashed soup onto the   'The child *be*-splashed the tablecloth
     tablecloth'   with soup'

Flößen 'pour' might be expected to alternate as well, but the verb denotes the motion of a liquid only into a container, and so is in conflict with the semantics of *be-*. Note that when *schwappen* 'slop' and *schwemmen* 'sweep' take their goal as direct object, they are not prefixed with *be-* but with the prepositional prefix *über* 'over'; cf. *überschwemmen* and *überschwappen*.

Comment: It might appear that the verbs *schießen* 'shoot', *rollen* 'roll', *schlagen* 'strike/beat', and *stoßen* 'push/thrust' alternate, since the verbs *beschießen*, *berollen*, *beschlagen*, and *bestoßen* exist and take an agent as subject. But this is not the case. *Berollen* is derived from the noun *Rolle* 'roller', which refers to an instrument used for painting; *beschlagen* and *bestoßen* are related to the PRESS verbs *schlagen* and *stoßen* (discussed in IV); and *beschießen* is derived from *schießen* 'shoot' and means 'put under fire'.[1]

There is yet another nonalternating verb, *schmettern* 'fling/bang', which does not fit any of the six categories described above. *Schmettern* denotes a particular manner in which an object is thrown, i.e., forcefully against a surface.

---

1. In accordance with this analysis, the sentences in (i-ii) below do not refer to situations in which the motion of the theme could be described by the intransitive forms of the verb, as shown by the ungrammaticality of the sentence in (iii).

(i)   Er beschlug die Leiste mit Ziernägeln. 'He *be*-beat the frame with studs'
(ii)   Er schlug (Ziernägel) auf die Leiste. 'He beat (studs) onto the frame'
(iii) *Die Ziernägel schlugen auf die Leiste. 'The studs beat onto the frame'

Overgeneralizations of BE-Prefixation

Do children make errors with the verbs just described? There is little evidence on this. A few ungrammatical *be*-verbs are listed by Augst (1984) in his overview of the vocabulary of four children at the age of 5, shortly before they enter school. His corpus contains more than 40 transparent *be*-verbs derived from verbs, nouns, and adjectives, and 7 of these are novel constructions, as shown in (20).

(20) *benähen* 'to *be*-sew' (from *nähen* 'to sew')
   beschmücken 'to *be*-decorate' (derived from either the noun *Schmuck* 'decoration/ jewellery' or the denominal verb *schmücken* 'to decorate')
   bewischen 'to *be*-wipe' (from *wischen* 'to wipe')
   belähmen 'to *be*-lame' (derived from either the adjective *lahm* 'lame' or the deadjectival verb *lähmen* 'to paralyze')
   beschmeicheln 'to *be*-flatter someone' (from *schmeicheln* 'to flatter')
   beäppeln (probably formed by analogy to *veräppeln* 'to make a joke about someone')
   beknickeln (?)

The translations given are tentative, since Augst does not provide information about the context in which the verbs were coined. As indicated in brackets, most of these verbs have an unprefixed or *ver*-prefixed grammatical counterpart. Unfortunately, without contextual information, it is impossible to determine whether the children interpreted the *be*-verbs differently from their base verbs. None of the errors involve locative verbs.

There is some evidence that *be*-prefixation is productively used to derive locative verbs from nouns specifying the theme (see 3.1, for discussion). (A similar example is shown in (20), *beschmücken*, which might have been derived from the noun *Schmuck*.) One such novel *be*-verb has been mentioned already in Chapter 2, *besuppt* (='souped'), coined by the two-year old Hilde Stern to refer to a spoon that got soup on it (Stern & Stern, 1907/28). Another example comes from Dutch, *bemuren* ('to supply with/surround with walls'), produced in the course of an elicited production study by a thirteen-year old subject (Smeedts, 1986).

Why are there so few reports of errors involving *be*-prefixation? The main reason seems to be that the available corpora of the speech of children acquiring German do not cover the relevant age ranges — detailed reports on the speech of children do not go beyond the age of four (Stern & Stern, 1907/28; Miller, 1976; Clahsen, 1982; see Appendix 2, for a description of these corpora), but productive knowledge of *be*-prefixation for changing the argument structure of locative verbs is probably not acquired before at least five. There are two reasons for thinking this.

First, coining novel *be*-verbs requires children to be able to derive new verbs through affixation, and this ability is typically not acquired before the age of five, often later. Clark (1993), for example, finds that children learning English do not use suffixation to derive novel verbs from nouns or adjectives until at least this age. (This suggests that H. Stern's novel coinage *besuppt* at the age of two was truly exceptional.) Similarly, Mills (1985) points out that affixation involving inseparable prefix verbs is a late acquisition in German-speaking children. Second, productive knowledge of *be*-prefixation requires understanding the semantic effect of the prefixation. In English — where semantic equivalents of *be*-prefixed locative verbs do not require affixation, so children would not be slowed down for this formal reason — the overgeneralized use of (unprefixed) locative verbs in goal-object construc-tions (e.g., **I spilled it of water*) is nevertheless late and quite rare (Melissa Bowerman, personal communication). The opposite type of error — use of goal-object verbs in theme-object constructions (e.g., **I filled water into the cup*) — occurs much earlier and more often (Bowerman, 1982b, 1988). The results of the experiments conducted by Gropen et al. (1991a, b) point in the same direction. As was noted in Section 2.5.2, children were much less willing or able to use nonalternating verbs like *pour* in the goal-object structure than to use nonalternating verbs like *fill* in the theme-object con-struction. According to the Preposition Incorporation account, this asymme-try between use of either structure is due to the fact that the verb in the goal-object structure is more complex than in the theme-object structure in that it has incorporated a preposition and so must accomodate the argument of that preposition. In the theme-object structure, in contrast, the preposition appears as a morphologically independent lexical item that takes its own argument.

Although we do not have enough data yet to trace how children acquiring German learn to prefix locative verbs with *be*-, it is clear that the operation does eventually become productive — cf. the novel coinages by adult speak-ers listed in (10) in Chapter 1. Whether there is a stage of overgeneralization to inappropriate verbs remains unclear.

6.3 Explaining the Restrictions

In what follows, I will try to explain why the verbs listed in the preceding section do not participate in the locative alternation, and how children can determine that they do not alternate. My analysis is motivated by the idea that the various reasons why a verb may not participate in the locative alternation can best be understood as a failure to meet one (or more) necessary conditions that are relevant for deriving the goal-object argument structure of a verb. The conditions are motivated by what has been said about the properties of the locative alternation in Chapter 3 and 4; the only exception is Condition 5 (cf. below), which is only partly motivated by what has been said so far about the alternation. I will briefly introduce the conditions and then discuss the verb classes each of them excludes.

The conditions are roughly ordered in terms of how essential they are for the locative alternation. This ordering may provide a first guideline as to how easily speakers may come up with contextual information or reconstruals of a nonalternating verb that allow them to accept it as a *be*-verb.

Condition 1   *The locative argument must be expressable in object position*
This condition is defining for the locative alternation and so needs no further comment.

Condition 2   *The locative argument must be indivisible with respect to the verbal predicate, and the satisfaction criteria must be met*
Once the locative argument is the direct object of the verb, it must be indivisible with respect to the verbal predicate (Löbner, 1990, 1996; cf. 3.2.2). The satisfaction criteria proposed by Wunderlich (1992; cf. 3.2.2) provide additional constraints on the locative alternation.

Condition 3   *The theme must either be specified as a structural (direct) argument or be omissable*
By definition, locative verbs take a theme. When these verbs take their locative argument as direct object, the theme cannot be expressed in that position, so it must either be expressed in subject position or be omissable. According to the Nonindividuation Hypothesis (cf. Chapter 4), transitive locative verbs must take an incremental theme in order to meet this condition.

Condition 4   *The verb must describe a process*
               Recall that the Nonindividuation Hypothesis states that transi-
               tive locative verbs must be turned into predicates that describe
               a process (or processes leading to a transition) in order to be
               able to incorporate a preposition and take their locative argu-
               ment as direct object. I will argue that the locative alternation
               may be more generally characterized as the functional compo-
               sition of a verbal process predicate with a preposition.

Condition 5   *The topological requirements of the locative alternation must
               be met*
               The topological requirements of the locative alternation are a)
               that the goal or location NP refer to the exterior of an object,
               and b) that the theme be conceived of as a point-like entity.
               The first of these requirements is language-specific, holding
               for German (and possibly Dutch), but not English: This is
               because of the topological restrictions imposed on *be*-verbs by
               the semantics of the prefix (cf. 3.1). The second requirement is
               independent of *be*-prefixation and so possibly not restricted to
               German (and Dutch). It is mainly motivated by the conditions
               under which causative verbs of position like *hängen* 'hang'
               may alternate (see below).

Condition 6.   *Pragmatically, it must make sense to use the goal-object form
               of verb*
               As already pointed out by Gropen et al. (1991b; cf. 2.5), the
               goal-object form of a verb focusses on the goal while
               defocussing the theme. This condition makes it unlikely that
               certain verbs will be used in the goal-object construction,
               although the corresponding *be*-forms would be grammatical.

Let us now see how the conditions can account for the restrictions on *be*-
prefixation in German.

Condition 1. The locative argument must be expressable in object position

This is the most essential condition to be met. Verbs that do not meet this
condition do not participate in the alternation under any circumstance. This
holds for directional verbs like *kommen* 'come' and *heben* 'lift'. The verbs do
not meet Condition 1 because they have incorporated an intransitive spatial

predicate, and so they cannot take their locative argument as direct object (see also Talmy, 1985, who suggests that their English counterparts have incorporated a path, and Miller & Johnson-Laird, 1976, who propose that they have incorporated a spatial adverb).

These verbs are interesting in the present context because native speakers of German find it almost impossible to interpret the object NP in a construction like *Er behebt den Tisch mit Taschen* 'He *be*-lifts the table with bags' as the goal of the motion. This distinguishes directional verbs from, e.g., accompanied motion verbs: A sentence like *Wegen des heftigen Schneefalls mußten selbst die Bürgersteige mit Schnee beschoben werden* 'Due to the heavy snowfall, even the sidewalks had to be *be*-pushed with snow' sounds almost grammatical.

Intransitive spatial predicates necessarily imply the existence of a location but, since they are intransitive, they cannot express this location syntactically (see Ehrich, 1982; Becker, Carroll, & Kelly, 1988; Wunderlich & Kaufmann, 1990, and Wunderlich & Herweg, 1991, for analyses of intransitive spatial predicates in German). In other words, the location is a semantic, but not a syntactic argument of the predicate. Intransitive spatial predicates may be either spatial adverbs like *oben* 'up' and *unten* 'down', or spatial adjectives like *hoch* 'high' and *niedrig/tief* 'low' (note that *unten* and *oben* specify only a location, not a path, in contrast to English *up* and *down*, which can specify either). Spatial adjectives imply the existence of a location because they must be interpreted *relative to a point* on the vertical dimension (Clark, 1973; Bierwisch & Lang, 1989; Lang, 1988, 1989).

That intransitive predicates cannot express the location syntactically can best be shown by comparing them to *transitive* spatial predicates — e.g., prepositions (cf. 3.2.2, the argument structure of prepositions). For example, the adverb *unten* 'down' in German is semantically identical to the preposition *unter* 'under': Both denote a *relation* between an object and a location — and so, semantically, take two arguments. But only the preposition can express both arguments syntactically.[2] Example (21a) below describes a relation between Marga and a table, and the corresponding NPs are both expressed syntactically. In contrast, for example (21b), we must infer the object with respect to which Marga is 'down' or 'below', since the adverb cannot express the locative argument syntactically, as shown in (21c).

---

2. A different terminology is proposed by Emonds (1972): 'intransitive prepositions' for adverbs and 'transitive prepositions' for what I am terming prepositions.

(21) a.   Marga ist unter dem Tisch. 'Marga is under the table'
     b.   Marga is unten. 'Marga is down/below'
     c.   *Marga ist unten dem Tisch. 'Marga is down/below the table'

Since intransitive spatial predicates necessarily imply the existence of a location, directional verbs that have incorporated them do as well, and this location is interpreted as the goal (which I will call 'implied goal'). But since the incorporated predicate is intransitive, this goal cannot be expressed syntactically. Why is it impossible to have both an implied goal and express the semantic argument of the incorporated preposition in object position? This is because a verb cannot specify that a theme moves or is moved to two different goals — each motion event can have only one goal. If there are two goals, there are two different (temporally bounded) events, and a verb can describe only one bounded event (see also Tenny, 1989, who argues that an event can be temporally bounded only once). Thus, the semantic argument of the incorporated preposition *must* be identified with the implied goal, and so cannot be expressed in object position. This means that in a sentence like *Er behebt den Tisch mit den Taschen* 'He *be*-lifts the table with the bags', *den Tisch* must be interpreted as the theme of the verb, so *mit den Taschen* will be interpreted as the instrument, not the theme; the sentence is ungrammatical in the goal-object reading.

In sum, directional verbs do not alternate because they cannot provide the needed goal argument in object position. I assume that this analysis also accounts for why directional verbs do not alternate in other languages. For example, neither English *lift* nor Dutch *tillen* 'lift' can take their goal as direct object: The goal-object reading of both *He lifts the table with the bags* and *Hij betilt de tafel met de tassen* are ungrammatical.

Let us take a look at *which* predicate is incorporated by different directional verbs. The deictic verbs of motion, e.g., *kommen* 'come' and *bringen* 'bring', describe motion to or away from a presupposed place that must be contextually determined. *Kommen*, for example, describes motion to a place that is either the speaker's actual place or the place of someone whose perspective the speaker takes (see also Clark, 1974; Fillmore, 1973, and Miller & Johnson-Laird, 1976). I therefore assume that *kommen* has incorporated a deictic adverb. In German, there is no deictic adverb that captures precisely the properties of the place presupposed in uses of *kommen*, and that could have been incorporated by the verb. The adverb *hier* 'here' is the most plausible candidate, but, unlike *kommen*, *hier* usually requires that the speaker be in the location referred to by this adverb, whereas this is not necessary for using *kommen* (cf. *Ich kann nicht zur Party kommen, aber Peter kommt.* 'I can't come to the party but Peter is coming'). But my argument that *kommen* has incorporated a deictic adverb does not rest on whether German actually has an independent adverb with the same semantic properties as *kommen,* but rather on whether the verb always requires presupposing the existence of a contextually determined location. I therefore assume that *kommen* has incorporated an abstract deictic adverb. This also holds for *gehen* 'go' in its directional sense. As for *bringen,* Clark (1974) and Miller and Johnson-Laird (1976) have proposed that *bring* is the causative form of *come* and means 'cause to come', and this analysis seems also plausible for German. Similarly, *holen* 'get/fetch' can be analyzed as 'go (x) and cause (y) to come'. Thus, both *bringen* and *holen* do not alternate for the same reason that *kommen* and the directional variant of *gehen* do not alternate: They have incorporated an abstract intransitive deictic adverb.

In contrast to the deictic verbs of motion, directional verbs that denote upward or downward motion — for example, *heben* — have incorporated a spatial adjective (*hoch/niedrig-tief* 'high/low'). Partial evidence for the incorporation of an adjective comes from English *lower,* which has incorporated the adjective *low.* As noted earlier, spatial adjectives like *high* and *low* imply the existence of a location since they must be interpreted *relative to a point* on the vertical dimension. But, like spatial adverbs, they cannot express the location syntactically. It seems that whether an object is considered to be high or low on the vertical dimension is determined relative to the original location of the theme; for example, even if I lift a barbell only three inch off the ground, I can still refer to the action as *heben.* This suggests that the meaning of *heben* can best be analyzed as 'cause to be higher' (rather than 'cause to be high').[3]

---

3. My analysis of directional verbs only holds for directional verbs in German. English, for example, has two types of directional verbs, Germanic (e.g., *rise, sink, fall*) and Latinate (e.g., *enter, exit, ascend, descend*) verbs. The verbs of Germanic origin behave like the directional verbs in German, i.e., cannot take the goal as direct object (cf. **He fell the floor*). In contrast, the verbs of Latinate origin do take the goal as direct object, cf. *He entered the building and ascended the stairs.* I assume that these verbs have incorporated a preposition (see Miller & Johnson-Laird, 1976, for a similar proposal). They are thus similar to verbs like *beladen* and the goal-object form of English *load,* which, according to the present analysis, also have incorporated a preposition (Wunderlich, 1987, 1992; cf. Chapter 3).

According to my analysis, children can infer that directional verbs do not alternate as soon as they know that these verbs have incorporated an intransitive spatial predicate. To know this, they must know *that* the verbs have incorporated a spatial predicate, and that the incorporated predicate is *intransitive*. I assume that children can infer that a spatial predicate is incorporated by learning the meanings of the verbs, i.e., this knowledge is entailed by knowledge of the verb meanings, although I can offer no specific account of how they can conclude this without morphological evidence. But, assuming that this assumption is correct, how can children determine that the incorporated predicate is *intransitive*? They can do so on the basis of the syntactic frames the verbs appear in: None of the verbs takes a goal as direct object, so the verbs cannot have incorporated a transitive spatial predicate — they must have incorporated an intransitive predicate. Once children have analysed the verbs in this way, they will automatically know that the verbs do not alternate.

Condition 2. The locative argument must be indivisible with respect to the verbal predicate, and the satisfaction criteria must be met

Löbner's (1990, 1996) Presupposition of Indivisibility and the satisfaction criteria proposed by Wunderlich (1992) are repeated again in (22-23):

(22) **Presupposition of Indivisibility**
Whenever a predicate is applied to one of its arguments, it is true or false of the argument as a whole.

(23) **Satisfaction criteria for the locative alternation**
a. For all y: y is a picture of Johnny Depp $\Rightarrow$ y is on the wall
b. For all z: z is a subregion of the wall $\Rightarrow$ there is a y: y is a picture of Johnny Depp and y is located in z

As stated in (23b), the location or goal referred to by the object NP of a *be*-verb can be conceived of as consisting of several subregions. (23b) explains the behavior of at least one class of nonalternating verbs if we assume that these subregions *may not be ordered* in any particular way, i.e., the sequence in which, e.g., the pictures of Johnny Depp are attached to the wall must be *arbitrary*.

If this assumption is correct, then it explains why causativizable motion verbs like *rollen* 'roll' do not alternate. These verbs denote uncontrolled motion. An entity that moves without control, e.g., a ball rolling down a street, is subject to the physical forces impinging on it, i.e., it cannot change the direction of its motion. This means that the various subregions of the street over which the ball is rolling are not reached in an arbitrary order; rather, their order is determined by the physical forces impinging on the ball. It seems to me, then, that in the majority of motion events described by verbs like *rollen*, the entity is seen as moving along a path. This is why these verbs cannot in general be prefixed with *be-* and take their goal as direct object: A path is an *ordered* series of subregions along which an entity moves. (Of course, controlled motion may likewise follow a path, but it need not; see below, for discussion.)

The role of path can be exemplified on the basis of the verb *schlagen* 'hit/ strike'. The verb may describe motion that does or does not imply a path, as shown in (24a) and (24b), respectively. The *be*-prefixed form of the verb is acceptable only for contexts like those in (24b).

(24) a. Ein Sturm kam auf, und die her-   *Ein Sturm kam auf, und die herunter-
unterfallenden Nüsse schlugen   fallenden Nüsse beschlugen unser Dach.
auf unser Dach.
'A storm rose, and the nuts that   'A storm rose, and the nuts that fell
fell down hit our roof'   down *be*-hit our roof'

    b. Der Dampf schlug gegen die   Der Dampf beschlug die Fensterscheibe.
Fensterscheibe.
'The steam struck the window-pane' 'The steam *be*-struck the window-pane'

The proposed analysis also accounts for why *schlagen* (for example) can take its locative argument as direct object in contexts like (24a) provided it is prefixed with a prepositional prefix rather than with *be-*. In example (17), *Der Dachziegel durchschlug die Fensterscheibe* 'The roof tile *through*-hit the window-pane', the preposition *durch* is incorporated. This preposition denotes a path, so the resulting verb *durchschlagen* requires that the subregions of, e.g., a window-pane be covered in a particular, nonarbitrary order. This corresponds to the type of motion that is at issue in this sentence.

Examples like those in (24) show that it would be incorrect to say that the class of causativizable motion verbs as such does not alternate. Rather, the verbs in this class are especially prone to describe the kind of motion that is incompatible with the requirements of *be*-prefixation, as these are spelled out in Condition 2. Members of this class that can describe motion not implying a path, as *schlagen* does in (24b), will be acceptable as *be*-verbs whenever no path is implied.

Condition 2 also explains why agentive intransitive motion verbs like *wandern* 'wander' may be prefixed with *be-* and take the locative argument as direct object. These verbs denote controlled motion, i.e., the subject NP is both the theme and the agent. These verbs are in principle compatible with the Presupposition of Indivisibility and the satisfaction criteria: If an agent wanders around in a park, he is free to move where he wants to. He may thus cover all relevant subregions of the park and do so in any order that befits him.

How can children determine that the intransitive forms of verbs like *rollen* do not, in general, alternate? To determine that constructions like **Die Billardkugeln*$_{theme}$ *berollen den Billardtisch* 'The billard balls *be*-roll the billard table' are ungrammatical, children must know that the direct arguments of a predicate must be indivisible with respect to the predication, and that the ordering of subregions of the goal or location referred to must be arbitrary. The Presupposition of Indivisibility, on which the satisfaction criteria are based, is a general condition on direct arguments, so children might well already have this knowledge by the time they acquire the locative alternation (perhaps it is even innate). As for the arbitrary ordering of subregions, it seems that children never observe *be*-verbs being used in contexts in which a path is implied, so they have no reason to assume that *be*-verbs describe motion implying a path. But they do have evidence that verbs like *überrollen* '*over*-roll' and *durchschlagen* '*through*-hit' describe motion implying a path — this evidence comes from what they know about the meanings of the corresponding prepositions *über* 'over' and *durch* 'through'. Most plausibly, then, they will conclude that there is a division of labor between *be*-prefixed verbs and verbs prefixed with a prepositional prefix: When no path is at issue, *be*-verbs are used, and when a path is at issue, verbs with a prepositional prefix are used.

Condition 3. The theme must either be specified as a direct argument or be omissable

By definition, locative verbs take a theme. When these verbs take their locative argument as direct object, the theme cannot be expressed in that position, so it must either be expressed in subject position or be omissable. (Intransitive verbs that meet Condition 2 (e.g., *wandern* 'wander') also meet Condition 3, since their theme is specified in subject position.) Let us first look at verbs whose theme is not omissable.

Recall that according to the Nonindividuation Hypothesis, transitive locative verbs allow their theme to be omissable only if they take an incremental theme. Some verbs do not alternate because they do not specify an incremental theme. This has already been shown for *ziehen* 'pull' in Chapter 4, and holds for all other verbs that are, like *ziehen*, accompanied motion verbs. There are two further classes of verbs that do not alternate because they do not take an incremental theme: PRESS verbs like *drücken* 'push/press' and STIR verbs like *schütteln* 'shake'. Since the verbs of these classes do not take an incremental theme, a process reading of the verbs does not render the theme omissable.

Condition 3 does not rule out verbs like *bedrücken* '*be*-press', derived from PRESS verbs, or verbs like *beschütteln* '*be*-stir', derived from STIR verbs, but it determines that the object NP of these verbs is the same as that of the base verbs. These *be*-verbs are — unlike **beschieben* — somewhat acceptable because their base verbs may appear with only one internal argument, which also is the direct object of the *be*-verbs. But *bedrücken* '*be*-press' and *beschütteln* '*be*-shake' cannot describe the motion of an object to a place, since *drücken* and *schütteln* do not take an incremental theme.

How can children determine that the verbs of these three categories do not alternate? By learning the meaning of the verbs (cf. the discussion in 4.2.3 on the kind of learning theories that can explain how children acquire this aspect of a verb's meaning). The semantics they will then associate with the theme arguments will be the semantics of a nonincremental theme, so they will know that the quantificational properties of the verbs' theme cannot be construed as irrelevant when the theme is not specified — which, as I have argued in Chapter 4, is a requirement for using a transitive verb in the goal-object argument structure.

Condition 3 rules out yet another class of verbs, i.e., the *causative* forms of verbs like *rollen* (whose theme must be a bounded entity). Causative *rollen* and similar verbs do not alternate because their theme cannot be deindividuated and omitted. Recall that in order for a transitive verb to take its goal as direct object, the quantificational properties of its theme must be construed as irrelevant for the theme to be omissable. However, causativizable verbs already have — by definition — an omissable argument, the agent. Thus, to interpret *berollen* as derived from the causative form of *rollen* (with the agent as subject and the goal as direct object), a speaker would have to deindividuate and omit the theme even though for *rollen*, it is the agent rather than the theme that is optional.

In contrast, the causative variants of *mass* verbs alternate — cf. *bespritzen* — because the theme of these verbs is already nonindividuated and so can easily be omitted. This is also shown by expletive constructions like *Hier spritzt/ tropft/rieselt es* 'It sprays/drips/drizzles here', where the pronoun *es* 'it' does not refer to the verbs' theme, but is, instead, an expletive pronoun whose sole purpose is to satisfy the syntactic requirement that sentences must have subjects.

How can children determine that the causative forms of verbs like *rollen* do not alternate? I have argued that causative constructions like *Er$_{agent}$ berollt den Billardtisch (mit Kugeln)* 'He *be*-rolls the pool table (with balls)' are ungrammatical because they require deindividuating and omitting the theme even though for these verbs it is the agent rather than the theme that is optional. I assume that children know that the causative forms of *rollen* etc., do not alternate as soon as they know that the agent is only an optional argument.

Condition 4. The verb must describe a process

Recall that, according to the Nonindividuation Hypothesis, transitive locative verbs must be (or be turned into) process predicates in order to be able to incorporate a preposition and take their locative argument as direct object. Maybe the locative alternation can be characterized more generally, for *both* transitive and intransitive verbs, as involving the functional composition of a verbal process predicate with a preposition. If so, then we can immediately account for why intransitive verbs of position cannot take their locative argument as direct object: They do not denote processes.[4] Children can determine that the intransitive verbs of position do not alternate once they know that the verbs do not denote processes.

Condition 5. The topological requirements of the locative alternation must be met

The locative alternation requires that the situation described by the verb have certain topological properties: The location or goal NP must refer to the

---

4. In English, intransitive verbs of position may be used in the progressive (cf. *The picture is hanging on the wall*), which suggests they do have process characteristics after all. I assume therefore that in order to combine with a preposition, a process predicate must specify some kind of *change* taking place over time.

exterior of an object, and the theme must be conceived of as a point-like entity.

As I have noted above, the first of these properties is due to the semantics of the *be*-prefix and so is specific to German (and possibly Dutch), but not English. As was noted in Chapter 3, the prefix requires that the object NP refer to the exterior of an object. The topological properties of INTO verbs like *stopfen* 'stuff' are therefore incompatible with the semantics of the prefix. That is, these verbs meet all the conditions discussed so far except this one — they describe motion only into a container or hollow space, and so are incompatible with the topological restrictions imposed on *be*-verbs by the semantics of the prefix.

How can children determine that the preposition incorporated in the *be*-verb does not correspond to the preposition *in*? They can do so because they hardly ever observe an association between *be*- and containers. Almost every time a child hears a sentence with a *be*-verb and figures out what it means, there is a spatial relationship between theme and goal that has to do with a surface, so she comes to associate *be*- with surface relationships only. That is, if she never observes a *be*-verb used to describe motion into a container, she has no reason to assume that *be*-verbs *could* describe motion into a container.[5]

But recall that a few *be*-verbs specify activities or events that can also be described by the base form of the *be*-verb and a PP headed by *in*: *befüllen* 'fill', *bewohnen* 'live in', *betreten* 'enter', and *besteigen* (as in *in den Bus steigen* 'climb into a bus'). Will these not suggest to the child that the preposition incorporated in *be*-verbs also encompasses relationships of containment? I think that these verbs are too idiosyncratic to suggest any systematic pattern. *Wohnen* 'live in a place' — the base verb of *bewohnen* — does not specify the (current) location of a person, but rather a habitual or institutional relationship between a person and a place that is independent of the person's current location (for example, I can live in Berlin but be currently in the U.S.). It seems legitimate, then, to assume that the child will not let her generaliza-

---

5. This account presupposes that children do not hypothesize semantic categories for lexical items that go far beyond what they have evidence for. Support for this assumption comes from research on semantic learning. Dromi (1987), for example, has shown that children only rarely overextend lexical items to semantic categories not observed in the input; mostly their categories are narrower than those of the target language, or about the right size. The assumption that children do not typically overextend semantic categories is also related to Pinker's (1989) notion of class-wise conservatism (cf. 2.5).

tions about *be*-prefixation be influenced by her analysis of *bewohnen*. *Betreten* is lexicalized, in that it can be used in only a few of the contexts in which *treten* 'step/kick' may be used. Unprefixed *treten* can be used in constructions like *jemandem gegen das Schienbein treten* 'kick someone's shin', *in die Matsche treten* 'step in the mud', and *in das Zimmer/auf die Bühne treten* 'enter the room/go onto the stage'. But *betreten* can only be used in contexts like the last, in which the agent changes location by making one or more steps. In these contexts, *treten* and *betreten* do not mean the same thing. *Treten* is a somewhat stilted way of saying that someone enters, e.g., a room, while *betreten* typically highlights the trespassing aspects associated with going to a place (as in signs like *Betreten verboten* 'Do not enter'). I assume, then, that the child will not attempt to analyse *betreten* on the basis of what she knows about *treten*. *Besteigen* '*be*-climb' is mostly used in contexts in which the object NP refers to the exterior of an object, as in *einen Berg besteigen* 'climb a mountain'. When the verb's object NP refers to cars or similar objects, the verb may therefore invite the child to reconceptualize the referent of the object NP as providing a surface to be mounted rather than suggesting that *be*- encompasses *in*-relationships as well. But arguing that reconceptualization takes place is somewhat ad hoc: Why would the child not be equally likely to take the existence of constructions like *das Auto besteigen* 'climb the car' as evidence that *be*-verbs can describe motion into a container or hollow space? Whether or not the 'surface' reconceptualization actually takes place, it seems unlikely that the child will take the existence of constructions like *das Auto besteigen* as evidence that *be*-verbs in general can correspond to *in*-PPs in addition to *auf*- and *an*-PPs. After all, there is only a single *be*-verb that unambiguously describes *in*-relationships, i.e., *befüllen* '*be*-fill'.

Be-verbs have yet to meet another topological requirement, i.e., that the theme be conceived of as a point-like entity. This restriction has not been motivated by what has been said about the locative alternation (in German and in other languages) in the preceding chapters. Rather, I would like to propose this restriction in view of the behavior of causative verbs of position.

Causative verbs of position provide perhaps the best example to demonstrate the role of contextual conditions. It seems that these verbs can alternate if they specify that the theme is attached to the goal object, and if the theme can be conceived of as a point (and so be a true 'figure' in the sense of Talmy, 1983). The verbs *kleben* 'glue' and *pappen* 'stick' specify a particular kind of attachment rather than a position (cf. 6.2), and they alternate freely. *Hängen* 'hang' and *stecken* 'stick' also always involve attachment. According to my intuition, *behängen* can be used in contexts in which the theme is coextensive with the goal like *Sie behängte die Wand mit Bildern* 'She *be*-hung the wall with pictures'; it is less acceptable in attachment contexts like ?*Sie behängte die Wäscheleine mit Handtüchern* 'She *be*-hung the clothes-line with towels', in which it is hard to ignore the vertical orientation of the theme. The kind of attachment required for *stecken* is usually in conflict with the topological requirements of the *be*-prefix (because it involves an *into* relation), but the verb alternates when the goal can be conceived of as a surface and the theme as a point, as in *Er besteckte den Hut mit Abzeichen* 'He *be*-stuck the hat with badges'; *bestecken* is less felicitous with a vertically extended theme, e.g., feathers — cf. ?*Er besteckte den Hut mit Federn* 'He *be*-stuck the hat with feathers'. Those cases in which *besetzen* '*be*-set' describes a spatial relation (so that its relationship to *setzen* 'set' is still transparent), e.g., *Sie besetzte ihre Jacke mit Perlen* 'She *be*-set her jacket with pearls' also suggest that a positional verb alternates only if attachment to the goal is specified and if the theme can be conceived of as a point — objects like pearls cannot have, after all, the position canonically associated with sitting.

The requirement that the theme be conceived of as a point explains why *stellen* 'make stand' and *lehnen* 'make lean' do not alternate: The position encoded by these verbs requires the theme to be vertically extended, which conflicts with the need to conceive of it as a point.

How can children determine whether a causative verb of position alternates? If my analysis is correct, then children need to know that the theme must be conceived of as a point. At the moment, I cannot offer a satisfying account for how children can find this out.

Condition 6. Pragmatically, it must make sense to use the goal-object form of a verb

This condition accounts for why *schmettern* 'fling/bang' is not a good candidate for the locative alternation. Compared to the more neutral verb *werfen* 'throw', *schmettern* provides *additional* manner information about *how* an object is thrown. This extra information renders the verb incompatible with the goal-object form: Choice of the goal-object form suggests that the speaker wants to focus on the goal, but choice of a verb that provides additional manner information over a more neutral verb suggests that she wants to focus on the theme.

As far as acquisition is concerned, there is no need for children to determine that verbs like *schmettern* do not alternate. Once they know the pragmatic reasons for using the goal-object form of a verb, and one they know the reason for using *schmettern* instead of *werfen*, they will, like adults, usually see no reason to use *schmettern* in the goal-object argument structure.

Summary of Reasons Why Some Verbs Fail to Participate in the Locative Alternation in German

In this and the preceding section, I have described and analyzed the locative verbs that do not participate in the locative alternation in German. Most verbs could be shown not to alternate because they fail to meet conditions that, according to the analysis of the alternation presented in Chapters 3 and 4, are essential to the alternation. Directional verbs do not alternate because they have incorporated an intransitive spatial predicate and so cannot take the locative argument as direct object. The Presupposition of Indivisibility provides a general condition on direct arguments (Löbner, 1990, 1996); together with the satisfaction criteria for *be*-verbs (Wunderlich, 1992), it rules out the goal-object form of *rollen* verbs. The topological restriction on *be*-verbs (which rules out the goal-object form of INTO verbs) was shown to be relevant for alternating verbs as well. (e.g., *das Auto bepacken* '*be*-pack the car' is fine but *den Kofferraum bepacken* '*be*-pack the trunk' is bad, cf. 3.1). Another condition that has been argued to be essential for the alternation is that a verb must provide a process predicate and that the quantificational properties of the theme of a transitive verb must be irrelevant, as I have proposed in my Nonindividuation Hypothesis in Chapter 4. The Nonindividuation Hypothesis explains the syntactic restrictions on several classes of nonalternating verbs: 1) accompanied motion verbs like *schieben* 'push' and the PRESS and STIR verbs do not specify an incremental theme, which means that under a process reading the quantificational properties of the theme do not become irrelevant; 2) intransitive verbs of position like *sitzen* do not alternate because they do not denote processes; and 3) the causative forms of verbs like *rollen* do not alternate because they require deindividuating and omitting the theme of a verb for which it is the agent rather than the theme that is optional. The Nonindividuation Hypothesis thus has shown itself to be empirically fruitful.

The behavior of only one class of nonalternating verbs could not be accounted for by principles shown to be essential for how the alternation works: Causativized verbs of position like *stellen* 'make stand'. I have argued that these verbs of position alternate only if the theme can be conceived of as a point.

I will refer to the claim that nonalternating verbs differ in which necessary condition they fail to meet as the Internal Structure Hypothesis. In the next chapter, I will present a comprehension experiment that tested one particular prediction of the Internal Structure Hypothesis: that children should not be able to interpret the object NP as the goal when the *be*-verb is derived from a directional verb.

Chapter 7

The Comprehension Experiment: Testing Children's Interpretations of *be*-Verbs

This chapter presents an experiment that tested children's interpretations of both grammatical and ungrammatical *be*-verbs. The grammatical *be*-verbs were derived from alternating mass and count verbs. These verbs served to further test the claim of the Nonindividuation Hypothesis that *be*-verbs derived from mass verbs are acquired earlier than *be*-verbs derived from count verbs (cf. Chapter 4). The ungrammatical *be*-verbs were derived from different categories of nonalternating verbs (cf. Chapter 6). These verbs served to test one particular prediction of the Internal Structure Hypothesis: that children should not be able to interpret the object NP as the goal when the *be*-verb is derived from a directional verb.

Directional verbs fail to meet the first, most basic, condition for participating in the locative alternation, the one that defines the alternation: that the locative argument must become the verb's object NP. To test this prediction of the Internal Structure Hypothesis, we must know if children will interpret the object NP of a novel *be*-verb as the verb's goal (or, more inclusively, as the locative argument) less often when the *be*-verb is based on a directional verb than when it is based on a verb that fails to alternate for a less fundamental reason, one that becomes relevant only after the goal has made its way to the direct object position. I therefore also included ungrammatical *be*-verbs that are derived from a causativizable motion verb (e.g., *bekullern* 'be-wobble'). The intransitive forms of causativizable motion verbs do not meet Condition 2 — the requirement that ensures that if the locative argument is the direct object, it must be indivisible with respect to the verbal predicate, and the order in which its various subregions are involved in the motion described by the verbal predicate must be arbitrary. The transitive counterparts of these verbs do not meet Condition 3, the requirement that the theme be expressed in subject position or be omissable. The Internal Structure Hypothesis predicts that children who know the meaning of the base verbs will more often fail to analyze the direct object as a locative argument for **beheben* 'be-lift' verbs than for **bekullern* 'be-wobble' verbs. As a further test of the prediction that only directional verbs fail to provide the needed locative argument in object position, three additional ungrammatical be-verbs were included: two derived from an accompanied motion verb (which do not meet Condition 3) and one from the verb *schmettern* 'bang/smash' (which does not meet Condition 6).

To test the Nonindividuation Hypothesis and the Internal Structure Hypothesis, I asked children a series of questions of the type "What are some things you can be-verb?" This question focusses on the referent of a verb's object NP, so children's answers should reveal what they take the object NP of a given be-verb to be.

The experiment was preceded by two pretests: one to assess children's knowledge of be-prefixation, and the other to test their knowledge of the meaning of the nonalternating verbs to be used in constructing ungrammatical be-verbs. (I use the phrase 'knowledge of be-prefixation' as shorthand for *knowledge of the syntactic effects BE-prefixation has on the argument structure of the base verb.*) According to my analyses (Chapter 6), nonalternating verbs do not alternate because of the particular way in which their semantics clash with the structural changes induced by be-prefixation. To test the Internal Structure Hypothesis, I therefore needed subjects who knew the meanings of the nonalternating verbs included in the study. But subjects also had to have acquired knowledge of be-prefixation. If they had not, we would not know whether their responses were due to a failure to analyze the be-prefix at all, or reflected the semantic properties of the nonalternating verbs.

7.1 The Experiment

7.1.1 *Subjects and Setting*[1]

Seventy-one elementary school children participated in the comprehension experiment: 12 children (4 boys, 8 girls) aged 6;9 to 7;11 (mean 7;5); 16 children (6 boys, 10 girls) aged 8;0 to 8;10 (mean 8;6); 24 children (10 boys, 14 girls) aged 9;0 to 9;11 (mean 9;7); 19 children (8 boys, 11 girls) aged 10;0

---

1. See Appendix 2 for my assumptions about the optimal age of subjects for the experiment.

to 11;10 (mean 10;6). Sixty-nine children lived in Kleve and two in Goch, two towns in Northrhine-Westfalia (the northwestern part of Germany). All subjects were native speakers of German.[2]

The two pretests and the main task were applied in a single session, which lasted about 40 minutes. The pretest assessing children's knowledge of *be*-prefixation (cf. 7.1.2) was applied first, followed by the pretest that assessed their knowledge of the meaning of the nonalternating verbs (cf. 7.1.3). The main task, which tested their interpretations of questions containing grammatical and ungrammatical *be*-verbs (cf. 7.1.4), immediately followed the pretests. Each child was tested individually. The children from Kleve were tested in a room in an elementary school, and those from Goch in the home of one of the children.

7.1.2 *Pretest I: Assessing Children's Knowledge of* BE-*Prefixation*

I assume that knowledge of *be*-prefixation consists of at least three parts:

(1) A *be*-verb takes its locative argument as direct object
(2) *Be*-verbs have incorporated a two-place prepositional predicate (Wunderlich, 1992; cf. Chapter 3)
(3) The incorporated preposition conjoins with a process predicate (cf. Chapter 4)

The pretest assessed this knowledge indirectly by testing whether children were able to interpret the object NP of a regular *be*-verb as the goal of the verb. The *be*-verbs that were used in the pretest were derived from transitive verbs to make them maximally comparable to the *be*-verbs to be used in the main task, which were based on transitive verbs or verbs that have a transitive variant (the causative verbs).

How can we establish whether children know that the direct object of a verb prefixed with *be*- must be the goal and not the theme? A stringent test is to determine whether they can interpret a *be*-verb correctly even when this interpretation conflicts with what they know about the action and the typical

---

2. As in the production experiment, I did not obtain information about whether the children were bilingual and/or spoke the dialect of the Kleve area in addition to High German. If differences in their linguistic background had influenced their behavior in the experiment, this would have increased the variance in the group, thus making it more difficult to obtain any systematic effect. To the extent that a systematic effect was obtained (see Section 7.4), differences in the linguistic background of children may be considered irrelevant.

themes and goals it involves. Such a conflict arises when the referent of the object NP is a typical theme for the verb but an atypical goal, as in 'He *be*-loads the hay' and 'She *be*-smears the paint'. In German, the prefix unambiguously signals that the hay and the paint are to be interpreted as the goal objects, even though these entities are more likely to be the themes in typical actions of loading and smearing. But it is not enough to present children with just any situation in which, for example, paint is the goal entity for an action of smearing. For example, if a boy smears dirt onto a freshly painted wall, it is fairly evident that the paint is the goal and not the theme. The interpretation of the prefix can best be tested if the action involves two entities that are equally likely to be the theme of the verb, but one of which happens to be the goal. In this case, the child must take the *be*-prefix into account in order to respond correctly. To assess the subjects' knowledge of *be*-prefixation, then, I designed a picture selection task that allowed me to bring the correct interpretation of the verb into conflict with the typical understanding of the action.

The Choice of Drawings

Two sets of drawings were constructed, each set containing eight individual 21cm x 15cm pictures that depicted the same action. The pictures in set A depicted actions of smearing, those of set B actions of pouring. The entities involved in smearing were paint, and those involved in pouring were juice. The themes and goals of a given picture set differed only in color. There were four colors per set, each color marking a goal twice and a theme twice across the eight pictures.

The eight smearing pictures of set A showed a boy sitting at a table with two pots of paint next to him. The two pots contained paint of different colors, corresponding to the theme and the goal of that picture. For example, a big blotch of grey paint was already spread out on a large sheet on the table, and the boy was smearing yellow paint over this blotch with his hands. The eight pouring pictures of set B showed a woman pouring some colored liquid from a pitcher into a flat bowl. The bowl already contained some liquid, which thus was the goal.

Procedure

Before the pictures of a given set were presented, the child was shown an independent 21cm x 31cm drawing that introduced the entities relevant for that particular set — four pots of paint or four pitchers of liquid. As the experimenter, I introduced each set by specifying the substances and their colors, and telling the child that these substances were relevant to the task to follow.

The introductory picture was then put away, and the 8 pictures of the set were arranged in front of the child so that he or she could inspect each of them with equal ease. The child's task was to respond to a number of instructions about the pictures. For example, for the pictures depicting *pouring (schütten),* the instructions were formulated as follows (I give the full text of the instructions for reasons that will become clear shortly):

(1) Zeige auf alle Bilder, auf denen der blaue Saft **be**schüttet wird. 'Point to all the pictures where the blue juice gets *be*-poured'
(2) Zeige auf alle Bilder, auf denen der gelbe Saft **be**schüttet wird. 'Point to all the pictures where the yellow juice gets *be*-poured'
(3) Zeige auf alle Bilder, auf denen der rote Saft **ge**schüttet wird. 'Point to all the pictures where the red juice gets *ge*-poured'
(4) Zeige auf alle Bilder, auf denen der Junge den braunen Saft schüttet. 'Point to all the pictures where the boy is pouring the brown juice'

The first two instructions tested whether children were able to correctly pick out the goal, and the last two tested whether they had correctly picked out the goal in response to the first two instructions only because the pictures were somehow unusual and so called for an unusual response.

The relative clause focussing on either the theme or the goal was formulated in the passive voice in the first three instructions, and in the active voice in the fourth instruction. In the active voice, *schütten* differs from *beschütten* in its number of syllables. Thus, if the active voice had been used throughout, the children might have responded correctly to the first two instructions only because they had noticed that the base verb was somehow changed, suggesting that an unusual response was called for, but not because they had correctly interpreted the prefix. The use of the passive in the first three instructions solved the problem of different numbers of syllables between *schütten* and *beschütten*, since the past participle of both the unprefixed and *be*-prefixed versions of the verb consists of a prefix plus the verb stem: **ge**schüttet for *schütten*, and **be**schüttet for *beschütten*. The participles in the first two instructions thus differed from that in the third only in their initial phoneme. In the third instruction (which, together with the fourth, served as a control), the base verb appeared in the passive voice in order to establish whether the children were able to switch to the correct theme interpretation merely on the basis of information about the prefix. If they were, the fourth instruction was skipped.[3]

Initially, I had intended to instruct children orally about what they should do. But in pilot testing, many more children than I had expected failed to respond correctly. That is, when I asked them to pick out the pictures in which, e.g., the red juice was getting *be*-poured, many children pointed to the pictures in which the red juice got *ge*-poured (i.e., they interpreted red juice as the theme). I was afraid that the children might simply not have noticed the prefix. To make this less likely, I decided to write the instructions down and have the child read each question aloud to me.

Each instruction was hand-written on an individual 10cm x 7cm card. The four cards for a picture set were stacked in front of the child, with the text facing down. The child was asked to pick up the topmost card and read it aloud. The youngest children, who were in their first year of school, sometimes had difficulty reading the text, so we read the card together. (The experiment took place at the end of the school year, so the children had already had some experience with reading.) Having subjects read the instructions had the additional advantage over the oral instructions that I could correct the children if they misread the text. In this way, I could be certain that their incorrect responses were not due to their not having noticed the *be*-prefix. Moreover, the requirement of reading the instructions meant that the children needed more time to understand what was expected of them, and so were less likely to rush into action and perhaps make a mistake unnecessarily.

The order of presentation of the picture sets was counterbalanced across subjects. The subjects' responses were recorded on a prepared response sheet.

---

3. Being designed to test whether children truly responded to the *be*-prefix, and not just to some change on the verb, the instructions became quite complex linguistically: They contained the passive forms of verbs and, in addition, relative clauses. Children may have therefore failed the pretest simply because the instructions were too difficult for them, but not because they did not know how to interpret the *be*-prefix. Accordingly, the pretest used in this experiment may have been overly conservative. Its results should therefore not be taken as evidence for when children learning German acquire *be*-prefixation but only as one means of ensuring that the children who *did* pass the pretest had acquired that knowledge. (I will return to the problem of an overly conservative pretest when discussing the results of the experiment.)

Results of the Pretest 'Knowledge of BE-Prefixation'

In order to pass the first pretest and be credited with knowledge of *be*-prefixation, children had to respond correctly to the first two questions of a picture set and also to either the third or the fourth question. The results are shown in Table 1, broken down by age. Eighteen of the 71 children did not pass the criterion, 13 of them because they did not select a goal picture for either of the two sets, and 5 because they did so for only one set. These subjects, 9 girls and 9 boys (6;9 to 10;10 years of age) could not be credited with sufficient knowledge of *be*-prefixation. Surprisingly, these children were not among the youngest subjects: Their mean age was 9;0 years. The 53 children who passed the pretest, 19 boys and 34 girls, were aged between 7;0 and 11;10 years; their mean age was 9;4 years.

7.1.3 Pretest II: Assessing Children's Knowledge of the Meaning of the Nonalternating Verbs

I assume that the nonalternating verbs included in the study do not alternate because of the particular way in which their semantics clash with the structural changes induced by *be*-prefixation. To test the predictions of the Internal Structure Hypothesis, I therefore had to make sure that the subjects knew the meanings of the nonalternating verbs included in the study: directional, causative, and accompanied motion verbs, and *schmettern*. These verbs were presented to children in the main task as ungrammatical *be*-verbs (e.g., **beheben*, **bewirbeln*). In selecting the nonalternating verbs, I took into account properties of both the base verbs and the resulting **be*-verbs.

Table 1: Number of subjects per age group who passed and failed Pretest 1

	AGE				
PRETEST I	6;9-7;11 (n=12)	8;0-8;10 (n=16)	9;0-9;11 (n=24)	10;10-11;10 (n=19)	total
pass	7	12	19	15	53
fail	5	4	5	4	18

Criteria for Selecting the Nonalternating Verbs

The base verbs had to correspond semantically as closely as possible to alternating verbs. For example, *fällen* 'fell' (= 'cause to fall') is a directional verb, but it is never used with a directional PP; therefore, *fällen* was not a good candidate for a **be*-verb since all the alternating motion verbs do take a directional PP. I also had to consider whether prefixing a candidate nonalternating verb with *be-* might result in a verb that is phonologically identical to some existing *be*-verb. For example, *rollen* 'roll' was not a candidate causative verb for the experiment because *berollen* exists as a grammatical *be*-verb: *berollen* is derived from the noun *Rolle* 'roller' and specifies the activity of painting a surface with a roller. A further criterion for selecting a verb was that it should be fairly common and likely to be known by children.

Two causative verbs of motion, 2 directional verbs, and 3 other non-alternating verbs were used for constructing the ungrammatical *be*-verbs. The causative verbs were *kullern* 'wobble' and *wirbeln* 'whirl'. Selecting the directional verbs was difficult since there are only few. I chose the verbs *heben* 'lift' and *senken* 'lower' because they are likely to be known by children and because they specify opposite directions. However, each of the verbs is problematic in some respects. The problem with *heben* is that it exists as a grammatical *be*-verb, *beheben*, which is used in idiomatic constructions like *einen Schaden beheben* 'remove a damage' (cf. Chapter 6). I assumed that children were not likely to know this *be*-verb, and that they would try to interpret **beheben* as a regular *be*-verb if the context invited them to do so. *Senken* is the causativized form of an intransitive verb, *sinken* 'sink'. It would be better if the directional verbs were not causativized variants of intransitive verbs, since this confounds the effects of directionality with those of causativization. However, in German, all transitive verbs specifying downward direction are derived from intransitive verbs: *Fällen* 'fell' is derived from *fallen* 'fall', and *tauchen* 'dip' comes from the phonologically identical *tauchen* 'dive'. Since *fällen* could not be used because it cannot take a PP, only *senken* remained.

I included three instead of two additional nonalternating verbs since I had not yet classified all nonalternating verbs at that time and I wanted to test the waters. As base verbs for these additional *be*-verbs, I used *schmettern* 'bang/smash', *schleppen* 'drag', and *schieben* 'push'. As noted in Chapter 6, *schmettern* does not fit into any of the six nonalternating verb classes I have identified. The verb emphasizes the particular manner in which an object is thrown, and it does not alternate because it would be pragmatically odd to defocus the theme in favor of the goal for a verb that emphasizes how the theme is caused to move. *Schleppen* and *schieben* are both accompanied motion verbs (cf. Chapter 6). The three types of nonalternating verbs included in the experiment are summarized in Table 2, along with frequency information about the base verbs taken from the CELEX database (see 5.2.2, for a description of the CELEX database).

The table shows that the directional verbs are much more frequent than the causative verbs. This may be problematic because it suggests that the subjects will have observed the correct theme-object argument structure of *heben* and *senken* more often than that of *kullern* and *wirbeln*, and so may be more reluctant to treat *beheben* and *besenken* as true *be*-verbs than *bekullern* and *bewirbeln*. However, the accompanied motion verbs *schleppen* and *schieben* are, like the directional verbs, much more frequent than the causative verbs. If amount of experience with the theme-object form of a nonalternating verb is indeed an important determinant of whether children treat its ungrammatical *be*-verb counterpart as a true *be*-verb, then subjects should be about as unwilling to interpret *beschieben* and *beschleppen* as true *be*-verbs as *beheben* and *besenken*. So if it turns out that — as predicted by the Internal Structure Hypothesis — *beschieben* and *beschleppen* (whose base verbs are frequent) are interpreted as *be*-verbs about as often as *bekullern* and *bewirbeln* (whose base verbs are infrequent), and more often than *beheben* and *besenken*, then we can safely assume that subjects' interpretations of the ungrammatical *be*-verbs of the two types do not just reflect relative amount of experience with the correct

Table 2: Nonalternating verbs used in Pretest II and in the main task, with frequency per 6,000,000 tokens

Causative Verbs	*kullern — *bekullern* 'wobble'	9
	*wirbeln — *bewirbeln* 'whirl'	39
Directional Verbs	*heben — *beheben* 'lift'	85
	*senken — *besenken* 'lower'	269
Control Verbs	*schmettern — *beschmettern* 'bang/smash'	11
	*schleppen — *beschleppen* 'drag'	137
	*schieben — *beschieben* 'push'	367

theme-object argument structure of the base verbs, but rather the influence of the specific semantic properties of verbs.

The Design of the Pretest

How can we assess whether children know the meaning of the nonalternating verbs included in the study? By determining whether they know the necessary conditions that an event must satisfy in order to count as an instance of the action or motion denoted by the verb. (In what follows, I will use the term 'action' to refer both to actions in the narrower sense as events involving an agent, and to motions.) For each of the seven nonalternating verbs to be used in the experiment, I specified what I took to be its necessary conditions (see below), and then videotaped actions that did or did not meet these conditions. (The extent to which other adult speakers of German agreed with my judgments is discussed shortly.) The child's task was to accept or reject each scene as a proper example of the action described by the verb.

For example, for the accompanied motion verb *schleppen* 'drag', I specified two necessary conditions: An agent carries a heavy object with effort, and keeps hold of the object throughout. A child who knows the meaning of *schleppen* should reject an action as an instance of *schleppen* if it does not satisfy one or both of these conditions, for example, if the object is so light that it is carried without much effort, or if the agent moves the object by releasing it from her hands.

The necessary conditions for the remaining verbs were defined as follows. For the causative verb *kullern* 'wobble', I specified two necessary conditions: An object must rotate irregularly around the longer of its two axes (*Längsachse*), and it must move or be caused to move without controlling the motion. An action is not an instance of *kullern* if an object that moves over the ground either rolls smoothly or does not turn around its axis (e.g., slides), if it moves through the air, or if it is turned under the continuous control of an agent. For *wirbeln* 'whirl', I assumed that an object must move through the air, turn around both of its axes, and move or be caused to move without controlling the motion. An action is not an instance of *wirbeln* if an object moves and turns around its axes but stays on the ground, if it moves through the air but only turns around one axis, or if it is turned around its axes under the continuous control of an agent. I decided that for the two causative verbs, children had to accept only the positive instance in which the object moved without external influence. They were then credited with knowing that, e.g., *wirbeln* is an intransitive verb that denotes a particular kind of uncontrolled motion, and it was considered irrelevant whether they also knew that the verb can be causativized to specify that an agent causes the object to move. This knowledge should be sufficient for them to be able to infer that **bewirbeln*, for example, is ungrammatical, since **bewirbeln* is ungrammatical regardless of whether it is taken to be derived from the intransitive form of the verb or from its causative, transitive form.

Heben 'lift' was defined as requiring an object to be taken off a (more or less) horizontal surface and moved upwards. An action is not an instance of *heben* if the object is moved downwards or laterally without being taken off the surface. *Senken* was defined as requiring an object to be moved downwards under the continuous control of an agent. Thus, if an object is dropped, is moved upwards, or is moved laterally, the action is not an instance of *senken*.

Schmettern 'smash/fling' was defined as requiring that an agent act on an object with his hands, imparting a lot of energy and thereby causing the object to move through the air and hit a surface hard. If an object is moved up into the air instead of against an object, or hits a surface without high impact, or is kicked, or simply drops onto another object with high impact, then the action is not an instance of *schmettern*. Finally, the accompanied motion verb *schieben* 'push' was defined as specifying that an agent imparts force to an object such that it moves away from her. An action is not an instance of *schieben* if the agent moves the object towards herself.

On the basis of these definitions, I decided on a series of actions that either satisfied the necessary conditions, and so were positive instances of a given verb, or that violated one necessary condition and were negative instances. The number of scenes needed per verb varied depending on how many necessary conditions there were to be violated and on whether one or two positive instances were shown. Each action was videotaped, with each scene lasting for about 6 seconds. All actions involving an agent were performed by a young woman.[4] Table 3 gives a summary and overview of the actions. A detailed description of these scenes is given in Appendix 5. The bold-faced labels immediately to the right of the verbs refer to the positive instances, i.e., to those instances which should be accepted by the child, and to the right of these are the labels referring to the negative instances, i.e., those that should be rejected.

The scenes testing a particular verb appeared one right after another, with positive and negative instances presented in random order, with the

---

4. I am grateful to Christy Bowerman for serving as the main actress in the videos.

Table 3: Summary of the actions used for assessing children's knowledge of the meanings of the nonalternating verbs in Pretest II

	ACTIONS					
VERBS	POSITIVE INSTANCES		NEGATIVE INSTANCES			
kullern 'wobble'	MOTION ONLY egg wobbles over carpet	MOTION+CAUSE egg caused to wobble	FLY egg flies thru air	SLIDE egg slides over carpet	ROLL egg rolls over carpet	TURN egg turned under cont. control
wirbeln 'whirl'	MOTION ONLY hat flies, turns around its axes	MOTION+CAUSE hat caused to fly and turn around its axes	TURN hat turned under cont. control	SPIN hat flies, turning only around horiz. axis		
heben 'lift'	LIFT stick is lifted		LOWER stick is lowered	PUSH stick is moved to new location, no lifting		
senken 'lower'	LOWER stick is lowered onto table	LOWER stick is lowered into bottle	PUSH stick is moved to new location, no lowering	DROP stick is dropped		LIFT stick is lifted
schleppen 'drag'	DRAG big sack is dragged over ground		SWING big sack is swung to new location	CARRY big sack is carried		
schmettern 'smash'	BOUNCE OFF ball smashed against wall, bouncing off	STAY ON WALL ball smashed against wall, remaining there	THROW ball thrown against wall, bouncing off	KICK ball kicked against wall, bouncing off	INTO AIR ball flung into air	FALL ball drops onto table, bounces off
schieben 'push'	PUSH cup pushed away from agent		PULL cup pulled toward agent			

qualification that the two positive instances of *kullern*, *wirbeln*, and *senken* did not appear in immediate succession. In addition to the seven test sets, there were three warm-up sets used to introduce the task. The films were always shown in the same order.[5]

---

5. The warm-up sets showed instances of *schneiden* 'cut', *gießen* 'pour', and *schreiben* 'write', in this order. The positive and negative instances of these verbs could be discriminated very easily. In the first scene testing cutting, the woman was jumping up and down, in the second she was tearing a sheet of paper apart, and in the third she was cutting a sheet of paper into pieces. The first scene testing pouring showed the woman drinking some liquid from a cup, and the

As in the videotapes for the elicited production experiment, each scene was preceded by a grey screen lasting for six seconds. The screen gave the same warning signal as in the production task — a white circle appearing in its center for about 625 msec (15 frames). After the warning signal, the grey screen appeared again for about 460 msec (11 frames) before the next scene started. Before the set of scenes testing the next verb started, there was a pause of 11 seconds, which again contained the same warning signal. The complete tape lasted about 8 minutes.

Adult Ratings

The definitions of necessary conditions for the verbs, and the selection of positive and negative instances, were based on my native-speaker intuitions about their meanings. To get a more objective evaluation, I asked a group of 31 high school students, all native speakers of German, to rate the scenes (presented in the order described above). They watched the films together in a single session, which lasted about 10 minutes. The films were shown on a large TV monitor standing in plain view on the upper shelf of a tall cabinet in the front of the room. Students rated the films individually, recording their judgments on a prepared response sheet. Each row of the sheet represented a different verb, ordered from top to bottom in the test sequence. Below each verb was printed a row of 6 *yes/no* pairs, so that the raters only needed to mark one member of a pair. Although only about a third of the scenes required 6 judgments, 6 response pairs were shown for all the verbs so that the raters could not predict from the number of pairs left how many judgments still had to be given. (This prevented raters' judging a scene as, for example, a positive instance of a verb only because they knew that it was the last scene to appear and because they hadn't accepted any of the prior scenes.)

The results of the rating are shown in Table 4. The percentages shown below the raw frequencies show the percentage of *no*-responses for scenes that I had classified as positive instances (bold-faced), and the percentage of *yes*-responses for the scenes that I had classified as negative instances — i.e., they show ratings that deviate from my own classifications.

---

second showed her pouring water from a tea kettle into a cup. In the first scene testing writing, the woman was putting several small foam balls into a bag, in the second she was writing on a sheet of paper, and in the third she was reading a book.

Table 4: Adult ratings of the actions used in Pretest II to assess children's knowledge of the meaning of the nonalternating verbs

	ACTIONS					
VERBS	POSITIVE INSTANCES		NEGATIVE INSTANCES			
kullern 'wobble'	MOTION ONLY	MOTION+CAUSE	FLY	SLIDE	ROLL	TURN
yes	30	25	0	1	18	1
no	1	6	31	30	13	30
%	3	19	0	3	58	3
wirbeln 'whirl'	MOTION ONLY	MOTION+CAUSE	TURN	SPIN		
yes	28	29	5	2		
no	3	2	26	29		
%	10	7	16	7		
heben 'lift'	LIFT		LOWER	PUSH		
yes	31		2	0		
no	0		29	31		
%	0		7	0		
senken 'lower'	LOWER-TO-TABLE	LOWER-INTO-BOTTLE	PUSH	DROP	LIFT	
yes	25	31	0	1	0	
no	6	0	31	30	31	
%	19	0	0	3	0	
schleppen 'drag'	DRAG		SWING	CARRY		
yes	31		0	1		
no	0		31	30		
%	0		0	3		
schmettern 'smash'	BOUNCE OFF	STAY ON WALL	THROW	KICK	INTO AIR	FALL
yes	29	26	0	2	5	3
no	2	5	31	29	26	28
%	7	16	0	7	16	10
schieben 'push'	PUSH		PULL			
yes	31		0			
no	0		31			
%	0		0			

The adults agreed with my classification of the scenes testing *heben*, *schleppen*, and *schieben*. This suggests that these scenes sufficiently discriminate between positive and negative instances of the verbs. But there is disagreement on some of the other verbs. Most strikingly, more than half the subjects found the negative instance 'roll' for *kullern*, which shows a ball rolling smoothly over the ground, to be an acceptable representation of the verb's meaning. Accordingly, I excluded this scene as a test of knowledge about the meaning of *kullern* in my analysis of the children's responses. Less clear are those cases in which 5 (16%) or 6 adults (19%) disagreed with my classification. Instead of setting an arbitrary criterion for when disagreement between the adults' classification and my own is sufficient to exclude a given scene from the analysis, I chose to decide on these scenes case by case in a theoretically motivated way. I explain decisions in Appendix 5.

Procedure

The children saw the films individually, immediately after the first pretest. The tape was shown on a middle-sized color TV monitor, and was started and stopped via remote control. The children sat about 1 1/2m away from the monitor, next to me, the experimenter, with a table between us. They were told that they would see a series of films and should tell the experimenter whether each film showed an instance of a particular action. The experimenter explained that they could see each film again if they weren't sure, and could take their time to decide. They were then shown the warm-up sets and were asked, after the last one, whether they knew what they were supposed to do. Many subjects were at first afraid that the task would be too difficult or that the films would pass by too quickly. But while watching the warm-up sets they usually discovered that they needn't worry. Their answers were recorded on a prepared response sheet.

Results of the Pretest 'Verb Knowledge'

To pass this second pretest, children had to appropriately accept or reject given scenes as representations of the action denoted by a verb. Table 5 summarizes the results of this pretest. Labels referring to scenes that will be excluded from the analyses on the basis of the adult ratings (see Appendix 5) are put in *square* brackets. Labels referring to scenes that showed positive instances of the causative verbs that did not have to be accepted (see above) are put in *round* brackets. As in Table 4, the percentages indicate the percentage of *no*-responses for scenes that I had classified as positive instances (bold-faced), and the percentage of *yes*-responses for the scenes that I had classified as negative instances.

Table 5: Children's ratings of the actions in Pretest II (Labels referring to scenes that were excluded on the basis of the adult ratings are given in square brackets; those referring to positive instances that did not have to be accepted are given in round brackets.)

	ACTIONS					
VERBS	POSITIVE INSTANCES		NEGATIVE INSTANCES			
kullern	MOTION ONLY	MOTION+CAUSE	FLY	SLIDE	ROLL	TURN
'wobble'						
yes	69	62	1	2	43	13
no	2	9	70	69	28	58
%	3	13	1	3	61	22
wirbeln	MOTION ONLY	MOTION+CAUSE	TURN	SPIN		
'whirl'						
yes	52	49	28	15		
no	19	22	43	56		
%	27	31	39	21		
heben	LIFT		LOWER	PUSH		
'lift'						
yes	71		1	3		
no	0		70	68		
%	0		1	4		
senken	LOWER-TO-TABLE	LOWER-INTO-BOTTLE	PUSH	DROP	LIFT	
'lower'						
yes	52	65	0	26	0	
no	19	6	71	45	71	
%	27	9	0	37	0	
schleppen	DRAG		SWING	CARRY		
'drag'						
yes	68		0	11		
no	3		71	60		
%	4		0	16		
schmettern	BOUNCE OFF	STAY ON WALL	THROW	KICK	INTO AIR	FALL
'smash'						
yes	48	40	14	12	30	22
no	23	31	57	59	41	49
%	32	44	20	20	42	31
schieben	PUSH		PULL			
'push'						
yes	69		21			
no	2		50			
%	3		30			

As shown in Table 5, one verb drew especially many unexpected ratings: *schmettern* 'smash'. To my surprise, many children accepted the scene in which a ball fell onto a table and bounced off again (abbreviated as FALL), which was designed to violate the presumed requirement that the motion be caused by an agent. It turned out that the children who accepted this scene took it to represent a particular reading of *schmettern*, on which *schmettern* is used as a technical term for referring to actions in which a table tennis ball is smashed onto the table with high impact. Since many children obviously had this reading of the verb in mind, I decided to exclude *schmettern* from the final analysis.

To be credited with knowledge of the meaning of a verb, a child had to correctly rate all of its critical scenes, i.e., all those that are not bracketed in Table 5 above (for *senken*, accepting one of the positive instances was sufficient). This is certainly a very strict criterion, but it is necessary. Recall that the scenes operationalize the *necessary* conditions for use of a given verb: If a child accepts a scene in which such a condition is violated, it is unclear what he thinks the verb means, so the relevance for the Internal Structure Hypothesis of his response to the *be*-version of the verb on the main task cannot be interpreted. Take, for example, the scene testing *schieben* 'push' in which an object is pulled. If a child accepts this scene as an instance of *schieben*, then he might think that *schieben* means simply 'cause to slide over a surface in any direction'. In this case, he may interpret *beschieben* as meaning 'rub a surface with an instrument', similar to the (somewhat acceptable) *be*-form of *reiben* 'rub'. (cf. Chapter 6). According to his understanding of the verb, then, *schieben* can alternate, but because his meaning for the word differs from that of adults, his assumptions about its alternation cannot be meaningfully compared with his assumptions about the alternation of verbs in other classes to which he does assign the correct meaning.

Of the 71 children who participated in the study, 22 knew the meaning of all six verbs (recall that *schmettern* was excluded), 12 boys and 10 girls (aged 7;7 to 11;10; mean age 8;4). Table 6 shows, for each of the nonalternating verbs tested, how many children of a given age group could or could not be credited with knowing its meaning.

Table 6: Number of subjects per age group who could or could not be credited with knowledge of the meaning of the nonalternating verbs

	AGE				
VERB	6;9-7;11 (n=12)	8;0-8;10 (n=16)	9;0-911 (n=24)	10;10-11;10 (n=19)	total
heben					
pass	9	16	24	18	67
fail	3	0	0	1	4
senken					
pass	9	15	24	19	67
fail	3	1	0	0	4
kullern					
pass	8	12	21	15	56
fail	4	4	3	4	15
wirbeln					
pass	2	9	13	14	38
fail	10	7	11	5	33
schleppen					
pass	8	12	23	16	59
fail	4	4	1	3	12
schieben					
pass	6	14	13	15	48
fail	6	2	11	4	23

Recall that to test the Internal Structure Hypothesis, two comparisons are decisive: how children interpret _be_-verbs derived from directional verbs versus from causative verbs, and how they interpret _be_-verbs derived from directional verbs versus from accompanied motion verbs. For the first comparison, we will need subjects who know the meanings of the directional and causative verbs, but it is irrelevant whether they know the meanings of the accompanied motion verbs. Twenty-eight of the 71 subjects knew the meanings of both the directional and the causative verbs. For the second comparison, we will need subjects who know the meanings of the directional and accompanied motion verbs, but it is irrelevant whether they know the meanings of the causative verbs. Of the 71 children, 32 knew the meanings of both the directional and the accompanied motion verbs. However, in each group, four subjects had to be excluded because they did not pass the first pretest, i.e., they could not be credited with sufficient knowledge of _be_-prefixation. Table 7 summarizes how many subjects in each age group could be included in the two comparisons.

Table 7: Number of subjects included in the comparisons 'Interpretation of BE-verbs derived from directional versus causative verbs' and 'Interpretation of BE-verbs derived from directional versus accompanied motion verbs'. (All these subjects passed Pretest I.)

	AGE				
VERB	6;9-7;11 (n=12)	8;0-8;10 (n=16)	9;0-911 (n=24)	10;10-11;10 (n=19)	total
Directional & causative verbs	1	4	10	9	24
Directional & accompanied motion verbs	3	8	11	10	32

7.1.4 *The Main Task: Testing the Internal Structure Hypothesis and the Nonindividuation Hypothesis*

The children's responses in the main task should reveal what they take to be the direct object of a *be*-verb. Following a procedure suggested by Melissa Bowerman, I constructed a questionnaire that contained questions of the general format "Was kannst du alles (*be*-verb)?" 'What are some things you can (*be*-verb)?' The questions invited subjects to list possible referents of the verb's object NP, thus giving information about the way they interpreted the verb. Subjects' answers to the questions were categorized with respect to whether they had listed a typical theme or a typical goal; the kinds of objects they listed for the verb in question served as the dependent variable in the experiment.

The questionnaire contained, as experimental items, both grammatical and ungrammatical *be*-verbs. The ungrammatical verbs, which will be called TARGET UNGRAMMATICAL BE-VERBS, were constructed from one of the 7 nonalternating verbs discussed in the preceding section. These verbs were included to test the Internal Structure Hypothesis. (Recall that responses to **beschmettern* will be disregarded due to a pervasive failure to construe the base verb in the intended way.) The grammatical *be*-verbs served to test the Nonindividuation Hypothesis, which predicts that *be*-verbs derived from mass verbs are acquired earlier than *be*-verbs derived from count verbs. The questionnaire contained 6 *be*-verbs derived from alternating mass verbs and 6 *be*-verbs derived from alternating count verbs. These *be*-verbs will be referred to as COUNT BE-VERBS and MASS BE-VERBS, respectively.

In addition to these 19 experimental items, the questionnaire contained various sorts of filler items. There were 4 additional grammatical *be*-verbs, 2 from a noun (*bekleistern* 'put paste on' and *benageln* 'put nails in') and 2 from an intransitive base verb (*bemalen* 'paint/decorate' and *bekritzeln* 'scribble on'). In addition, there were 3 ungrammatical or only marginally acceptable *be*-verbs (*beklemmen, from *klemmen* 'jam'; *bestopfen, from *stopfen* 'stuff'; and ?*bedrücken*, from *drücken* 'press'). The purpose of these last three was to draw the subjects' attention away from the target ungrammatical *be*-verbs.

The questionnaire also contained a number of verbs that were prefixed not with *be-* but with *ver-*. *Ver*-fillers were included in part because I wanted to prevent a set effect that might have arisen if subjects had been presented solely with *be*-verbs. A set effect might cause subjects to list goals in response to a particular question only because they had been listing goals in answering the preceding question(s), and not because they were really analyzing the structure of the *be*-verb in question. *Ver*-verbs seemed useful to forestall such a set effect because the prefix *ver-* often affects the argument structure of a transitive motion verb in the opposite way from *be-*. That is, the *ver*-verbs used as fillers in this experiment take only one internal argument, the theme of the base verb, which is expressed in object position, and the locative argument is no longer an argument of the verb. A good example is the verb *laden* 'load', whose *ver*-prefixed form, *verladen*, means 'entrain/ship' — cf. *Die Männer luden die Container auf das Schiff* 'The men loaded the containers onto the ship' versus *Die Männer verluden die Container (*auf das Schiff)* 'The men *ver*-loaded the containers (*onto the ship)'.[6] Including *ver*-verbs also allowed me to explicitly invite subjects to reflect on how the prefixation of a verb changes the verb's meaning. This invitation provided a natural transition from the second pretest to the main task and, in addition, was supposed to draw the subjects' attention to how the prefix *be-* in particular affects the interpretation of the verb. In order to make the set of *ver*-verbs comparable to the set of *be*-verbs, I included both grammatical and ungrammatical *ver*-verbs.

---

6. Sometimes, *ver*-prefixation affects the argument structure of the base verb in a way that is similar to that of *be*-prefixation (see Stiebels, 1996, for a detailed analysis of the various effects of *ver*-prefixation). The resulting verbs differ from *be*-verbs in that they always denote a change of state. An example is given in (i):

(i) Der Hund pinkelte auf die Begonien. 'The dog peed onto the begonias'
    Der Hund verpinkelte die Begonien. 'The dog *ver*-peed (i.e., soaked by peeing) the begonias'

The *ver*-verbs used as fillers in the experiment may *only* be used as theme-object verbs, and so I am reasonably certain that they did serve the purpose of preventing a set effect.

Table 8 summarizes the experimental and filler items used in the questionnaire, along with frequency information for the mass and count *be*-verbs taken from the CELEX database. (See 7.1.3, for frequency information about the base verbs of the target ungrammatical *be*-verbs.)

Table 8: Experimental and filler items in the questionnaire, with frequency of the mass and count be-verbs included in the study per 6,000,000 tokens.

Target ungrammatical *be*-verbs
*bekullern (kullern 'wobble')
*bewirbeln (wirbeln 'whirl')
*beheben (heben 'lift')
*besenken (senken 'lower')
*beschmettern (schmettern 'smash')
*beschleppen (schleppen 'drag')
*beschieben (schieben 'push')

Mass *be*-verbs		**Count *be*-verbs**	
bespritzen '*be*-splash'	8	*bedecken* '*be*-cover'	66
bestreichen '*be*-streak'	5	*belegen* '*be*-lay'	226
bestreuen '*be*-strew'	7	*beladen* '*be*-load'	23
begießen '*be*-pour'	7	*bepacken* '*be*-pack'	4
besprühen '*be*-spray'	1	*bewerfen* '*be*-throw'	18
betropfen '*be*-drip'	0	*bekleben* '*be*-glue'	3

Grammatical fillers
bekleistern 'put paste on'
benageln 'put nails in'
bekritzeln 'scribble on'
bemalen 'paint/decorate'
verstreuen 'scatter'
verspritzen 'squirt/spatter'
versprühen 'spray'
verstreichen 'spread'
verbiegen 'twist/distort'
verladen 'load/ship/entrain'

Ungrammatical fillers
*beklemmen (klemmen 'jam')
*bestopfen (stopfen 'stuff')
*bedrücken (drücken 'press')

*verschmeißen (schmeißen 'throw')
*verlösen (lösen 'loosen')
*verplatschen (intr. *platschen* 'splash')
*verholen (holen '(go and) get/fetch')
*verfüllen (füllen 'fill')[7]

---

7. The Dutch translation equivalents of *verfüllen* and *verholen* — *vervullen* ('fill/fulfill/pervade') and *verhalen* ('tell/narrate' or 'recover a loss from someone') — are grammatical. Since Kleve is close to the Dutch border, these verbs might be grammatical in the dialect of Kleve as well. According to my informant Barbara Stiebels, however, *verfüllen* and *verholen* are not part of the Kleve dialect.

Table 8 shows that count *be*-verbs are more frequent than mass *be*-verbs. This should make it more difficult to find the predicted difference in children's interpretations of the two types of *be*-verbs, i.e., that mass *be*-verbs are interpreted correctly more often than count *be*-verbs.

Order of presentation. Two versions of the questionnaire were constructed, the second differing from the first only in that it listed 6 of the 7 target ungrammatical *be*-verbs in the reverse order. Unfortunately, the target *be*-verb *beschieben always appeared at the end of the list. The reason for this was that the list of questions turned out to be fairly long, so I initially decided to use only two of the three additional nonalternating verbs instead. But I decided to add a question containing *beschieben whenever possible at the end of the list and always to keep *beschmettern and *beschleppen further up in the questionnaire. A second flaw in the design was that, due to experimenter oversight, the order of mass *be*-verbs and count *be*-verbs was not counterbalanced across the lists.

Except for *beschieben, the experimental items were sequenced in groups of three. In each group, a pair of grammatical *be*-verbs preceded an ungrammatical *be*-verb, in the order mass *be*-verb/count *be*-verb in the first, third, and fifth group, and count *be*-verb/mass *be*-verb in the second, fourth, and sixth group. The first experimental item was a mass *be*-verb; it was preceded by 4 filler items. The remaining filler items were presented in between the groups of experimental items. The basic order of verbs is given in Table II in the appendix. Half the children received the questionnaire in the first order, and half in the second order.

Procedure

The main task started immediately after the two pretests (the first assessing children's knowledge of *be*-prefixation, the second their knowledge of the meaning of the nonalternating verbs). Recall that in the second pretest, children were shown a series of films showing various actions of lifting, whirling etc.. The instructions for the main task referred back to these films: For each of the verbs the children had been tested on, I asked them to list objects that could be lifted (whirled, etc.). The verbs from the pretest were, then, first presented in their (grammatical) base forms. Following this, I asked subjects to list objects that could be scribbled, glued, and nailed, again using unprefixed verbs; these verbs appeared again later as filler *be*-verbs. Two further questions also contained unprefixed verbs — *schmieren* 'smear' and *schütten* 'pour2', which had been used in the first pretest (I will use 'pour1' to refer to *gießen*, one of the mass *be*-verbs). These five questions were asked so that the child would not assume that only the verbs from the films were relevant in the main task. I then drew the child's attention to the fact that some verbs may be 'changed', which I illustrated by pointing out that *schmieren* 'smear' may be turned into both *verschmieren* 'spread' and *beschmieren* 'be-smear', and, similarly, that *schütten* 'pour2' may be turned into both *beschütten* '*be*-pour' and *verschütten* 'spill'. After asking whether the child knew these changed forms of the verbs, I asked him (her) to list objects that could be *beschmiert, verschmiert*, etc. In this way, I tried to call the child's attention to the contrast between the base form of a verb and its various prefixed forms, and to help him (her) pay attention to what was relevant in the subsequent interview. I then started the questionnaire.

I usually varied the questions a little, sometimes asking, "Was kann man alles (verb)?" 'What are some things one can (verb)?', and sometimes the more colloquial "Was kannst du alles (verb)?" 'What are some things you can (verb)?'; in addition, I occasionally used the passive voice. Throughout the interview, no questions were asked as to whether children judged the verbs to be grammatical. The children's responses were tape-recorded.

7.2 Experimental Hypotheses

The theoretical predictions of the Internal Structure Hypothesis and the Nonindividuation Hypothesis can now be reformulated as more specific hypotheses about the outcome of the main task I have just described. The Internal Structure Hypothesis predicts that subjects will list one or more goal NPs in their response to a question less often when the ungrammatical *be*-verb in the question is constructed from a directional verb than when it is constructed from either a causative verb or an accompanied motion verb. The null hypothesis is that nonalternating verbs do not differ systematically with respect to properties that keep them from participating in the locative alternation, so subjects will list one or more goal NPs in their response to a question equally often for questions containing verbs of the three types.

The Nonindividuation Hypothesis predicts that subjects will list one or more goal NPs in their response to a question less often when the question contains a count *be*-verb than when it contains a mass *be*-verb. The null hypothesis is that *be*-verbs derived from count verbs are not systematically

harder to comprehend than *be*-verbs derived from mass verbs, so subjects will
list one or more goal NPs equally often for verbs of the two types.

7.3 Results

Scoring

The children's pattern of responses to each of the questions containing an
experimental item was classified into one of seven categories according to the
types of objects they listed. I was only interested in the part of their answer
that contained noun phrases naming things you can *be*-verb, and, in fact, the
answers consisted predominantly of these. Each noun phrase was counted as
an individual unit. Sometimes children also described how an action could be
carried out, and these descriptions were used as additional information about
how to classify the object NP(s). Two of the categories were motivated by the
particular hypotheses tested in the experiment, i.e., whether the child listed a
goal or a theme. The remaining five were established for the responses that fit
neither of these two categories. The categories used were:

(1) Goal	The child lists one or more objects that typically function as goals in the action denoted by the verb. Example: "Flowers, trees, and walls" in response to "What are things you can *be*-spray [*bespritzen*]?"
(2) Goal & other	Some but not all the NPs refer to typical goals. Example: "Walls, cars, water" in response to "What are things you can *be*-spray?"
(3) Theme	The child lists one or more objects that are typically moved/trans-ferred in the action denoted by the verb. Example: "Balls and hats" in response to "What are things you can *be*-whirl [**bewirbeln*]?"
(4) Instrument	The child lists objects that are typically used as instruments in the action denoted by the verb. Example: "A spray gun" in response to "What are things you can *be*-spray?"
(5) Verb-specific	The response shows that the child's interpretation of the verb is idiosyncratic. Example: "Presents" in response to "What are things you can *be*-pack [*bepacken*]?" (This response indicates that the child interpreted the verb as meaning *ein-packen* 'wrap in'.)
(6) Unclassifiable	The NPs listed cannot be classified unambiguously. Example: When asked "What are things you can *be*-push [**beschieben*]?", the child answers "Pigs, at soccer, then I push that away from them".
(7) No response	The child does not list any object.

After classifying the response patterns to the questions containing the experimental items, I asked an independent judge to categorize them from 8 randomly selected interview transcripts. To compute the agreement between the corater's and my classification, I collapsed categories 4, 5, 6, and 7 — i.e., responses that referred to neither a theme nor a goal object — into one category. In 94% of the cases, the co-rater and I agreed on the classification of the responses.

7.3.1 Responses to the Ungrammatical Target BE-Verbs

The Internal Structure Hypothesis predicts that subjects will list goal NPs less often when the ungrammatical *be*-verb in the question is constructed from a directional verb than when it is constructed from either a causative verb or an accompanied motion verb. Recall that of the children who passed Pretest I (knowledge of *be*-prefixation), 24 children knew the meanings of both the directional and the causative verbs, and 32 knew the meanings of both the directional and the accompanied motion verbs.

Only Categories 1, 2, 3, and 7 of the classificatory scheme were needed to classify the subjects' responses to these particular questions. Table 9 shows, for each target ungrammatical *be*-verb, how often the subjects listed goals, goals and other objects, or themes, or gave no response.

Table 9: Responses to the target ungrammatical causative verbs (n=24; mean age 9;7), and to the target ungrammatical directional and accompanied motion verbs (n=32; mean age 9;3)

VERB	RESPONSE			
	goal	goal & other	theme	no response
Causative verbs				
bekullern	15	1	8	
bewirbeln	4	2	18	
Directional verbs				
beheben	5		27	
besenken	1		31	
Accompanied motion verbs				
beschieben	8		24	
beschleppen	19	1	11	1

Except in response to *be*-verbs constructed from *kullern* and *schleppen*, children mostly listed themes rather than goals. They hardly ever listed goals when the question contained a *be*-verb derived from a directional verb. *Be*-verbs constructed from *wirbeln* and *schieben* elicited goal responses in about a third of the cases.

To test whether the differences between the verb types shown in Table 9 were significant, I collapsed the 4 response categories of the table into 2 basic categories: GOAL and GOAL&OTHER were treated as *goal responses*, and THEME and NO RESPONSE were treated as *other responses*. The data were then subjected to a t-test for paired samples, comparing *be*-verbs containing a directional verb both to *be*-verbs containing a causative verb (n=24), and to *be*-verbs containing an accompanied motion verb (n=32). Children were less likely to list goals for *be*-verbs containing a directional verb than for *be*-verbs containing a causative verb (p. < .001, for $t_{df=23}$ = -4.73; two-tailed), and also than for *be*-verbs containing an accompanied motion verb (p. < .001, for $t_{df=31}$ = -5.27; two-tailed).

7.3.2 *Responses to the Mass* BE-*Verbs and the Count* BE-*Verbs*

According to the Nonindividuation Hypothesis, children will list one or more goal NPs less often when the question contains a count *be*-verb than when it contains a mass *be*-verb. Table 10 shows, for each verb, how often children's responses contained goals, themes, and/or objects that were neither goals nor themes.

According to the experimental hypothesis, the responses should be dichotomized as was done before in the analysis of the responses to the ungrammatical target *be*-verbs, i.e., as either *goal responses* (including GOAL and GOAL&OTHER responses) versus *other responses*. But dichotomizing the responses in this way would not have done justice to the data, and in fact might provide illegitimate support for the Nonindividuation Hypothesis. The problem is that only the count *be*-verbs, and in particular, the verbs *bekleben* '*be*-glue' and *bepacken* '*be*-pack', drew verb-specific or unclassifiable responses; moreover, the verb-specific responses were acceptable on a liberal interpretation of the *be*-verbs in question. This suggested that some yet unanalyzed properties of the verbs influenced the subjects' interpretation. In order not to penalize the subjects for interpreting the verbs in a way that I had not expected, I therefore decided to collapse the categories shown in Table 10 somewhat differently than before: Instead of collapsing them into *goal re-*

Table 10: Responses to mass and count BE-*verbs from all children (n=71)*

	VERB	RESPONSE						
	goal	goal& other	theme	instrument	verb specific	unclassi- fiable	no response
Mass *be*-verbs							
bespritzen	69	2					
bestreichen	69	2					
besprühen	68	1	2				
begießen	70	1					
bestreuen	58	4	9				
betropfen	63	5	2	1			
Total	397	15	13	1			
Count *be*-verbs							
beladen	63	3	5				
bekleben	51	2	8		5	3	2
bewerfen	66	2	2	1			
bepacken	58	2	4		7		
bedecken	70		1				
belegen	64	3	2		1		1
Total	372	12	22	1	13	3	3

sponses versus *other responses*, I collapsed them according to whether they reflected a *correct* or an *incorrect* interpretation of the verb (cf. below).

As *correct* responses I considered: goal responses, goal&other, verb-specific, and unclassifiable responses. I classified goal&other responses as correct because they showed that the child had correctly analyzed the verb for at least one response, and verb-specific responses because the particular responses given were acceptable on a liberal interpretation of the *be*-verbs in question. I considered unclassifiable responses as correct because I assumed that my not understanding the child was my fault, not the child's. This collapsing works against my predictions rather than in favor of them, since the responses to the count *be*-verbs contained 28 goal&other, verb-specific, and unclassifiable responses, whereas those to the mass *be*-verbs contained only 15 goal&other, and, as noted above, no verb-specific or unclassifiable responses (cf. Table 10). The second category contained what I considered *incorrect* responses: theme and instrument responses as well as nonresponses. Instrument responses were considered incorrect because none of the *be*-verbs is compatible with an interpretation of its object NP as an instrument, and failure to respond was considered incorrect because I interpreted it as evidence that the child had not been able to interpret the verb.

For each group of subjects, the responses were subjected to a t-test for paired samples. The results show that children interpreted count *be*-verbs less often correctly than mass *be*-verbs, a result which approaches significance (p. < .06, for $t_{df=70} = 1.91$; two-tailed). But recall that among the subjects were both children who had and those who had not shown sufficient knowledge of *be*-prefixation to pass the first pretest. Do both subgroups interpret count *be*-verbs correctly less often than mass *be*-verbs, or are count *be*-verbs especially difficult for those eighteen children who had not shown sufficient knowledge of *be*-prefixation? To find out, I broke down children's responses on the basis of whether they had passed the first pretest: Table 11 shows the responses of the 18 children who did not pass, and Table 12 the responses of the 53 children who did pass.

Table 11: Responses to mass and count BE-*verbs from children with insufficient knowledge of be-prefixation (n=18; mean age 9;0)*

	VERB	RESPONSE				
	goal	goal& other	theme	verb specific	unclassi- fiable	no response
Mass *be*-verbs						
bespritzen	17	1				
bestreichen	17	1				
besprühen	18					
begießen	18					
bestreuen	13	1	4			
betropfen	16	2				
Total	99	5	4			
Count *be*-verbs						
beladen	15	1	2			
bekleben	10		4	2	1	1
bewerfen	16		2			
bepacken	13	1	2	2		
bedecken	18					
belegen	13	2	2	1		
Total	85	4	12	5	1	1

Table 12: Responses to mass and count BE-verbs from children with sufficient knowledge of BE-prefixation (n=53; mean age 9;4)

	VERB	RESPONSE					
	goal	goal& other	theme	instrument	verb specific	unclassi- fiable	no response
Mass *be*-verbs							
bespritzen	52	1					
bestreichen	52	1					
besprühen	50	1	2				
begießen	52	1					
bestreuen	45	3	5				
betropfen	47	3	2	1			
Total	298	10	9	1			
Count *be*-verbs							
beladen	48	2	3				
bekleben	41	2	4		3	2	1
bewerfen	50	2		1			
bepacken	45	1	2		5		
bedecken	52		1				
belegen	51	1					1
Total	287	8	10	1	8	2	2

The responses of each group of subjects were subjected to a t-test for paired samples. The results show that the children who had not passed the pretest were less likely to correctly interpret count *be*-verbs than mass *be*-verbs (p. < .02, for $t_{df=17} = 2.68$; two-tailed). Interestingly, the children who had passed the pretest showed no such difference: They were just as likely to correctly interpret count *be*-verbs as they were to correctly interpret mass *be*-verbs (p. < .77, for $t_{df=52} = .30$; two-tailed).[8]

---

8. It may be surprising that the subjects who did not pass the first pretest interpreted mass *be*-verbs more often correctly than count *be*-verbs. The pretest contained only mass *be*-verbs. Why would we expect that children who did not pass *this* test would find mass *be*-verbs easier than count *be*-verbs in the *main task*? Both the pretest and the main task drew on children's understanding of *be*-verbs, but the pretest was more difficult than the main task. To pass the pretest, children had to consider the linguistic properties of the verbs in the instructions as more important than what they knew about the typical themes of the verbs. It seems likely that only children with a very solid understanding of *be*-prefixation will be able to take linguistic information more seriously than contextual information. Children with only partial knowledge of *be*-prefixation may more easily allow contextual information to guide their responses. In the main task, subjects could fully rely on whatever knowledge of *be*-prefixation they had already acquired, and did not have to pit information about the prefix against their knowledge of typical themes for a verb. The main task was thus much easier than the pretest, which explains why some subjects failed to interpret the mass *be*-verbs in the pretest correctly even though they interpreted those in the main task correctly.

7.4 Discussion

The experiment just presented tested two (compatible) hypotheses about the acquisition of the locative alternation — the Internal Structure Hypothesis and the Nonindividuation Hypothesis. The Internal Structure Hypothesis predicts that children will interpret the object NP of an ungrammatical *be*-verb as the verb's locative argument less often when the verb is constructed from a directional verb than when it is constructed from a causative verb. The results support this hypothesis: Subjects almost never attributed canonical *be*-verb semantics to a *be*-verb derived from a directional verb. They did so significantly more often for *be*-verbs derived from causative or accompanied motion verbs, which shows that the subjects' reluctance to attribute canonical *be*-verb semantics to *be*-verbs derived from directional verbs cannot be explained by a more general unwillingness to interpret ungrammatical *be*-verbs in a canonical way.

The Nonindividuation Hypothesis predicts that children will find it easier to interpret the object NP of a *be*-verb as the verb's goal when the *be*-verb is derived from a mass verb than from a count verb. The results also support this hypothesis, although the outcome is due mainly to the responses of the 18 children who did not pass the first pretest and so did not have a firm knowledge of *be*-prefixation.

One might argue that the pretest simply distinguished between linguistically more advanced children and linguistically less advanced children rather than tapping the subjects' knowledge of *be*-prefixation per se. Even if this interpretation of the pretest were correct, the results would still support the Nonindividuation Hypothesis, since they would show that linguistically less advanced children find it easier to interpret mass *be*-verbs correctly than count *be*-verbs.

But is it possible that children's better performance with mass verbs than with count verbs is due to an experimental artifact? The first pretest, which assessed children's knowledge of *be*-prefixation, contained only mass verbs, *schütten* 'pour2' and *schmieren* 'smear', and these were also included in the introduction to the main task.[9] Count verbs were not included in the introduc-

---

9. I included only mass verbs in the first pretest because actions specified by mass *be*-verbs can be represented pictorially more easily than actions specified by count verbs. Recall that the children had to interpret instructions containing *be*-verbs on the basis of individual pictures that were or were not instances of the action specified in the instructions. Actions denoted by mass

tion to the main task. It might be argued, then, that children had been trained on changing the argument structure of mass verbs but not count verbs. While children with sufficient knowledge of *be*-prefixation did not need any training to interpret *be*-verbs of any type correctly, the 18 subjects with insufficient knowledge did need training, according to this criticism, and indeed profitted from it — and, as a result, they interpreted mass *be*-verbs correctly more often than count *be*-verbs, in seeming support of the Nonindividuation Hypothesis.

This alternative explanation for my findings is dubious, however. First, note that the *be*-forms of the mass verbs in the first pretest (which were then repeated in the main task instructions) were not themselves used as experimental items in the main task. So in order to have benefitted from training on the mass *be*-verbs, children would have had to generalize to mass *be*-verbs as a class, which seems unlikely. More critically, however, in order to have been trained on the mass *be*-verbs, children would have had to receive feedback that would 'teach' them that the object NP of the verbs must be interpreted as the goal — but such feedback was never provided. It seems safe to conclude, then, that the results of this experiment, like those of the production experiment discussed in Chapter 5, provide support for the Nonindividuation Hypothesis.

The results of the present experiment have implications for the analysis of locative verbs that has been offered by Pinker (1989; cf. 2.5). Recall that Pinker assumes that for a verb to participate in the locative alternation, it must specify both a specific change of location and a specific change of state. For a morphologically marked alternation like that of German, specifying these two types of specific changes should be both a necessary and a sufficient condition for alternating. Pinker does not distinguish between verbs that do not meet this condition: Verbs that only specify a specific change of location should all be equally ungrammatical in the goal-object form, and verbs that only specify a specific change of state should all be equally ungrammatical in the theme-object form.

---

be-verbs can consist of a single, uninterrupted activity of, e.g., smearing, which can easily be depicted by a single picture. But *be*-verbs derived from count verbs typically require the base verb to be interpreted iteratively as denoting a series of subevents (see Chapter 4). I assumed that children would not typically interpret a single picture as representing a series of subevents, and so I was afraid that a pretest involving such a picture might not test what children know about *be*-prefixation, but rather how well they can cope with poor pictorial representations of actions.

None of the nonalternating verbs tested in the present experiment meet the necessary conditions that Pinker defines for participating in the locative alternation: Although they specify a specific change of location, they do not specify a specific change of state. (Pinker does not in fact even discuss their English translation equivalents as candidate verbs for participating in the alternation; see Pinker, 1989, p. 124 ff.). Still, children did not treat the verbs alike: *be*-verbs derived from a directional verb were less often treated as canonical *be*-verbs than *be*-verbs derived from a causative or accompanied motion verb. This shows that details of the internal structure of verbs additional to, or different from, those proposed by Pinker are important to the alternation.

To determine that *directional* verbs do not alternate, it is sufficient simply to know their meaning. I have argued that these verbs have incorporated an intransitive spatial predicate and so cannot provide the needed goal in object position. Children who know the meanings of the verbs know that the verbs have incorporated such a predicate, and so will automatically infer that the goal cannot be expressed in object position. This analysis is strongly supported by the results of the present experiment: Even though subjects were presented with ungrammatical *be*-verbs derived from directional verbs, they were not willing or able to treat them as canonical *be*-verbs.

In contrast, subjects *were* to some extent willing to give a canonical *be*-verb interpretation to ungrammatical *be*-verbs derived from causative and accompanied motion verbs. Since the two accompanied motion verbs — *schieben* and *schleppen* — take *nonincremental* themes, this finding may seem to call into question my claim (Section 4.2) that once children understand the basic syntactic machinery of the locative alternation, they will automatically realize that such verbs cannot alternate. The claim would indeed be undermined if the children had *produced* verbs like *beschieben* and *beschleppen*, or judged them to be grammatical. But recall that the study solicited children's *interpretations* of verbs presented to them by the experimenter. These interpretations do not in themselves establish whether children thought the verbs were grammatical, since, even when speakers find a derived form ungrammatical, they can still often give it a canonical interpretation (e.g., *to *unhang (a picture)* would mean to reverse an action of hanging, e.g., to take a picture down). The interpretations show only that for these verbs the canonical *be*-verb reading was (somewhat) available to children, whereas for ungrammatical *be*-forms of directional verbs it was not. The reasons why we might predict such a difference in the availability of the reading were discussed in Section 6.3 and at the beginning of this chapter.

In sum, the comprehension experiment showed that knowing the meaning of directional verbs is sufficient for establishing that these verbs do not alternate. Further research is needed to determine whether a child who knows the meaning of causative and accompanied motion verbs likewise suffices to infer that the verbs do not alternate.

Chapter 8

Summary and Conclusions

In this study, I have analyzed the structure and acquisition of the locative alternation in German. The locative alternation is a change in the argument structure of verbs of motion and position (locative verbs), as is shown for English in (1) and for German in (2); in German, the alternation usually involves prefixing the verb with *be-*.

(1) He sprays paint on the wall. He sprays the wall with paint.
(2) Er spritzt Farbe an die Wand. Er bespritzt die Wand mit Farbe.

Like most argument structure changes, the locative alternation in German is both productive and constrained: New *be*-verbs can be derived from many candidate verbs, but not all. The alternation therefore raises a learnability problem: How can children acquire a productive rule for changing the argument structure of locative verbs, while at the same time determining the verbs to which the rule may not be applied? This study tries to answer this question.

In Chapter 1, I introduce the reader to the phenomenon of argument structure alternations by discussing the locative alternation along with three other cross-linguistically relevant argument structure alternations: passivization, causativization, and the dative alternation. These alternations all have in common that they apply to some but not all candidate verbs. I report studies in the literature showing that attempts to explain how children determine the restrictions must take account of the so-called 'No Negative Evidence' problem: Children receive little or no corrective feedback when they make grammatical errors, so they must rely on some other means to determine which verbs undergo a particular alternation and which verbs do not.

In Chapter 2, I discuss several theories of the acquisition of argument structure alternations. I start out with Baker's (1979) claim that children do not develop productive rules for changing the argument structure of verbs at all, but instead simply register the syntactic frames they have actually heard

the verbs appear in. I then summarize evidence from both diary and experimental studies against Baker's claim: Children use verbs in syntactic frames
that adults find ungrammatical and are therefore unlikely to have modeled
(e.g., *"Don't say me that or you'll make me cry"; *"Can I fill some salt into
the bear?", Bowerman, 1988), which suggests that they do acquire productive
techniques for assigning argument structures to verbs, and sometimes assign
an incorrect argument structure to a verb. The theories that are discussed in
the remainder of the chapter all take children's productivity into account.

In his theory of Discovery Procedures, Braine (1971, 1988; Braine et al.,
1990) proposes that children make errors not because they incorrectly apply a
productive rule for changing a verb's argument structure, but because they fall
back on default argument structures when they do not really know a verb's
specific argument structure(s). He suggests that they acquire the correct
restrictions on argument structures by learning verb-specific information that
comes to prevail over general information or default argument structures.
However, Braine's theory has some important weaknesses. Among other
things, it incorrectly predicts that adult speakers are conservative, i.e., do not
assign novel argument structures to existing verbs.

According to the Criteria Approach (Mazurkewich & White, 1984;
Pinker, 1984), children do acquire productive rules for argument structure
alternations, and make errors because their rules are initially overly general.
Children cut back on their overgeneralizations by gradually annotating the
rule with criteria that specify the kinds of verbs to which it applies. Taking a
different tack, Randall (1987, 1990, 1992) argues that children do not need to
modify the rule itself but only to identify the verbs to which it applies.
According to her Catapult Hypothesis, innate principles of Universal Grammar block the application of the dative and the locative alternations to verbs
with only one obligatory internal argument. Errors may initially occur when a
learner has wrongly assigned two internal arguments to a verb, but they will
cease once the learner has determined the verb's correct number of arguments.
The Criteria Approach and the Catapult Hypothesis both face theoretical and
empirical problems. An important theoretical problem of the Catapult Hypothesis, for example, is that it does not show how children can distinguish
between arguments that are optional and arguments that are obligatory but
may occasionally be omitted for pragmatic reasons. The major empirical
problem for both approaches is the existence of negative exceptions: verbs
that do not alternate even though they satisfy all the proposed conditions on

the alternation (Bowerman, 1987, 1988; Pinker, 1989).

The most plausible approach to date has been Pinker's (1987, 1989) Lexicosemantic Structure Theory. Like Randall, Pinker assumes that children do not need to modify their rule but must learn to identify the verbs to which it applies, but, unlike Randall, he proposes that children identify these verbs not by learning their syntactic properties but by learning their *meanings*. Knowledge of a verb's meaning is decisive, since the meaning directly determines the syntactic frames the verb may occur in: A verb that may occur in one syntactic frame may occur in an alternative frame only if its meaning can be changed so that it is compatible with the second frame. Pinker's theory is representative of many recent approaches to argument structure alternations in which alternations are assumed to be caused by a change in the meaning of the verb (see Rappaport & Levin, 1985, 1988; Levin & Rappaport Hovav, 1992, among others).

In applying this theory to the acquisition of the locative alternation, Pinker and his collaborators (Gropen, 1989; Gropen et al., 1991a,b) argue that children are equipped with an innate rule that links affected arguments to direct object position (the Object Affectedness Linking Rule). They therefore know that for a verb to alternate, it must specify both its theme and its goal as affected: the theme because it undergoes a specific change of location, and the goal because it undergoes a specific change of state. The claim that the goal must be specified to change state in order to be expressed as direct object accounts for the phenomenon, first observed by Anderson (1971), that when the goal is the direct object, it must be interpreted holistically.

But Pinker's and Gropen et al.'s account of the locative alternation faces empirical problems. First, if goal arguments must be specified to change state to become the direct object, then goal-object sentences should be achievements or accomplishments and should combine only with temporal frame adverbials (e.g., *spray the wall **within an hour**.*) But in fact they also combine with durational adverbials (e.g., *spray the wall **for an hour***). Second, in German, it is clear that the goal need *not* be specified to change state in order to be expressed as direct object (cf. *Er bewirft die Wand mit Steinen* 'He be-throws the wall with stones'). This suggests that the Object Affectedness Linking Rule constrains the verbs that participate in the locative alternation incorrectly. As a potential solution to the problem raised by the German data, I discuss Lebeaux's (1988) theory of Affectedness. In trying to account for how the passive is acquired, Lebeaux has argued that children initially restrict this argument structure change to verbs whose direct object argument is specified as affected. When they later discover that the alternation is morphologically marked, however, they will extend it to verbs that do not specify an affected object. Applying Lebeaux's reasoning about the role of markedness to the locative alternation, we could predict that children will first produce goal-object forms of locative verbs only when the goal is affected; if, however, the verb is morphologically marked, as in German, they will eventually relax this restriction.

Even though Pinker's and Gropen et al.'s Affectedness Hypothesis can, then, in principle be modified in a way that accounts for German, I do not believe that the account is correct. In the main body of this study, I present and develop an alternative account of the structure and acquisition of the locative alternation. First, I summarize the main properties of the alternation in German. I then present the Preposition Incorporation account proposed by Wunderlich (1992; Brinkmann & Wunderlich, 1996; cf. Chapter 3), which provides the basis for my own account. Wunderlich argues that in order to take its goal as direct object, a locative verb must incorporate a preposition. The preposition becomes the most deeply embedded predicate in the predicate-argument structure of the new verb, so by default its argument, the goal, becomes the direct object of the verb. The holistic interpretation of the goal, which is taken by Pinker and Gropen et al. as evidence that the verb has changed its meaning, is only a by-product of the syntactic change: When the goal is a direct argument of the verb, it follows from Löbner's (1990, 1996) Presupposition of Indivisibility that it must be *indivisible* with respect to the predicate. Wunderlich's Preposition Incorporation account shows how we can explain the locative alternation without positing that the verb changes its meaning, and without needing to invoke a linking rule whose sole purpose is to link affected arguments to direct object position.

But why do alternating transitive verbs allow the theme *not* to be expressed in object position? To answer this question, I propose the Nonindividuation Hypothesis (Chapter 4). The Nonindividuation Hypothesis states that for a verb to take its goal as direct object, the quantificational properties of the theme must be irrelevant. The theme may then be construed as nonindividuated when it is not specified, i.e., as an unbounded amount of stuff or objects. This allows speakers to infer that the actual identity of the theme is unknown or irrelevant, and so they may simply presuppose the existence of some stuff or objects involved in the action described by the verb. The theme thus does not need to be expressed syntactically, and this renders the object position available for the goal. The quantificational properties of an unspecified theme can be considered irrelevant only when, by virtue of its meaning, the verb takes an incremental theme, i.e., a theme that is gradually involved in the action described by the verb (see Dowty, 1991, and Krifka, 1986, 1989a, on the concept of incremental theme). Speakers can construe the quantificational properties of an incremental theme as irrelevant by interpreting the verb as a predicate that specifies a process or a process leading to a transition.

According to the Nonindividuation Hypothesis, the goal-object form can be derived more easily from some verbs than from others. In particular, verbs that describe only the motion of substances and are atelic (termed here mass verbs) are easier: Their theme is typically nonindividuated to begin with and they already describe a process. In contrast, verbs that describe the motion of both substances and bounded objects and are telic (count verbs) are more difficult: To deindividuate the verb's theme, the speaker must interpret the verb iteratively, i.e., as describing a series of telic events that together form a larger, temporally unbounded event. The Nonindividuation Hypothesis thus predicts that children will acquire the goal-object construction earlier for mass verbs than for count verbs. It further predicts that children, once they have come to grips with the basic syntactic machinery of the alternation, will automatically know that verbs that do not take an incremental theme do not participate in the alternation.

In Chapter 5, I describe a production experiment that pits the Nonindividuation Hypothesis against Gropen et al.'s and Lebeaux's Affectedness hypotheses. Four kinds of verbs were defined by crossing the *goal affected/ not affected* distinction with the *mass verb/count verb* distinction: +AFF and -AFF mass verbs, and +AFF and -AFF count verbs. Fifty-nine children, divided into 3 age groups between 6 and 10 years of age, and 27 adults, divided into 2 age groups, participated in the experiment. A pretest established, for the children and for the younger group of adults, whether or not the subjects interpreted the verbs as specifying an affected goal. The main task was designed to create felicitous conditions for producing goal-object constructions using verbs of the four types. Subjects were shown a series of video films depicting actions and asked to describe the films to a listener. Within a set of scenes, the actor(s) and theme stayed constant, but the actions and color of the goal objects changed; the changing information had to be communicated to the listener.

The results support the predictions of the Nonindividuation Hypothesis, but not the two Affectedness hypotheses: The children of the two youngest age groups used the goal-object form more often for mass than for count verbs, but were not at all influenced by affectedness. Affectedness did play a dominant role for the older children and the adults, but the difference between mass and count verbs continued to influence subjects in whether they used a goal-object construction. For the oldest children mass verbs had an advantage regardless of whether the verb specified an affected goal, but for adults the advantage was limited to -AFF verbs. The results indicate that children learn how to make the goal the direct object of the verb without reference to a linking rule based on affectedness, but that the affectedness of the goal is a factor that influences adults' decision to *use* a goal-object construction.

Chapters 6 and 7 focus on the locative verbs of German that do not participate in the alternation, or else are only marginally acceptable as *be*-verbs. Chapter 6 analyzes why they are so restricted, and Chapter 7 presents a comprehension experiment that tested a particular prediction that follows from this analysis. Several different classes of nonalternating verbs were identified, and the restrictions on most of them were shown to follow directly from the principles that are needed to state how the alternation works. On the basis of these principles, I propose the Internal Structure Hypothesis, which states that a verb's inability to participate in the locative alternation can best be understood in terms of its failure to meet one (or more) of a set of necessary conditions that are relevant for deriving the goal-object argument structure. Directional verbs (e.g., *heben* 'lift') fail to meet the first, most basic condition for participating in the alternation: that the locative argument must be able to become the direct object of the verb. These verbs have incorporated an *intransitive* spatial predicate rather than a preposition, so they cannot express the goal syntactically. The remaining nonalternating verbs could in principle provide a locative argument in object position, but they fail to meet one or more additional conditions.

Thus, to be acceptable as the direct object of a verb, the locative argument must be indivisible with respect to the verbal predicate, and the verb must further meet the satisfaction criteria of the locative alternation proposed by Wunderlich (1992) on the basis of Löbner's Presupposition of Indivisibility. This rules out verbs whose theme is inferred as moving along a path. In particular, it rules out intransitive verbs of motion describing uncontrolled motion (e.g., *rollen* 'roll'), i.e., whenever the uncontrolled motion implies a path. Locative verbs further have to allow their theme to be omissable or else be expressed in subject position. The Nonindividuation Hypothesis explains why this condition is not met by accompanied motion verbs (e.g., *schieben* 'push'), PRESS verbs (e.g., *drücken* 'press'), and STIR verbs (e.g., *schütteln* 'shake'): These verbs do not alternate because they do not take an incremental theme. The hypothesis also accounts for why the condition is not met by causative verbs that denote the motion of bounded objects (e.g., transitive *rollen* 'roll'): For these verbs, the deindividuation of the theme is blocked as a means to render the theme omissable, since for these verbs, it is the agent that is optional rather than the theme. (Causative verbs denoting the motion of substances, e.g., *spritzen* 'smear', do participate in the locative alternation, because their theme is nonindividuated already.) Intransitive verbs of position (e.g., *liegen* 'lie') do not alternate because they violate a fundamental tenet of the Nonindividuation Hypothesis: that in order to alternate, a predicate must specify a *process*. Because of the topological requirements of the locative alternation, most members of yet two other classes of verbs do not alternate, causative verbs of position (e.g, *legen* 'lay') and INTO verbs (e.g., *stopfen* 'stuff'). Since verbs like *schmettern* 'smash' provide additional information about the manner in which an object is (e.g.) thrown, they focus on the theme and so are unlikely to appear in the goal-object structure, which is used by speakers to focus on the goal. They thus fail to meet the condition that it must make pragmatic sense to use the goal-object form of a verb.

According to the Internal Structure Hypothesis, directional verbs are the *only* verbs that cannot provide the needed locative argument in object position. The hypothesis thus predicts that children will interpret the object NP as the goal less often when an (ungrammatical) *be*-verb is derived from a directional verb than when it is derived from, e.g., a causative verb. This prediction was tested by presenting 71 children, divided into three age groups between 6 and 11 years, with questions of the format "What are some things you can (verb)?". This type of question focusses on the referent of the verb's object NP, so children's answers reveal what semantic role they assign to the direct object. The questions contained an ungrammatical *be*-verb derived from a directional, a causative or an accompanied motion verb. Besides testing the Internal Structure Hypothesis, the experiment provided an additional test of the Nonindividuation Hypothesis — this time tapping comprehension rather than production — by including a set of questions that contained grammatical *be*-verbs derived from alternating mass versus count verbs. Two pretests were also conducted, one to assess children's knowledge of *be*-prefixation and the other their knowledge of the meanings of the nonalternating verbs used in the main task.

As predicted, children were far less likely to list one or more goal NPs for a *be*-verb derived from a directional verb (e.g., **besenken* '*be*-lower') than for a *be*-verb derived from a causative verb (e.g., **bekullern* '*be*-wobble') or an accompanied motion verb (e.g., **beschieben* '*be*-push'). This suggests that to determine that directional verbs do not alternate, it is enough for children to know the meanings of the verbs. In contrast, even when they know the meanings of causative and accompanied motion verbs, they may still be willing to construe the verbs in a way that seemingly fits the conditions for alternating. The experiment also provided further support for the Nonindividuation Hypothesis: Children whose knowledge of *be*-prefixation was still weak (as established by their failure to pass the first pretest) were more likely to interpret a *be*-verb correctly as taking its goal as its direct object when it was derived from a mass verb than when it was derived from a count verb.

These results not only support the Internal Structure Hypothesis but also cast further doubt on Pinker's analysis of locative verbs. None of the nonalternating verbs included in the comprehension study specifies a state change of the goal, so none satisfies what he has proposed as a necessary condition for participating in the alternation. Since they fail equally, and for the same reason, we would not expect children to treat them systematically differently. The fact that they did means that structural properties of verbs in addition to those cited as relevant by Pinker must be taken into account in efforts to explain why some verbs do not alternate.

In summary, the research presented in this study offers a new way to account for the structure and acquisition of the locative alternation. Wunderlich's Preposition Incorporation account shows that we can explain the structure of the locative alternation without postulating that a verb must change its meaning in order to change its argument structure. The production experiment supports his analysis: Children used the goal-object form of a verb regardless of whether the verb specified a state change of the goal. The Nonindividuation Hypothesis developed and tested in this thesis emphasizes the role of the theme rather than the goal. Both the production and the comprehension experiments show that the hypothesis correctly predicts the order of acquisition of the alternation for different types of motion verbs. The Nonindividuation Hypothesis also captures an important restriction on the alternation: Transitive verbs can alternate only if their theme can be moved out of the object position to make way for the goal. Directional verbs fail to alternate for an even more basic reason: They cannot in any event provide the goal in object position. The comprehension experiment shows that children do not mistake directional verbs for alternators even if they are encouraged by the presence of the prefix *be-* to do so, but they do sometimes mistake causative and accompanied motion verbs for alternators. These findings support the Internal Structure Hypothesis, which states that verbs can alternate only if they meet a set of conditions that are essential to the alternation, and that verbs that do not meet them all may differ in *which* of these condition(s) they fail to meet.

Appendices

Appendix 1

Alternating and Nonalternating Verbs in German Referred to in the Study

1. Alternating Verbs

1.1 Transitive Locative Verbs

BASE VERBS		BE-PREFIXED VERBS		VERBS PREFIXED WITH A PREPOSITIONAL PREFIX	
füllen	'fill'	*?befüllen*	'*be*-fill'		
gießen	'pour'	*begießen*	'*be*-pour'		
kleckern	'spill'	*bekleckern*	'*be*-spill'		
rieseln	'drizzle/sprinkle'	*berieseln*	'*be*-sprinkle'		
schmieren	'smear'	*beschmieren*	'*be*-smear'		
schütten	'pour'	*beschütten*	'*be*-pour'		
spritzen	'spray'	*bespritzen*	'*be*-spray'		
sprühen	'spray'	*besprühen*	'*be*-spray'		
streichen	'streak/brush'	*bestreichen*	'*be*-brush'		
streuen	'strew'	*bestreuen*	'*be*-strew'		
ballern	'smash'	*beballern*	'*be*-smash'		
decken	'cover'	*bedecken*	'*be*-cover'		
hängen	'hang'	*behängen*	'*be*-hang'		
kleben	'glue'	*bekleben*	'*be*-glue'		
laden	'load'	*beladen*	'*be*-load'		
packen	'pack'	*bepacken*	'*be*-pack'		
werfen	'throw'	*bewerfen*	'*be*-throw'		
wickeln	'coil'			*umwickeln*	'*around*-coil'

1.2 *Intransitive Locative Verbs*

steigen	'climb'	*besteigen*	'*be*-climb'
treten	'step into'	*betreten*	'enter'
wohnen	'live in'	*bewohnen*	'live in'
joggen	'jog'		
rollen	'roll'		
schlagen	'hit'		
segeln	'sail'		

durchjoggen	'*through*-jog'
überrollen	'*over*-roll'
durchschlagen	'*through*-hit'
umsegeln	'*around*-sail'

1.3 *Other Semantic Classes of* BE-*Verbs*

Verbs of Active Perception

fühlen	'feel around on'	*befühlen*	'*be*-feel'
riechen	'sniff at'	*beriechen*	'*be*-sniff'
schnobern	'sniff at'	*beschnobern*	'*be*-sniff'
schnuppern	'sniff at'	*beschnuppern*	'*be*-sniff'
tasten	'touch around on'	*betasten*	'*be*-touch'

Verbs of Material Manipulation

arbeiten	'work at'	*bearbeiten*	'*be*-work'
kritzeln	'scribble on'	*bekritzeln*	'*be*-scribble'
malen	'paint on'	*bemalen*	'*be*-paint'
schnitzen	'cut at'	*beschnitzen*	'*be*-cut'

Verbs of Speech

kakeln	'waffle over '	*bekakeln*	'*be*-waffle'
reden	'speak about'	*bereden*	'*be*-speak'
schwatzen	'speak about'	*beschwatzen*	'*be*-speak'
sprechen	'speak about'	*besprechen*	'*be*-speak'

Verbs of Emotion

staunen	'gape at'	*bestaunen*	'*be*-gape'
trauern	'mourn'	*betrauern*	'bemourn'
weinen	'cry about'	*beweinen*	'*be*-cry'
schluchzen	'weep'		

durchschluchzen '*through*-weep'

1.4 *Other* BE-*Verbs with a Nonlocative Meaning*

erben	'inherit'	*beerben*	'*be*-inherit s.o.'
kochen für	'cook for'	*bekochen*	'*be*-cook s.o.'
rauben	'rob s.o. of s.th.'	*berauben*	'*be*-rob s.o.'
schenken	'give as a gift'	*beschenken*	'*be*-gift s.o.'

1.5 *Denominal* be-*Verbs*

BE-VERB		BASE NOUN	
bebildern	'illustrate'	*Bild*	'picture'
behexen	'bewitch'	*Hexe*	'witch'
bepflastern	'put a bandaid on'	*Pflaster*	'plaster/bandaid'
beschmutzen	'deface/disfigure'	*Schmutz*	'spot/dirt'
beseitigen	'remove'	*Seite*	'side'
durchbluten	'supply with blood'	*Blut*	'blood'
durchschiffen	'travel through by ship'	*Schiff*	'ship'
überdachen	'cover with a roof'	*Dach*	'roof'
übertünchen	'whitewash'	*Tünche*	'varnish'
ummauern	'enclose with walls'	*Wand*	'wall'
unterkeilen	'drive a wedge under something'	*Keil*	'wedge'

2. be-**Prefixed Verbs Judged to be Novel Coinages**

BE-VERB		BASE VERB/NOUN/ADJECTIVE	
beäppeln		cf. *veräppeln*	'make a joke about s.o.'
bedudeln	'*be*-play/play for s.o.'	*dudeln*	'fiddle'
beknickeln	(?)	(?)	
bekuscheln	'*be*-snuggle'	*kuscheln*	'snuggle toward s.o.'
belähmen	'*be*-lame'	*lahm/lähmen*	'lame/paralyze'
benähen	'*be*-sew'	*nähen*	'sew'
bereiten	'*be*-ride'	*reiten*	'ride'
beschmeicheln	'*be*-flatter s.o.'	*schmeicheln*	'flatter'
beschmücken	'*be*-decorate'	*Schmuck-schmücken*	'jewellery/decorate'
bestreifen	'*be*-patrol'	*(durch)-streifen*	'patrol'
besuppt	'*be*-souped'	*Suppe*	'soup'
betextet	'*be*-texted'	*Text*	'text'
bewischen	'*be*-wipe'	*wischen*	'wipe'

3. **Nonalternating Verbs**

INTO *Verbs*		*Directional Verbs*	
klemmen	'pinch/squeeze'	*bringen*	'bring'
quetschen	'jam'	*fallen-fällen*	'fall-fell'
stechen	'stick/prick'	*gehen*	'go'
stopfen	'stuff'	*heben*	'lift'
zwängen	'wedge/jam'	*hieven*	'heave'
		holen	'get/fetch'
		kommen	'come'
		sinken-senken	'sink-lower'
		steigen	'rise/climb'
		tauchen	'dive-dip'

Accompanied Motion Verbs		*Stir Verbs*		*Press Verbs*	
schieben	'push'	*kneten*	'knead'	*drücken*	'press/push'
schleppen	'schlepp'	*rühren*	'stir'	*hacken*	'hack'
tragen	'carry'	*rütteln*	'shake/jog'	*klopfen*	'beat/knock'
ziehen	'pull'	*schütteln*	'shake'	*pressen*	'press'
				reiben	'rub'

Causativizable Verbs (non-directional)

fließen-flößen	'flow/float-pour into'
fluten	'flood'
kippen	'tip over'
klappen	'clap-fold'
kugeln	'roll like a ball'
kullern	'wiggle/roll like a raw egg'
prallen	'bounce'
rollen	'roll'
schießen	'shoot'
schlagen	'strike/beat'
schleifen	'slide/drag'
schleudern	'skid/fling'
schnellen	'jerk'
schwimmen-schwemmen	'swim-sweep'
schwingen-schwenken	'swing-swing'
stoßen	'push/thrust'
treiben	'drift'
wirbeln	'whirl'

hängen	'hang'
lehnen	'lean'
liegen-legen	'lie-lay'
sitzen-setzen	'sit-set'
stecken	'stick/pin'
stehen-stellen	'stand-put' (lit: 'make stand')

Appendix 2

Assumptions about the Optimal Age of the Subjects in the Experiments

I made decisions about the optimal age of subjects for the experiments I conducted after considering various sources. First, I searched for the use of *be*-verbs in corpora of naturalistic speech data from children acquiring German. The data I considered include the very extensive corpus collected by Miller (1976) from his daughter Simone, which was available at the Max Planck Institute for Psycholinguistics. The recordings cover the period of 1;9 (one year; nine months) to 4;0 years of age. In addition, I analyzed the Clahsen corpus (Clahsen, 1982), which comprises monthly recordings of the speech of the three siblings, Julia, Daniel, and Mathias, and is available in the CHILDES data base (MacWhinney & Snow, 1990; MacWhinney, 1991). Julia was recorded from age 1;9 to 2;6; and her twin brothers from 2;9 to 3;6. The children occasionally produced verbs prefixed with *be-* in the period under investigation, but almost all of these verbs have idiomatic, nontransparent meanings.

Second, I consulted the verbs listed in Augst's (1984, p. 173-175) overview of the vocabulary of 4 children at the age of 5, shortly before they enter school. The Augst-corpus contains more than 40 transparent *be-*verbs derived from verbs, nouns, and adjectives, including 6 novel constructions (e.g., *bewischen*, from *wischen* 'wipe'; *benähen*, from *nähen* 'sew'). About half of the transparent *be-*verbs have a local meaning, and 8 of them are derived from transitive verbs of motion (e.g., *begießen*, from *gießen* 'pour'; *bewerfen*, from *werfen* 'throw'). Unfortunately, Augst does not state how often these verbs were used and whether they were used by more than one child. Nevertheless, his list shows that by age 5, children are likely to know at least some *be-*verbs derived from transitive motion verbs and are developing a productive rule of *be-*prefixation.

Third, I conducted a pilot study with children from 6 to 11 years. In this study, I read aloud simple sentences containing a transitive verb of motion in its base form, e.g., *Hans legt den Käse auf die Brötchen* 'Hans lays the cheese on the rolls', and the child's task was to convert the verb into a *be-*verb and changing the order of the postverbal NPs accordingly, e.g., *Hans belegt die Brötchen mit dem Käse* 'Hans *be-*lays the rolls with the cheese.' Each child was trained on the task until he or she could reorder several sentences in succession without mistake. Despite this training phase, many children still faced considerable difficulties in prefixing the verb and reordering the sentences. This suggested that elementary school children have not mastered *be-*prefixation well enough to deal with it on a metalinguistic level.

The optimal age for the subjects in the production experiment (cf. Chapter 5) was further determined on the basis of the pretest assessing children's knowledge of *be-*prefixation in the comprehension experiment (Chapter 7), which was conducted before the production experiment. The main purpose of the comprehension experiment was to test the subjects' willingness to change the argument structure of different kinds of nonalternating verbs. I decided to conduct this experiment with elementary school children because, for the purposes of the experiment, I wanted a sufficiently large group of subjects that had acquired a good productive knowledge of *be-*prefixation. Of the 71 children who participated in the comprehension experiment (between 6;9 and 11;10 years of age; mean age 9;2), 18 (25%) subjects (aged between 6;9 and 10;10; mean age 9;0) did not pass the pretest on knowledge of *be-*prefixation. This suggested that elementary school children indeed differ considerably in what they know about *be-*prefixation, as the pilot study had indicated.

Drawing these various sources of evidence together, I concluded that children aged between 5 and 10 years would still be in the process of acquiring the locative alternation and would, therefore, be likely to show a developmental pattern that I could use to test my empirical predictions.

Appendix 3

Why Two Different Tests were Used in the Pretest of the Production Experiment to Assess Subjects' Interpretation of the +AFF and -AFF Verbs

In 5.5, I discuss some problems associated with the 'bias' test used for assessing children's interpretation of the -AFF, and with the 'sensitivity' test used for assessing their interpretation of the +AFF verbs. But why did I use two different tests in the first place? Because each test would have been problematic if it had been applied to verbs of the other type. A 'bias' test is simply not appropriate for assessing subjects' knowledge of +AFF verbs (which specify both manner and endstate): It can only show which aspect of a verb's meaning the subject takes to be *more* important, even though he might know that both are important. A 'sensitivity' test for the -AFF verbs would not have been useful either: It would have assessed subjects' knowledge of the manner aspect of these verbs, but I was not interested in this — only in whether they thought that endstate was important. But why did I not use the sensitivity test to determine *only* whether subjects erroneously took endstate to be important for the -AFF verbs? Because to do so would have involved presenting children with a choice between two candidate endstates, *neither* of which is in fact associated with the verb for adults, and this seemed utterly misleading. Imagine, for example, that you have to choose between two perfect instances of throwing, one in which a dry sponge hits a drawing board without leaving any traces and another in which a wet sponge hits the board and leaves spots. If you know what *throw* means, the question which of these represents *throwing* just does not make any sense. Even worse, the question might invite children to think that endstate is relevant to *throw* after all, since it suggests that it is sensible to distinguish the two drawings. Given these shortcomings of using the same test for both types of verbs, I decided to test the two verb types differently.

Appendix 4

Picture Sets Used in the Pretest of the Production Experiment (Chapter 5) for Assessing Subjects' Interpretation of the +AFF and -AFF Verbs

PANEL 1 (MANNER)   PANEL 2 (ENDSTATE)

+AFF/MASS verbs

schmieren 'smear'
SCENARIO 1
boy brushing paint onto sheet of paper   some dots on paper
boy brushing paint onto sheet of paper   tree painted on paper
boy brushing paint onto sheet of paper   paint all over paper

boy brushing paint onto sheet of paper   some dots on paper
boy drawing on sheet with a pen   some dots on paper
boy smearing paint on sheet with hands   some dots on paper

SCENARIO 2

girl shovelling sand onto bench of sand-pit	small heaps of sand on bench
girl making sand cakes on bench	small heaps of sand on bench
girl smearing sand onto bench with hands	small heaps of sand on bench
girl shovelling sand onto bench of sand-pit	small heaps of sand on bench
girl shovelling sand onto bench of sand-pit	one cake of sand on bench
girl shovelling sand onto bench of sand-pit	sand all over bench

spritzen 'spray'
SCENARIO 1

girl dripping water from plastic bag onto garbage bin	some puddles on bin
girl spraying water with water pistol onto garbage bin	some puddles on bin
girl pouring2 water from bucket onto garbage bin	some puddles on bin
(*pouring2* means an action described in German as *schütten*)	
girl dripping water from plastic bag onto garbage bin	some puddles on bin
girl dripping water from plastic bag onto garbage bin	splashes all over bin
girl dripping water from plastic bag onto garbage bin	bin all wet

SCENARIO 2

girl dripping water from sponge onto boy	some drops on boy
girl dripping water from sponge onto boy	splashes all over boy
girl dripping water from sponge onto boy	drenched boy
girl dripping water from sponge onto boy	some drops on boy
girl splashing water from hose onto boy	some drops on boy
girl pouring2 water from bucket onto boy	some drops on boy

PANEL 1 (MANNER)	PANEL 2 (ENDSTATE)

+AFF/COUNT verbs

laden 'load'
SCENARIO 1

crane lowering stone onto one edge of truck	a small pile of stones on truck
crane lowering stone onto one edge of truck	a few stones on truck
crane lowering stone onto one edge of truck	truck full
crane lowering stone onto one edge of truck	truck full
crane dropping stone onto truck from midair	truck full
crane loading stone onto truck	truck full

SCENARIO 2

fork-lift truck gliding box onto trolley	a suitcase and some boxes on trolley
fork-lift truck dropping box onto trolley	a suitcase and some boxes on trolley
fork-lift truck loading box on trolley	a suitcase and some of boxes on trolley

fork-lift truck gliding box onto trolley	a suitcase and a couple of boxes on trolley
fork-lift truck gliding box onto trolley	box on trolley
fork-lift truck gliding box onto trolley	trolley full of luggage

packen 'pack'
SCENARIO 1

boy holding newspaper bundle on string over bicycle bag	bundle in bag
boy throwing newspaper bundle into bicycle bag	bundle in bag
boy putting newspaper bundle in bicycle bag (holding it firm by both hands)	bundle in bag
boy holding newspaper bundle by string over bicycle bag	bundle in bag
boy holding newspaper bundle by string over bicycle bag	bundle halfway in bag
boy holding newspaper bundle by string over bicycle bag	bundles stacked and bound onto bag

SCENARIO 2

man holding box by string, putting it on trailer	two boxes on trailer
man holding box by string, putting it on trailer	one box on trailer
man holding box by string, putting it on trailer	boxes stacked and bound on trailer
man holding box by string, putting it on trailer	two boxes on trailer
man swinging box onto trailer	two boxes on trailer
man holding box firmly in arms, putting it on trailer	two boxes on trailer

PANEL 1 (MANNER)	PANEL 2 (ENDSTATE)

-AFF/MASS verbs

gießen 'pour'
SCENARIO 1

girl pouring water from watering can on 1/2 blown-up ball	water in dent on top of ball
girl dripping water from bag on 1/2 blown-up ball	water in dent on top of ball
girl pouring water from watering can on 1/2 blown-up ball	puddle of water in front of ball

SCENARIO 2

girl pouring water from watering can onto slanted corrugated sheet iron	puddles of water on sheet iron
girl pouring water from watering can onto slanted corrugated sheet iron	puddle of water in front of sheet iron
girl dripping water from bag onto slanted corrugated sheet iron	puddles of water on sheet iron

rieseln 'sprinkle'
SCENARIO 1

boy sprinkling sand onto chute	big pile of sand on chute
boy sprinkling sand onto chute	pile of sand in front of chute
boy pouring2 sand from bucket onto chute	big pile of sand on chute

SCENARIO 2

boy and girl sprinkle sand onto belly of man on beach	pile of sand on belly
boy and girl pour sand from bucket onto belly of man	pile of sand on belly
boy and girl sprinkle sand onto belly of man	piles of sand next to belly

-AFF/COUNT verbs

werfen 'throw'
SCENARIO 1

two boys throwing sponges at blackboard	wet blackboard
two boys kicking sponges at blackboard	wet blackboard
two boys throwing sponges at blackboard	dry blackboard

SCENARIO 2

two boys throwing soap at showerstall	wet showerstall
two boys throwing soap at showerstall	wet showerstall
two boys kicking soap at showerstall	dry showerstall

ballern 'smash/fling'
SCENARIO 1

two boys smashing balls with sticks at wall of house	dirty wall
two boys smashing balls with sticks at wall of house	clean wall
two boys rolling balls with sticks against wall of house	dirty wall

SCENARIO 2

two boys smashing cans with sticks against boarding	wet boarding
two boys rolling cans with sticks against boarding	wet boarding
two boys smashing cans with sticks against boarding	clean boarding

FILLER ITEM

reißen 'tear' (+AFF)
SCENARIO 1

boy tearing a sheet of paper apart	2 halves of paper with ragged edges
boy tearing a sheet of paper apart	2 halves of paper with clean edges
boy cutting paper	2 halves of paper with ragged edges

SCENARIO 2

boy tearing a sheet of paper apart	2 halves of paper with ragged edges
boy separating paper with little saw	2 halves of paper with ragged edges
boy tearing a sheet of paper apart	2 halves of paper with somewhat uneven edges

Appendix 5

Descriptions of the Scenes Used in Pretest II in the Comprehension Experiment to Assess Children's Knowledge of the Meaning of the Nonalternating Verbs

The following scenes were used to test whether children knew the necessary conditions an action must meet in order to be an instance of a given verb. After each description, the abbreviations used to refer to the scenes in Tables 3-5 in Chapter 7 are given in brackets.

Kullern 'wobble'
MOVING OBJECT
A 12cm white styrofoam egg, which had a blue ribbon (about 1cm wide) taped around its longer axis so that its axis of rotation was perceptible.

POSITIVE INSTANCES
1. Egg rolls over a grey carpet in a wobbling manner, with no agent present (*motion only*).
2. Agent causes egg to move as in 1. (*motion+cause*).

NEGATIVE INSTANCES
1. Egg flies through the air (*fly*).
2. Egg slides over the carpet without rotating (this was done by pulling the object on a nylon string that was invisible on the carpet) (*slide*).
3. Egg rolls over the carpet without wobbling (*roll*).
4. Egg rotates around its long axis under the continuous control of an agent (*turn*).

Wirbeln 'whirl'
MOVING OBJECT
A black hat

POSITIVE INSTANCES
1. Hat moves through the air turning around both its axes (*motion only*).
2. Agent causes hat to move as in 1. (*motion+cause*).

NEGATIVE INSTANCES
1. Hat rotated under continuous control of agent without being displaced (*turn*).
2. Hat moves through the air turning only around its horizontal axis (*shoot*).

Heben 'lift'
MOVING OBJECT
30cm stick

POSITIVE INSTANCE
1. Agent takes stick off table (*lift*).

NEGATIVE INSTANCES
1. Agent lowers stick (*lower*).
2. Agent slowly pushes stick toward a second table without taking it off the first table (*push*). (The tables stood about 3cm apart, so that the initial and final location of the stick could clearly be distinguished.)

Senken 'lower'
MOVING OBJECT
30cm stick

POSITIVE INSTANCES
1. Agent holds stick horizontally, slowly lowering it onto a table (*lower (table)*)
2. Agent first holds stick vertically, right above a transparent bottle, and then slowly lowers it into the bottle (*lower (bottle)*). (Some speakers find this a much better instance of *senken* than 1.)

NEGATIVE INSTANCES
1. Agent slowly pushes stick onto another table (the tables stood about 3cm apart from each other).
2. Agent drops stick into the bottle (*drop*).
3. Agent slowly moves stick upwards (*lift*).

Schleppen 'drag'
MOVING OBJECT
Sack

POSITIVE INSTANCE
1. Agent holds a big sack with both hands and drags it several meters with obvious difficulty over the ground because of the sack's weight (*drag*).

NEGATIVE INSTANCES
1. Agent swings sack away from her (*swing*).
2. Agent carries sack over the same distance with obvious ease (*carry*).

Schmettern 'smash/fling'
MOVING OBJECT
Balls

POSITIVE INSTANCES
1. Agent bangs a small rubber ball against a white board; it bounces off immediately (*bounce off*).
2. Agent bangs a small ball, made of material that deforms under pressure but then slowly regains shape, against a white board; ball remains stuck on the surface (*stay on wall*). (In this instance, the imparting of force required for actions of smashing was dissociated from the effect that the object bangs off the goal object.)

NEGATIVE INSTANCES
1. Agent throws rubber ball against board without much impact (*throw*).
2. Agent kicks ball against board (*kick*).
3. Agent throws ball forcefully into the air (*into air*).
4. Rubber ball drops onto table from an angle of about 45 degrees and bounces off again (*fall*).

Schieben 'push'
MOVING OBJECT
Cup

POSITIVE INSTANCE
1. Agent sits at a table, pushing a cup away from her with her hand (*push*).

NEGATIVE INSTANCE
1. Agent pulls cup toward her by its handle (*pull*).

Appendix 6

Evaluating the Adult Ratings of the Video Films in Pretest II of the Comprehension Experiment

In the second pretest of the comprehension experiment, children's knowledge of the meanings of the nonalternating verbs included in the study was assessed by showing them video-taped scenes that did or did not represent instances of the actions described by the verbs. The scenes were rated for their fit to the verbs by a group of 31 young adults (7.1.3). For some scenes, a minority of five or six adults disagreed with my classification. Here, I motivate my decisions for including or excluding these scenes from the analysis.

Kullern 'wobble'
Six adults rejected the intended positive instance of *kullern* in which the agent initiates the egg's motion. I decided that it was not necessary for children to accept this scene to be credited with knowledge of *kullern*. If a child rejects it on grounds that she does not know that *kullern* may be causativized, she should still not attribute canonical *be*-verb semantics to **bekullern* (analogous, for example, to *bewandern* '*be*-wander') as long as she knows that *kullern* denotes uncontrolled motion. This aspect of her knowledge was assessed by her judgment of the *motion only* scene. That is, regardless of whether a child thinks that *kullern* is an intransitive verb and describes uncontrolled motion (as assessed by her acceptance of the *motion only* scene) or a transitive, causativized verb (as assessed by her acceptance of the *motion+cause* scene), her representation of the verb should be incompatible with the locative alternation.

Wirbeln 'whirl'
Five adults accepted the intended negative instance of *wirbeln* in which the hat was rotated under the continuous control of the agent, but not displaced. If we take these adults' rating to indicate that displacement is not crucial to the meaning of *wirbeln*, we would simply have to use another verb, since causative *wirbeln* would then not be a causative verb of *motion* at all, and the account presented in Chapter 6 of why these verbs do not alternate would not apply to it. I therefore decided that the scene was crucial: Children had to reject it. Those children who accepted the scene might have acquired one possible meaning of the verb (in the sense that they behaved like the minority of adults), but my account of why causative motion verbs do not alternate has nothing to say about how these children will process **bewirbeln*.

Senken 'lower'
Six adults rejected the intended positive instance of *senken* in which the stick was lowered onto a table, and accepted only the scene in which it was lowered into a bottle. I decided that acceptance of either scene of lowering was sufficient, since both represent the downward motion aspect of the verb.

Appendix 7

Order of Experimental and Filler Items Presented to Children in the Main Task of the Comprehension Experiment

The experimental items in the table are bold-faced. There were two different orders of presentation, the second one differing from the one shown here in the sequencing of the first six target ungrammatical *be*-verbs. Their order of appearance in the second order is shown in brackets. (Recall that **beklemmen* [from *klemmen* 'pinch/squeeze'] and **bestopfen* [from *stopfen* 'stuff'] served as filler items.)

(1)	*verstreuen*	'ver-strew'	
(2)	*bekleistern*	'be-paste'	
(3)	**beklemmen*	'be-squeeze'	
(4)	*verbiegen*	'ver-bow'	
(5)	**bespritzen**	'be-splash'	(mass *be*-verb)
(6)	**beladen**	'be-load'	(count *be*-verb)
(7)	***beschmettern**	'be-smash'	(derived from *schmettern*) (23)
(8)	*versprühen*	'ver-spray'	
(9)	**verfüllen*	'ver-fill'	
(10)	*bemalen*	'be-paint'	
(11)	**bekleben**	'be-glue'	(count *be*-verb)
(12)	**bestreichen**	'be-streak'	(mass *be*-verb)
(13)	***bekullern**	'be-wobble'	(derived from a causative verb) (29)
(14)	**verholen*	'ver-fetch'	
(15)	**bestopfen*	'be-stuff'	
(16)	**besprühen**	'be-spray'	(mass *be*-verb)
(17)	**bewerfen**	'be-throw'	(count *be*-verb)
(18)	***besenken**	'be-lower'	(derived from a directional verb) (35)
(19)	*verladen*	'ver-load'	
(20)	**verlösen*	'ver-loosen'	
(21)	**bepacken**	'be-pack'	(count *be*-verb)
(22)	**begießen**	'be-pour'	(mass *be*-verb)
(23)	***beschleppen**	'be-drag'	(derived from an accompanied motion verb) (7)
(24)	*verstreichen*	'ver-streak'	
(25)	**verplatschen*	'ver-splash'	
(26)	*benageln*	'be-nail'	
(27)	**bestreuen**	'be-strew'	(mass *be*-verb)

(28)	**belegen**	'be-lay'	(count be-verb)
(29)	***beheben**	'be-lift'	(derived from a directional verb) (13)
(30)	*verspritzen*	'ver-splash'	
(31)	***verschmeißen**	'ver-throw'	
(32)	***bedrücken**	'be-press'	
(33)	**bedecken**	'be-cover'	(count be-verb)
(34)	**betropfen**	'be-drip'	(mass be-verb)
(35)	***bewirbeln**	'be-whirl'	(derived from a causative verb) (18)
(36)	*bekritzeln*	'be-scribble'	
(37)	***beschieben**	'be-push'	(derived from an accompanied motion verb)

Appendix 8

Instruction for the Main Task of the Comprehension Experiment

"Also, jetzt haben wir ja eine ganze Reihe von Filmen gesehen, über 'schleppen', 'kullern', 'senken', usw, ne? Was kann man denn noch alles schleppen? (Repeated for *kullern, senken, wirbeln, heben, schmettern, schieben*). (...) Gucken wir uns jetzt mal ein paar andere Wörter an. Was kann man zum Beispiel alles kritzeln (Repeated for *kleben, nageln, schütten, schmieren*)? (...) Jetzt kann man diese Wörter ja auch verändern. Aus 'schütten' kann man z.B. 'verschütten' machen, aber auch 'beschütten', und aus 'schmieren' kann man 'beschmieren' und 'verschmieren' machen. Kennst du diese Wörter schon? (...) Was kann man denn alles verschütten? (Repeated for *beschütten, beschmieren, verschmieren*) (...) Mal gucken, was man noch alles machen kann. Was kann man z.B. alles ..."

Translation

'So, now we have seen quite a number of films, about 'drag', 'wobble', 'lower', and so forth. What else can you drag (*wobble, lower, whirl, lift, smash, push*)? (...) Now, let's have a look at some other words. For example, what are some things you can draw/ scribble? (*glue, nail, pour2, smear*) (...) One can also change these words now. For example, you can turn 'pour2' into 'ver-pour2', but also into 'be-pour2', and you can turn 'smear' into 'be-smear' and 'ver-smear', can't you? Do you know these words already? (...) Now, what are some things you can 'ver-pour2'? (BE-pour2, BE-smear, VER-smear.) (...) Let's see what else one can do. For example, what are some things you can ...'

References

Anderson, M. (1979). Noun phrase structure. Unpublished doctoral dissertation, University of Connecticut, Storrs.

Anderson, R.W., & Shirai, Y. (1994). Discourse motivations for some cognitive acquisition principles. *Studies in Second Language Acquisition, 16*, 133-156.

Anderson, S. R. (1971). On the role of deep structure in semantic representation. *Foundations of Language, 6*, 197-219.

Aronoff, M. (1976). *Word formation in generative grammar.* Cambridge, MA: MIT Press.

Augst, G. (Ed.) (1984). *Kinderwort. Der aktive Kinderwortschatz (kurz vor der Einschulung).* Frankfurt, Germany: Peter Lang.

Baayen, R.H., Piepenbrock, R., & van Rijn, H. (1993). *The CELEX lexical database (CD-ROM).* Linguistic Data Consortium, University of Pennsylvania, Philadelphia, PA.

Baker, C.L. (1979). Syntactic theory and the projection problem. *Linguistic Theory, 10*, 533-581.

Baker, C.L. (1981). Learnability and the English auxiliary system. In C.L. Baker & J.J. McCarthy (Eds.), *The logical problem of language acquisition.* Cambridge, MA: MIT Press.

Baker, C.L. (1992). Review of 'Learnability and cognition: The acquisition of argument structure', by Steven Pinker. *Language, 68*, 402-413.

Baker, M.C. (1988). *Incorporation: A theory of grammatical function changing.* Chicago: University of Chicago Press.

Baker, M.C. (1992). Thematic conditions on syntactic structures: Evidence from locative applicatives. In I.M. Roca (Ed.), *Thematic structure: Its role in grammar.* Dordrecht, The Netherlands: Foris.

Becker, A., Carroll, M., & Kelly, A. (1988). *Reference to space.* ESF Project, Vol. 4, Strasbourg & Heidelberg.

Behrend, D.A. (1990). The development of verb concepts: Children's use of verbs to label familiar and novel events. *Child Development, 61*, 681-696.

Behrens, H. (1993). Temporal reference in German child language. Form and function in early verb use. Unpublished doctoral dissertation, Vrije Universiteit Amsterdam, Amsterdam.

Berwick, R.C. (1985). *The acquisition of syntactic knowledge.* Cambridge, MA: MIT Press.

Bickerton, D. (1981). *Roots of language.* Ann Arbor, MI: Karoma Publishers.

Biederman, I. (1987). Recognition-by-component: A theory of human image understanding. *Psychological Review, 94*, 115-147.

Bierwisch, M. (1983). Semantische und konzeptuelle Repräsentation lexikalischer Einheiten. In R. Ruzicka & W. Motsch (Eds.), *Untersuchungen zur Semantik.* Berlin, Germany: Akademie-Verlag.

Bierwisch, M. (1988). On the grammar of local prepositions. In M. Bierwisch, W. Motsch, & I. Zimmermann (Eds.), *Syntax, Semantik und Lexikon.* Berlin, Germany: Akademie-Verlag.

Bierwisch, M., & Lang, E. (Eds.) (1989). *Dimensional adjectives: Grammatical structure and conceptual interpretation.* Berlin, Germany: Springer-Verlag.

Bohannon, J.N., & Stanowicz, L. (1988). The issue of negative evidence: Adult responses to children's language errors. *Developmental Psychology, 24*, 684-689.

Booij, G. (1992). Morphology, semantics, and argument structure. In I.M. Roca (Ed.), *Thematic structure: Its role in grammar.* Dordrecht, The Netherlands: Foris.

Bowerman, M. (1974). Learning the structure of causative verbs: A study in the relationship of cognitive, semantic, and syntactic development. In *Papers and Reports on Child Language Development, 8*, 142-178. Stanford University Department of Linguistics, Stanford, CA.

Bowerman, M. (1977). The acquisition of rules governing "possible lexical items": Evidence from spontaneous speech errors. *Papers and Reports on Child Language Development, 13*, 148-156. Stanford University Department of Linguistics, Stanford, CA.

Bowerman, M. (1982a). Evaluating competing linguistic models with language acquisition data: Implications of developmental errors with causative verbs. *Quaderna di Semantica, 3*, 5-66.

Bowerman, M. (1982b). Reorganizational processes in lexical and semantic development. In E. Wanner & L.R. Gleitman (Eds.), *Language acquisition: The state of the art.* Cambridge: Cambridge University Press.

Bowerman, M. (1982c). Starting to talk worse: Clues to language acquisition from children's late speech errors. In S. Strauss (Ed.), *U-shaped behavioral growth.* New York: Academic Press.

Bowerman, M. (1983). How do children avoid an overly general grammar in the absence of feedback about what is not a sentence? *Papers and Reports on Child Language Development, 22*, 23-35. Stanford University Department of Linguistics, Stanford, CA.

Bowerman, M. (1987). Commentary: Mechanisms of language acquisition. In B. MacWhinney (Ed.), *Mechanisms of language acquisition.* Hillsdale, NJ: Lawrence Erlbaum.

Bowerman, M. (1988). The 'no negative evidence' problem: How do children avoid constructing an overly general grammar? In J.A. Hawkins (Ed.), *Explaining language universals.* Oxford, MA: Basil Blackwell.

Braine, M.D.S. (1971). On two types of models of the internalization of grammars. In D.I. Slobin (Ed.), *The ontogenesis of grammar.* New York: Academic Press.

Braine, M.D.S. (1988). Modeling the acquisition of linguistic structure. In Y. Levy, I.M. Schlesinger, & M.D.S. Braine (Eds.), *Categories and processes in language acquisition.* Hillsdale, NJ: Lawrence Erlbaum.

Braine, M.D.S., Brody, R.E., Fisch, S.M., Weisberger, M.J., & Blum, M. (1990). Can children use a verb without exposure to its argument structure? *Journal of Child Language, 17,* 313-342.

Braine, M.D.S., & Brooks, P.J. (1995). Verb argument structure and the problem of avoiding an overgeneral grammar. In M. Tomasello & W.E. Merriman (Eds.), *Beyond names for things.* Hillsdale, NJ: Lawrence Erlbaum.

Breiman, L., Friedman, J.H., Olshen, R.A., & Stone, C.J. (1984). *Classification and regression trees.* New York: Chapman & Hall.

Bresnan, J. (1978). Computational psycholinguistics. Course taught at MIT, 1st term. Cited in Gropen, J., Pinker, S., Hollander, M., Goldberg, R., & Wilson, R. (1989), The learnability and acquisition of the dative alternation in English. *Language, 65,* 203-257.

Bresnan, J. (1982). The passive in lexical theory. In J. Bresnan (Ed.), *The mental representation of grammatical relations.* Cambridge, MA: MIT Press.

Brinkmann, U. (1993). Nonindividuation versus affectedness: What licenses the promotion of the prepositional object? In E.V. Clark (Ed.), *Proceedings of the 25th Annual Child Language Research Forum,* Stanford University, Stanford, CA.

Brinkmann, U., & Wunderlich, D. (1996). How to loose semantic weight: Accounting for the locative alternation by preposition incorporation. Unpublished manuscript, Heinrich-Heine-Universität, Düsseldorf.

Brown, R. (1973). *A first language: The early stages.* Cambridge, MA: Harvard University Press.

Brown, R., & Hanlon, C. (1970). Derivational complexity and order of acquisition in child speech. In J.R. Hayes (Ed.), *Cognition and the development of language.* New York: Wiley.

Burnage, G. (1990). *CELEX. A guide for users.* Centre for Lexical Information, Katholieke Universitiet Nijmegen, Nijmegen, The Netherlands.

Campos, H. (1986). Indefinite object drop. *Linguistic Inquiry, 17,* 354-359.

Carlson, G.N. (1980). *Reference to kinds in English.* New York: Garland Publishing.

Carrier, J., & Randall, J.H. (1992). The argument structure and syntactic structure of resultatives. *Linguistic Inquiry, 23,* 173-234.

Carrier, J., & Randall, J.H. (to appear). *From conceptual structure to syntax.* Dordrecht, The Netherlands: Foris.

Carrow, M. (1968). The development of auditory comprehension of language structures in English. *Journal of Speech and Hearing Disorders, 33,* 99-111.

Carter, R.J. (1976). Some linking regularities. Unpublished manuscript, University of Paris VIII, Vincennes. In B. Levin & C. Tenny (Eds.) (1988), *On linking: Papers by Richard Carter.* Lexicon Project Working Papers 25. Cambridge, MA: MIT Center for Cognitive Science.

Chomsky, N. (1962). A transformational approach to syntax. In A.A. Hill (Ed.), *Proceedings of the 1958 conference of problems of linguistic analysis in English.* Austin, Texas.

Chomsky, N. (1965). *Aspects of the theory of syntax.* Cambridge, MA: MIT Press.

Chomsky, N. (1981). *Lectures on government and binding.* Dordrecht, The Netherlands: Foris.

Chomsky, N. (1986a). *Knowledge of language, its nature, origin, and use*. New York: Praeger.

Chomsky, N. (1986b). *Barriers*. Cambridge, MA: MIT Press.

Chomsky, N. (1993). A minimalist program for linguistic theory. In K. Hale & S.J. Keyser (Eds.), *The view from building 20*, Cambridge, MA: MIT Press.

Chomsky, N. (1995). Bare phrase structure. In H. Campos & P. Kempchinsky (Eds.), *Evolution and Revolution in Linguistic Theory*. Washington, DC: Georgetown University Press.

Chomsky, N., & Halle, M. (1968/1991). The sound pattern of English. Cambridge, MA: MIT Press.

Chomsky, N., & Lasnik, H. (1977). Filters and control. *Linguistic Inquiry, 8*, 425-504.

Clahsen, H. (1982). *Spracherwerb in der Kindheit: Eine Untersuchung zur Entwicklung der Syntax bei Kleinkindern*. Tübingen, Germany: Gunter Narr.

Clahsen, H. (1984). Der Erwerb von Kasusmarkierungen in der deutschen Kindersprache. *Linguistische Berichte, 89*, 1-31.

Clark, E.V. (1974). Normal states and evaluative viewpoints. *Language, 50*, 316-332.

Clark, E.V. (1983). Meanings and concepts. In P.H. Mussen (Ed.), *Handbook of child psychology, Vol. 3*. New York: John Wiley & Sons.

Clark, E.V. (1987). The principle of contrast: A constraint on language acquisition. In B. MacWhinney (Ed.), *Mechanisms of language acquisition*. Hillsdale, NJ: Erlbaum.

Clark, E.V. (1993). *The lexicon in acquisition*. Cambridge: Cambridge University Press.

Clark, E.V., & Clark, H.H. (1979). When nouns surface as verbs. *Language, 55*, 767-811.

Clark, H.H. (1973). Space, time, semantics, and the child. In T.E. Moore (Ed.), *Cognitive development and the acquisition of language*. New York: Academic Press.

Clark, L.A., & Pregibon, D. (1992). Tree-based models. In J.M. Chambers & T.J. Haskie (Eds.), *Statistical models in S*. Pacific Grove, CA: Wadsworth & Brooks/Cole Advanced Books & Software.

Croft, W. (1991). *Syntactic categories and grammatical relations*. Chicago: University of Chicago Press.

Croft, W. (1993). Aspect, countability and the conceptual unity of instantiation. Unpublished manuscript, Max Planck Institute for Psycholinguistics, Nijmegen.

Czepluch, H. (1987). Lexikalische Argumentstruktur und syntaktische Projektion: zur Beschreibung grammatischer Relationen. *Zeitschrift für Sprachwissenschaft, 6*, 3-36.

Czepluch, H. (1988). Kasusmorphologie und Kasusrelationen: Überlegungen zur Kasustheorie am Beispiel des Deutschen. *Linguistische Berichte, 116*, 275-310.

Cziko, G. A. (1989). A review of the state-process and punctual-nonpunctual distinctions in children's acquisition of verbs. *First Language, 9*, 1-31.

Demetras, M.J., Post, K.N., & Snow, C.E. (1986). Feedback to first language learners: The role of repetitions and clarification questions. *Journal of Child Language, 13*, 275-292.

Dowty, D.R. (1972). *Studies in the logic of verb aspect and time reference in English*. Studies in Linguistics 1, University of Texas, Austin, Texas.

Dowty, D.R. (1979). *Word meaning and Montague grammar. The semantics of verbs and times in generative semantics and in Montague's PTQ*. Dordrecht, The Netherlands: Reidel.

Dowty, D.R. (1991). Thematic proto-roles and argument selection. *Language, 67,* 547-619.

Dromi, E. (1987). *Early lexical development.* Cambridge: Cambridge University Press.

Ehrich, V. (1982). *Da* and the system of spatial deixis in German. In J. Weissenborn & W. Klein (Eds.), *Here and there: Cross-linguistic studies on deixis and demonstration.* Amsterdam: John Benjamins.

Eisenbeiß, S. (1994). Kasus und Wortstellungsvariationen im deutschen Mittelfeld. Theoretische Überlegungen und Untersuchungen zum Erstspracherwerb. In B. Haftka (Ed.), *Was determiniert Wortstellungsvariation? Studien zu einem Interaktionsfeld von Grammatik, Pragmatik und Sprachtypologie.* Opladen, Germany: Westdeutscher Verlag.

Eisenbeiß, S., & Penke, M. (1996). Children checking Checking Theory. Paper presented at the conference *What children have to say about linguistic theory,* Utrecht, The Netherlands, June 28-30.

Emonds, J.E. (1972). Evidence that indirect object movement is a structure-preserving rule. *Foundations of Language, 8,* 546-561.

Eroms, H.-W. (1980). *Be-Verb und Präpositionalphrase.* Heidelberg, Germany: Winter.

Fanselow, G. (1987). *Konfigurationalität.* Tübingen, Germany: Gunter Narr.

Fiengo, R. (1981). *Surface structure: The interface of autonomous components.* Cambridge, MA: Harvard University Press.

Fillmore, C.J. (1968). The case for case. In E. Bach & R.T. Harms (Eds.), *Universals in linguistic theory.* New York: Holt, Rinehart, and Winston.

Fillmore, C.J. (1973). May we come in? *Semiotica, 9,* 98-115.

Fillmore, C.J. (1977). The case for case reopened. In P. Cole & J.M. Saddock (Eds.), *Syntax and semantics, Vol. 8: Grammatical relations.* New York: Academic Press.

Fillmore, C.J. (1978). On the organization of semantic information in the lexicon. In D. Farkas, W.M. Jacobson, & K.W. Todrys (Eds.), *Papers from the parassession on the Lexicon.* Chicago Linguistics Society, Chicago, April 14-15.

Fischer, S. (1971). The acquisition of verb-particle and dative constructions. Unpublished doctoral dissertation, Massachusetts Institute of Technology, Cambridge, MA.

Fisher, C., Gleitman, L.R., & Gleitman, H. (1991). On the semantic content of subcategorization frames. *Cognitive Psychology, 23,* 331-392.

Fodor, J.D., & Crain, S. (1987). Simplicity and generality of rules in language acquisition. In B. MacWhinney (Ed.), *Mechanisms of language acquisition.* Hillsdale, NJ: Lawrence Erlbaum.

Fraser, B. (1971). A note on the spray paint cases. *Linguistic Inquiry, 2,* 604-607.

Gentner, D. (1978). On relational meaning: The acquisition of verb meaning. *Child Development, 49,* 988-998.

Gleitman, L. R. (1990). The structural sources of verb meaning. *Language Acquisition, 1,* 3-55.

Gold, E.M. (1967). Language identification in the limit. *Information and Control, 10,* 447-474.

Green, G.M. (1974). *Semantics and syntactic regularity.* Bloomington, Indiana: Indiana University Press.

Grice, H.P. (1975). Logic and conversation. In P. Cole & J.L. Morgan (Eds.), *Syntax and semantics, Vol. 3: Speech acts.* New York: Academic Press.

Grimshaw, J. (1990). *Argument structure*. Cambridge, MA: MIT Press.

Grimshaw, J. (1994). Lexical reconciliation. *Lingua, 92*, 411-430.

Grimshaw, J., & Vikner, S. (1993). Obligatory adjuncts and the structure of events. In E. Reuland & W. Abraham (Eds.), *Knowledge and Language, Vol. 2*. Dordrecht, The Netherlands: Kluwer.

Gropen, J. (1989). Learning locative verbs: How universal linking rules constrain productivity. Unpublished doctoral dissertation, Massachusetts Institute of Technology, Cambridge, MA.

Gropen, J., Pinker, S., Hollander, M., Goldberg, R., & Wilson, R. (1989). The learnability and acquisition of the dative alternation in English. *Language, 65*, 203-257.

Gropen, J., Pinker, S., Hollander, M., & Goldberg, R. (1991a). Syntax and semantics in the acquisition of locative verbs. *Journal of Child Language, 18*, 115-151.

Gropen, J., Pinker, S., Hollander, M., & Goldberg, R. (1991b). Affectedness and direct objects: The role of lexical semantics in the acquisition of verb argument structure. *Cognition, 41*, 153-195.

Gruber, J. (1965). Studies in lexical relations. Doctoral dissertation, Massachusetts Institute of Technology, Cambridge, MA. Reprinted as *Lexical structures in syntax and semantics*. Amsterdam: North-Holland (1976).

Günther, H. (1974). *Das System der Verben mit* BE- *in der deutschen Sprache der Gegenwart*. Tübingen, Germany: Niemeyer.

Günther, H. (1987). Wortbildung, Syntax, *be*-Verben und das Lexikon. *Beiträge zur Geschichte der deutschen Sprache und Literatur, 109*, 179-201.

Haegeman, L. (1991/1994). *Introduction to government and binding theory*. Oxford, MA: Basil Blackwell.

Haider, H. (1984). Mona Lisa lächelt stumm – über das sog. deutsche 'Rezipientenpassiv'. *Linguistische Berichte, 89*, 32-42.

Haider, H. (1985). The case of German. In J. Toman (Ed.), *Studies in German Grammar*. Dordrecht, The Netherlands: Foris.

Haider, H. (1986). Fehlende Argumente: vom Passiv zu kohärenten Infinitiven. *Linguistische Berichte, 101*, 3-33.

Hale, K., & Keyser, S.J. (1986). Some transitivity alternations in English. *Lexicon Project MIT Working Paper, 7,* Massachusetts Institute of Technology, Cambridge, MA.

Hale, K., & Keyser, S.J. (1993). On argument structure and the lexical expression of syntactic relations. In K. Hale & S.J. Keyser (Eds.), *The view from building 20*. Cambridge, MA: MIT Press.

Hall, B. (1965). Subject and object in Modern English. Doctoral dissertation, Massachusetts Institute of Technology, Cambridge, MA. Reprinted as *Subject and object in Modern English*. New York: Garland (1979).

Herweg, M. (1988). Zur Semantik einiger lokaler Präpositionen des Deutschen. LILOG-Report, 21, IBM, Hamburg, Germany.

Herweg, M. (1991). Perfective and imperfective aspect and the theory of events and states. *Linguistics, 29*, 969-1010.

Hirsh-Pasek, K., Treiman, R., & Schneiderman, M. (1984). Brown and Hanlon revisited: Mothers' sensitivity to ungrammatical forms. *Journal of Child Language, 11*, 81-88.

Hochberg, J.G. (1986). Children's judgements of transitivity errors. *Journal of Child Language, 13*, 317-334.

Hoekstra, T., & Mulder, R. (1990). Unergatives as copular verbs: Locational and existential predication. *Linguistic Review, 7*, 1-79.

Hopper, P.J., & Thompson, S.A. (1980). Transitivity in grammar and discourse. *Language, 56*, 251-299.

Hout, A. van (1994). Projection based on event structure. In P. Coopmans, M. Everaert, & J. Grimshaw (Eds.), *Lexical specification and lexical insertion*. Hillsdale, NJ: Lawrence Erlbaum.

Hout, A. van (1996). Event semantics of verb frame alternations. A case study of Dutch and its acquisition. Unpublished doctoral dissertation, Katholieke Universiteit Brabant, Tilburg, The Netherlands.

Hyams, N. (1986). *Language acquisition and the theory of parameters*. Dordrecht, The Netherlands: Reidel.

Ingham, R. (1992). Review of 'Learnability and cognition: The acquisition of argument structure', by Steven Pinker. *Journal of Child Language, 19*, 205-211.

Jackendoff, R.S. (1972). *Semantic interpretation in generative grammar*. Cambridge, MA: MIT Press.

Jackendoff, R.S. (1975). Morphological and semantic regularities in the lexicon. *Language, 51*, 639-671.

Jackendoff, R.S. (1977). *X-bar syntax: A study of phrase structure*. Cambridge, MA: MIT Press.

Jackendoff, R.S. (1987). The status of thematic relations in linguistic theory. *Linguistic Inquiry, 18*, 369-411.

Jackendoff, R.S. (1990). *Semantic structures*. Cambridge, MA: MIT Press.

Jackendoff, R.S. (1991). Parts and boundaries. *Cognition, 41*, 9-45.

Juffs, A. (1996). *Learnability and the lexicon. Theories and second language acquisition research*. John Benjamins: Amsterdam.

Kaufmann, I. (1989). Direktionale Präpositionen. In C. Habel, M. Herweg, & K. Rehkämper (Eds.), *Raumkonzepte in Verstehensprozessen*. Tübingen, Germany: Niemeyer.

Kaufmann, I. (1993). Semantic and conceptual aspects of the preposition *durch*. In C. Zelinski-Wibbelt (Ed.), *The semantics of prepositions: From mental processing to natural language processing*. Berlin, Germany: de Gruyter.

Kaufmann, I. (1995): *Konzeptuelle Grundlagen semantischer Dekompositionsstrukturen. Die Kombinatorik lokaler Verben und prädikativer Komplemente*. Tübingen, Germany: Niemeyer.

Keenan, E.O. (1976). Towards a universal definition of "subject." In C. Li (Ed.), *Subject and topic*. New York: Academic Press.

Kefer, M. (1980). A note on lexical entries. *Linguistic Inquiry, 11*, 429-431.

Kiparsky, P. (1989): Agreement and linking theory. Unpublished manuscript. Stanford University, Stanford, CA.

Kiparsky, P. (1992): Structural case. Unpublished manuscript, Wissenschaftskolleg, Berlin, Germany.

Kirsner, R.S. (1985). Iconicity and grammatical meaning. In J. Haiman (Ed.), *Iconicity in syntax*. Amsterdam: John Benjamins.

Kirsner, R.S. (1986). On being empirical with indirect objects: The subtleties of *aan*. In J. van Oosten & J.P. Snapper (Eds.), *Dutch Linguistics at Berkely: Papers presented at the Dutch Linguistics Colloquium held at the University of California, Berkely on November 9th, 1985*. Berkely, CA: The Dutch Studies Program.

Kirsner, R.S., Verhagen, A., & Willemsen, M. (1985). Over PP's, transitiviteit en het zgn. indirekt objekt. *Spektator, 14,* 341-347.

Klein, W. (1994). *Time in language*. London: Routledge.

Krifka, M. (1986). *Massennomina. Mit einem Exkurs zu Aktionsarten.* Forschungsbericht 117 des Sonderforschungsbereichs 99. Universität Konstanz, Konstanz, Germany.

Krifka, M. (1989a). *Nominalreferenz und Zeitkonstitution. Zur Semantik von Massentermen, Pluraltermen und Aspektklassen.* München, Germany: Wilhelm Fink.

Krifka, M. (1989b). Nominalreferenz, Zeitkonstitution, Aspekt, Aktionsart: Eine semantische Erklärung ihrer Interaktion. In W. Abraham & T. Janssen (Eds.), *Tempus-Aspekt-Modus. Typologie der lexikalischen und grammatischen Formen in den germanischen Sprachen.* Berlin, Germany: Mouton.

Kühnhold, J., & Wellmann, H. (1973). *Deutsche Wortbildung: Das Verb.* Düsseldorf, Germany: Schwann.

Labelle, M. (1991). The semantic representation of denominal verbs. Paper presented at the *Workshop on lexical specification and lexical insertion*. Research Institute for Language and Speech, Utrecht, The Netherlands, December 9-11.

Landau, B., & Gleitman, L.R. (1985). *Language and experience*. Cambridge, MA: Harvard University Press.

Lang, E. (1988). Gestalt und Lage räumlicher Objekte: Semantische Struktur und kontextuelle Interpretation von Dimensionsadjektiven. In J. Bayer (Ed.), *Grammatik und Kognition. Psycholinguistische Untersuchungen.* Opladen, Germany: Westdeutscher Verlag.

Lang, E. (1989). Primärer Orientierungsraum und inhärentes Proportionsschema: Interagierende Kategorisierungsraster bei der Konzeptualisierung räumlicher Objekte. In C. Habel, M. Herweg, & K. Rehkämper (Eds.), *Raumkonzepte in Verstehensprozessen.* Tübingen, Germany: Niemeyer.

Lebeaux, D. (1988). The feature +affected and the formation of the passive. In W. Wilkins (Ed.), *Syntax and semantics, Vol. 21: Thematic relations.* New York: Academic Press.

Leisi, E. (1953). *Der Wortinhalt. Seine Struktur im Deutschen und Englischen.* Heidelberg, Germany: Quelle und Meyer.

Levin, L. (1985). Operations on lexical forms: Unaccusative rules in Germanic languages. Unpublished doctoral dissertation, Massachusetts Institute of Technology, Cambridge, MA.

Levin, B. (1993). *English verb classes and alternations: A preliminary investigation.* Chicago: University of Chicago Press.

Levin, B., & Rappaport, M. (1988): Non-event *er*-nominals: A probe into argument structure. *Linguistics, 26,* 1067-1983.

Levin, B., & Rappaport Hovav, M. (1991). Wiping the slate clean: A lexical semantic exploration. *Cognition, 41,* 123-151.

Levin, B., & Rappaport Hovav, M. (1992). The lexical semantics of verbs of motion: The perspective from unaccusativity. In I.M. Roca (Ed.), *Thematic structure: Its role in grammar*. Dordrecht, The Netherlands: Foris.

Löbner, S. (1990). *Wahr neben Falsch: Duale Operatoren als die Quantoren natürlicher Sprache*. Tübingen, Germany: Niemeyer.

Löbner, S. (1996). Polarity in natural language: Towards an integrated theory of predication, quantification and negation in particular and characterizing sentences. To appear in *Linguistics and Philosophy*.

Lord, C. (1979). "Don't you fall me down": Children's generalizations regarding cause and transitivity. *Papers and Reports on Child Language Development, 17*. Stanford University Department of Linguistics, Stanford, CA.

MacWhinney, B. (1991). *The CHILDES-project: Tools for analyzing talk*. Hillsdale, NJ: Erlbaum.

MacWhinney, B., & Snow, C. (1990). The Child Language Data Exchange System: An update. *Journal of Child Language, 17*, 457-472.

Maienborn, C.M. (1990). *Position und Bewegung: Zur Semantik lokaler Verben*. IWBS Report 138, IBM, Hamburg, Germany.

Maienborn, C.M. (1992). Zur Verarbeitung lokaler Adjunkte. In G. Görz (Ed.), *Tagungsband KONVENS 92*. Berlin, Germany: Springer.

Maienborn, C.M. (1994). Kompakte Strukturen. Direktionale Präpositionen und nicht-lokale Verben. In S. Felix, C. Habel, & G. Rickheit (Eds.), *Kognitive Linguistik. Repräsentation und Prozesse*. Opladen, Germany: Westdeutscher Verlag.

Marantz, A.P. (1982). On the acquisition of grammatical relations. *Linguistische Berichte, 80-82*, 32-69.

Marantz, A.P. (1984). *On the nature of grammatical relations*. Cambridge, MA: MIT Press.

Maratsos, M.P., Gudeman, R., Gerard-Ngo, P., & DeHart, G. (1987). A study in novel word learning: The productivity of the causative. In B. MacWhinney (Ed.), *Mechanisms of language acquisition*. Hillsdale, NJ: Lawrence Erlbaum.

Maratsos, M.P., Kuczaj, S.A. II, Fox, D.E., & Chalkley, M. (1979). Some empirical studies in the acquisition of transformational relations: Passives, negatives, and the past tense. In W.A. Collins (Ed.), *Minnesota Symposium on Child Psychology, Vol. 12*. Hillsdale, NJ: Lawrence Erlbaum.

Marcus, G.F. (1993). Negative evidence in language acquisition. *Cognition, 46*, 53-85.

Mazurkewich, I., & White, L. (1984). The acquisition of the dative alternation: Unlearning overgeneralizations. *Cognition, 16*, 261-283.

Miller, G.A., & Johnson-Laird, P.N. (1976). *Language and perception*. Cambridge, MA: Harvard University Press.

Miller, M.. (1976). *Zur Logik der frühkindlichen Sprachentwicklung*. Stuttgart, Germany: Ernst Klett.

Mills, A. (1985). The acquisition of German. In D.I. Slobin (Ed.), *The crosslinguistic study of language acquisition*. Hillsdale, NJ: Lawrence Erlbaum.

Mittwoch, A. (1982). On the difference between *eating* and *eating something*: Activities versus accomplishments. *Linguistic Inquiry, 13*, 113-122.

Moravcsik, E.A. (1978). On the case marking of objects. In J.H. Greenberg (Ed.), *Universals of human language, Vol. 4: Syntax*. Stanford, CA: Stanford University Press.

Morgan, J.L., & Travis, L.L. (1989). Limits on negative information in language input. *Journal of Child Language, 16,* 531-552.

Naigles, L. (1990). Children use syntax to learn verb meanings. *Journal of Child Language, 17,* 357-374.

Naigles, L. (1991). Review of 'Learnability and cognition: The acquisition of argument structure', by Steven Pinker. *Language and Speech, 34,* 63-79.

Naigles, L., Fowler, A., & Helm, A. (1992). Developmental shifts in the construction of verb meanings. *Cognitive Development, 7,* 403-427.

Naigles, L., Gleitman, L.R., & Gleitman, H. (1992). Children acquire word meaning components from syntactic evidence. In E. Dromi (Ed.), *Language and development.* Norwood, NJ: Ablex.

Neumann, D. (1987). *Objects and spaces. A study in the syntax and semantics of the German case system.* Tübingen, Germany: Gunter Narr.

Nishigauchi, T., & Roeper, T. (1987). Deductive parameters and the growth of the empty categories. In T. Roeper & E. Williams (Eds.), *Parameter setting.* Dordrecht, The Netherlands: Reidel.

Oehrle, R.T. (1976). The grammatical status of the English dative alternation. Unpublished doctoral dissertation, Massachusetts Institute of Technology, Cambridge, MA.

Ojeda, A.E. (1993). *Linguistic individuals.* CSLI lecture notes 31, Stanford University, Stanford, CA.

Olsen, S. (1994). Lokativalternation im Deutschen und Englischen. *Zeitschrift für Sprachwissenschaft, 13,* 210-235.

Olsen, S. (1995). Alternative grammatische Realisierung lokativer Komplemente. *Sprache und Pragmatik, 36,* 1-26.

Ostler, N.D.M. (1980). A theory of case linking and agreement. Unpublished manuscript, Indiana University Linguistics Club, Bloomington, Indiana.

Paul, H. (1920). *Deutsche Grammatik. Vols. 1-5.* Halle, Germany.

Pelletier, F.J., & Schubert, L.K. (1989). Mass expressions. In D. Gabbay & F. Guenther (Eds.), *Handbook of philosophical logic, Vol. 4.* Dordrecht, The Netherlands: Reidel.

Penner, S. (1987). Parental responses to grammatical and ungrammatical child utterances. *Child Development, 58,* 376-384.

Pinker, S. (1982). A theory of the acquisition of lexical interpretive grammars. In J. Bresnan (Ed.), *The mental representation of grammatical relations.* Cambridge, MA: MIT Press.

Pinker, S. (1984). *Language learnability and language development.* Cambridge, MA: Harvard University Press.

Pinker, S. (1987). The bootstrapping problem in language acquisition. In B. MacWhinney (Ed.), *Mechanisms of language acquisition.* Hillsdale, NJ: Erlbaum.

Pinker, S. (1989). *Learnability and cognition: The acquisition of argument structure.* Cambridge, MA: MIT Press.

Pinker, S. (1994). How could a child use verb syntax to learn verb semantics? *Lingua, 92,* 377-410.

Pinker, S., Lebeaux, D.S., & Frost, L.A. (1987). Productivity and constraints in the acquisition of the passive. *Cognition, 26,* 195-227.

Pustejovski, J. (1991). The syntax of event structure. *Cognition, 41,* 47-81.

Quine, W. (1960). *Word and object.* Cambridge, MA: MIT Press.

Randall, J. (1987). Indirect positive evidence: Overturning overgeneralizations in language acquisition. Indiana University Linguistics Club, Bloomington, Indiana.

Randall, J. (1990). Catapults and pendulums: The mechanisms of language acquisition. *Linguistics, 28,* 1381-1406.

Randall, J. (1992). The catapult hypothesis: An approach to unlearning. In J. Weissenborn, H. Goodluck, & T. Roeper (Eds.), *Theoretical issues in language acquisition: Continuity and change in development.* Hillsdale, NJ: Lawrence Erlbaum.

Rappaport, M. (1983). On the nature of derived nominals, In L. Levin, M. Rappaport, & A. Zaenen (Eds.), Papers in lexical functional grammar. Indiana University Linguistics Club, Bloomington, Indiana.

Rappaport, M., & Levin, B. (1985). A case study in lexical analysis: The locative alternation. Unpublished manuscript, MIT Center for Cognitive Science, Cambridge, MA.

Rappaport, M., & Levin, B. (1988). What to do with theta-roles. In W. Wilkins (Ed.), *Syntax and semantics, Vol. 21: Thematic Relations.* San Diego, CA: Academic Press.

Rappaport Hovav, M., & Levin, B. (1992): -*er* nominals: Implications for a theory of argument structure. In E. Wehrli & T. Stowell (Eds.), *Syntax and semantics, Vol. 26: Syntax and the lexicon.* New York: Academic Press.

Reinhart, T. (1981). Definite NP anaphora and c-command. *Linguistic Inquiry, 12,* 605-635.

Reis, M. (1985). Mona Lisa kriegt zuviel — vom sog. Rezipientenpassiv im Deutschen. *Linguistische Berichte, 96,* 140-155.

Rietveld, T., & van Hout, R. (1993). *Statistical techniques for the study of language and language behavior.* Berlin, Germany: Mouton de Gruyter.

Rispoli, M. (1990) Lexical assignability and perspective switch: The acquisition of verb subcategorization for aspectual inflections. *Journal of Child Language, 17,* 375-392.

Rispoli, M. (1992) Discourse and the acquisition of *eat. Journal of Child Language, 19,* 581-595.

Roeper, T., Lapointe, S., Bing, J., & Tavakolian, S. (1981). A lexical approach to language acquisition. In S. Tavakolian (Ed.), *Language acquisition and linguistic theory.* Cambridge, MA: MIT Press.

Rumelhart, D., & McClelland, J. (1986). On learning the past tense of English verbs. Implicit rules or parallel distributed processing? In J. McClelland, D. Rumelhart, & the PDP research group (Eds.), *Parallel distributed processing: Explorations in the microstructure of cognition.* Cambridge, MA: MIT Press.

Saile, G. (1984). *Sprache und Handlung.* Braunschweig, Germany: Friedrich Vieweg & Sohn.

Schwartz-Norman, L. (1976). The grammar of 'content' and 'container'. *Journal of Linguistics, 12,* 279-287.

Siegel, D. (1974). Topics in English morphology. Unpublished doctoral dissertation, Massachusetts Institute of Technology, Cambridge, MA.

Simpson, J. (1983). Resultative attributes. In A. Zaenen, M. Rappaport, & B. Levin (Eds.), Papers in lexical-functional grammar. Indiana University Linguistics Club, Bloomington, Indiana.

Sjöström, S. (1990). Spatial relations: Towards a theory of spatial verbs, prepositions, and pronominal adverbs in Swedish. *Gothenburg Monographs in Linguistics, 8.*

Slobin, D.I. (1985). Crosslinguistic evidence for the language-making capacity. In D. I. Slobin (Ed.), *The child's construction of language*. London: Academic Press.

Slobin, D.I. (1995). Why are grammaticizable notions special? – A reanalysis and a challenge to Learning Theory. Paper presented at the conference *Language Acquisition and Conceptual Development*, Max Planck Institute for Psycholinguistics, Nijmegen, November 14-17. To appear in S. C. Levinson & M. Bowerman (Eds.), *Language acquisition and conceptual development*. Cambridge: Cambridge University Press.

Smeedts, W.A.J. (1986). *De beheersing van de woordvorming: een sociolinguistisch onderzoek bij Vlaamse dertienjarigen*. Leuven, Belgium: Universitaire Pers Leuven.

Snyder, W., & Stromswold, K. (1997). The structure and acquisition of the English dative constructions. *Linguistic Inquiry, 28,* 281-317.

Stern, C., & Stern, W. (1907/1928). *Die Kindersprache*. Leipzig, Germany: Barth (reprint: Darmstadt, Germany: Wissenschaftliche Buchgesellschaft).

Stiebels, B. (1991). *Präpositionsinkorporierung und das Problem der Partikelverben im Deutschen*. M.A. thesis, Heinrich-Heine-Universität, Düsseldorf, Germany.

Stiebels, B. (1996). *Lexikalische Argumente und Adjunkte: Zum semantischen Beitrag von verbalen Präfixen und Partikeln*. Berlin, Germany: Akademie-Verlag.

Stiebels, B. & Wunderlich, D. (1994): Morphology feeds syntax: The case of particle verbs. *Linguistics, 32,* 913-968.

Talmy, L. (1978). Figure and ground in complex sentences. In J. Greenberg (Ed.), *Universals of human language, Vol. 4: Syntax*. Stanford, CA: Stanford University Press.

Talmy, L. (1983). How language structures space. In H. Pick & L. Acredolo (Eds.), *Spatial orientation: Theory, research, and application*. New York: Plenum.

Talmy, (1985). Lexicalization patterns: Semantic structure in lexical forms. In T. Shopen (Ed.), *Language typology and syntactic description, Vol. 3: Grammatical categories and the lexicon*. Cambridge: Cambridge University Press.

Tenny, C.L. (1987). Grammaticalizing aspect and affectedness. Unpublished doctoral dissertation, Massachusetts Institute of Technology, Cambridge, MA.

Tenny, C.L. (1989). The aspectual interface hypothesis. Lexicon Project Working Papers 31, Center for Cognitive Science, Massachusetts Institute of Technology, Cambridge, MA.

Tenny, C.L. (1992). The aspectual interface hypothesis. In I. Sag & A. Szabolsci (Eds.), *Lexical matters*. CSLI lecture notes 24, Stanford University, Stanford, CA.

Tracy, R. (1986). The acquisition of case morphology in German. *Linguistics, 24,* 47-78.

Urbas, M. (1990). Denominale Verben: Semantische und konzeptuelle Aspekte. Unpublished M.A. thesis, Heinrich-Heine-Universität, Düsseldorf, Germany.

Van Valin, R.D. (1990). Semantic parameters of split intransitivity. *Language, 66,* 221-260.

Vendler, Z. (1957). Verbs and times. *Philosophical Review, 84,* 327-352.

Verkuyl, H.J. (1971). *On the compositional nature of the aspects*. Dordrecht, The Netherlands: Reidel.

Verkuyl, H.J. (1993). *A theory of aspectuality: The interaction between temporal and atemporal structure*. Cambridge: Cambridge University Press.

Wahrig, G. (1982). Deutsches Wörterbuch. Mosaik Verlag.

Wasow, T. (1981). Comments on the paper by Baker. In C.L. Baker & J.J. McCarthy (Eds), *The logical problem of language acquisition*. Cambridge, MA: MIT Press.

Wegener, H. (1985). "Er bekommt widersprochen." Argumente für die Existenz eines Dativpassivs im Deutschen. *Linguistische Berichte, 96,* 127-139.

Wegener, H. (1991). Der Dativ — ein struktureller Kasus? In G. Fanselow & S. Felix (Eds.), *Strukturen und Merkmale syntaktischer Kategorien*. Tübingen, Germany: Gunter Narr.

Weist, R.M., Wysocka, H., Witkowska-Stadnik, K., Buczowska, E., & Konieczna, E. (1984). The defective tense hypothesis: On the emergence of tense and aspect in child Polish. *Journal of Child Language, 11,* 347-374.

Wexler, K. (1979). Untitled presentation at the Workshop on learnability. Laguna Beach, California, June 4-8. Cited in Pinker, S. (1984). *Language learnability and language development.*

Wexler, K., & Culicover, P. (1980). *Formal principles of language acquisition*. Cambridge, MA: MIT Press.

Wexler, K., & Manzini, M.R. (1987). Parameters and learnability in binding theory. In T. Roeper & E. Williams (Eds.), *Parameter setting*. Dordrecht, The Netherlands: Reidel.

Wierzbicka, (1985). Oats and wheat: The fallacy of arbitrariness. J. Haiman (Ed.), *Iconicity in syntax*. Amsterdam: John Benjamins.

Wilkins, W. (Ed.) (1988). *Syntax and semantics, Vol. 21: Thematic relations*. New York: Academic Press.

Williams, E. (1981). Language acquisition, markedness and phrase-structure. In S.L. Tavakolian (Ed.), *Language acquisition and linguistic theory*. Cambridge, MA: MIT Press.

Wunderlich, D. (1983). On the compositionality of German prefix verbs. In R. Bäuerle, C. Schwarze, & A. von Stechow (Eds.), *Meaning, use, and the interpretation of language*. Berlin, Germany: Springer.

Wunderlich, D. (1985). Raumkonzepte. Zur Semantik der lokalen Präpositionen. In Th.T. Ballmer & R. Posner (Eds.), *Nach-Chomskysche Linguistik*. Berlin, Germany: de Gruyter.

Wunderlich, D. (1987). An investigation of lexical composition. The case of German *be-*verbs. *Linguistics, 25,* 283-331.

Wunderlich, D. (1991). How do prepositional phrases fit into compositional syntax and semantics? *Linguistics, 29,* 591-621.

Wunderlich, D. (1992). CAUSE and the structure of verbs. Arbeiten des SFB *Theorie des Lexikons*, Heinrich-Heine-University, Düsseldorf, Germany.

Wunderlich, D. (1997). Cause and the structure of verbs. *Linguistic Inquiry, 28,* 27-68.

Wunderlich, D., & Herweg, M. (1991). Lokale und Direktionale. In A. von Stechow & D. Wunderlich (Eds.), *Handbuch Semantik*. Berlin, Germany: de Gruyter.

Wunderlich, D., & Kaufmann, I. (1990). Lokale Verben und Präpositionen – semantische und konzeptuelle Aspekte. In S.W. Felix, S. Kanngießer, & G. Rickheit (Eds.), *Sprache und Wissen: Studien zur kognitiven Linguistik*. Opladen, Germany: Westdeutscher Verlag.

Author Index

Subject Index

In the series LANGUAGE ACQUISITION AND LANGUAGE DISORDERS (LALD) the following titles have been published thus far or are scheduled for publication:

1. WHITE, Lydia: *Universal Grammar and Second Language Acquisition.* 1989.
2. HUEBNER, Thom and Charles A. FERGUSON (eds): *Cross Currents in Second Language Acquisition and Linguistic Theory.* 1991.
3. EUBANK, Lynn (ed.): *Point Counterpoint. Universal Grammar in the second language.* 1991.
4. ECKMAN, Fred R. (ed.): *Confluence. Linguistics, L2 acquisition and speech pathology.* 1993.
5. GASS, Susan and Larry SELINKER (eds): *Language Transfer in Language Learning. Revised edition.* 1992.
6. THOMAS, Margaret: *Knowledge of Reflexives in a Second Language.* 1993.
7. MEISEL, Jürgen M. (ed.): *Bilingual First Language Acquisition. French and German grammatical development.* 1994.
8. HOEKSTRA, Teun and Bonnie SCHWARTZ (eds): *Language Acquisition Studies in Generative Grammar.* 1994.
9. ADONE, Dany: *The Acquisition of Mauritian Creole.* 1994.
10. LAKSHMANAN, Usha: *Universal Grammar in Child Second Language Acquisition. Null subjects and morphological uniformity.* 1994.
11. YIP, Virginia: *Interlanguage and Learnability. From Chinese to English.* 1995.
12. JUFFS, Alan: *Learnability and the Lexicon. Theories and second language acquisition research.* 1996.
13. ALLEN, Shanley: *Aspects of Argument Structure Acquisition in Inuktitut.* 1996.
14. CLAHSEN, Harald (ed.): *Generative Perspectives on Language Acquisition. Empirical findings, theoretical considerations and crosslinguistic comparisons.* 1996.
15. BRINKMANN, Ursula: *The Locative Alternation in German. Its structure and acquisition.* 1997.
16. HANNAHS, S.J. and Martha YOUNG-SCHOLTEN (eds): *Focus on Phonological Acquisition.* 1997.